The Role of Culture
and Cultural Context

A volume in
Evaluation and Society
Series Editor: Katherine E. Ryan

Evaluation and Society

Katherine E. Ryan, Series Editor

Exploring Evaluator Role and Identity (2002)
  edited by Katherine E. Ryan and Thomas A. Schwandt

Evaluating Educational Reforms: Scandinavian Perspectives (2003)
  edited by Peder Haug and Thomas A. Schwandt

The Role of Culture and Cultural Context: A Mandate for Inclusion, the Discovery of Truth, and Understanding in Evaluative Theory and Practice (2005)
  edited by Stafford Hood, Rodney Hopson, and Henry Frierson

The Role of Culture and Cultural Context

A Mandate for Inclusion, the Discovery of Truth and Understanding in Evaluative Theory and Practice

Edited by

Stafford Hood
Arizona State University

Rodney Hopson
Duquesne University

and

Henry Frierson
University of North Carolina–Chapel Hill

INFORMATION AGE
PUBLISHING

Greenwich, Connecticut • www.infoagepub.com

Library of Congress Cataloging-in-Publication Data

The role of culture and cultural context : a mandate for inclusion, the
    discovery of truth and understanding in evaluative theory and practice
    / edited by Stafford Hood, Rodney Hopson Duquesne, and Henry
    Frierson.
     p. cm.
    Includes bibliographical references.
    ISBN 1-59311-358-7 (pbk.) – ISBN 1-59311-359-5 (hardcover)
    1. Educational evaluation–Social aspects–United States. 2. Educa-
tional equalization–United States.   I. Hood, Stafford. II. Hopson,
Rodney K. (Rodney Kofi) III. Frierson, Henry T. (Henry Taylor),
1944-   .
    LB2822.75.R66 2005
    379.1'58–dc22

                                                              2005017203

Copyright © 2005 Information Age Publishing Inc.

Printed in the United States of America

CONTRIBUTING AUTHORS

Sofia Aburto   WESTED

Sharon Nelson-Barber   WESTED

Katrina L. Bledsoe   The College of New Jersey

Nona M. Burney   Roosevelt University (Chicago, IL)

Dedra Eatmon   University of North Carolina–Chapel Hill

Henry T. Frierson   University of North Carolina–Chapel Hill

Jennifer C. Greene   University of Illinois at Urbana–Champaign

Melvin Hall   Northern Arizona University

Mary Hermes   University of Minnesota–Duluth

Denice Ward Hood   Northern Arizona University

Stafford Hood   Arizona State University

Rodney Hopson   Duquesne University

Michelle Jay   University of North Carolina–Chapel Hill

Elmima Johnson   National Science Foundation

Karen E. Kirkhart   Syracuse University

Joan LaFrance   Mekinak Consulting

Gaetano Senese   Northern Arizona University

Elise Trumbull   WESTED

Mary E. Weems   John Carroll University

Carolyne J. White   Rutgers University

CONTENTS

CHAPTER 1

INTRODUCTION

This is Where We Stand

Stafford Hood, Rodney Hopson, and Henry Frierson

The contributors to this volume value their apparent differences and celebrate the opportunity to stand on common ground in crafting this volume. We, as editors, openly proclaim our first principle: without nuanced the consideration of cultural context in evaluations conducted within communities of color and/or poverty there can be no good evaluation. We long ago laid to rest the need to seek validation from known and unknown faces to legitimize our work, purpose, or responsibility. We accept and willingly act upon our responsibility as researchers, evaluators, scholars, and socially responsible professionals to serve communities of color and the underserved that have been traditionally disenfranchised in *our* American society. Culturally responsive evaluation is a powerful tool that has not been employed in the evaluation community at large. Moreover, there is a growing knowledge base about the practice of culturally responsive evaluation that can assist us in making our efforts more sensible, robust, and useful. We contend that if evaluators consider and become more responsive to cultural context and adopt strategies that are congruent with cultural understandings, the face of educational evaluation can be profoundly changed for the better.

The Role of Culture and Cultural Context in Evaluation, pages 1–5
Copyright © 2005 by Information Age Publishing

This edited volume does not promise to deliver answers to all, most, or even many of the complex answers facing the evaluation community regarding the role of culture and cultural context in evaluation theory and practice. This is not a scientific undertaking. We are not ready for concerns with prediction, explanation, or control. However, we are ready for serious explorations. Even if the evaluation community cannot articulate the necessary and sufficient conditions for a culturally relevant evaluation, it does know several of the desiderata. Our aim in this volume is to reflect evaluation theory, history, and practice within the context of culture with illustrative examples.

For too long the broad, established evaluation community has either ignored or been reluctant to engage in a meaningful scholarly dialogue about the roles of culture and context in evaluation. Rapidly changing demographics in the United States and the world make our efforts at once daunting and inescapable. We must not continue to dodge the issue of cultural competence and acknowledgment in educational evaluation. We must move forward and the time is *now.* Disagreements about how to approach the issue are welcome. We feel that the evaluation community should assiduously mount efforts to address issues related to training culturally competent evaluators, designing culturally competent evaluations, and enhancing the usefulness of those efforts.

This volume seeks to address select questions drawn from the matrix of the complex issues related to culturally responsive evaluation. We ask, should evaluation be culturally responsive? Is the field heading in the right direction in its attempt to become more culturally responsive? What is culturally responsive evaluation today and what might it become tomorrow? Are there compelling examples of culturally responsive evaluation practice to be emulated? Are culturally responsive evaluations more effective than evaluations without such considerations? What strategies can be pursued to ensure more evaluators of color are trained and become active participants in the evaluation community? Should evaluators who work in communities of color be required to exhibit an acceptable level of cultural competence beyond their technical know-how?

And finally we ask, what should be the nature of training in preparing evaluators with the cultural and technical competence needed to evaluate programs in culturally diverse settings? These are but a few of the right questions to be pursued. There are more, of course. We regard this as firing the first salvo.

We have not come to the thinking we share overnight. A story may illustrate the early beginnings of this volume. About a quarter century ago one of the editors had an early flash of insight regarding cultural competence in educational evaluators. He was conducting an evaluation in the Minneapolis public schools teamed with an older, skillful white evaluator. He recalls being disappointed to see what his colleague seemed to miss when they visited a school, spoke with black principals, and watched instruction in classrooms that served underclass children of color. To complicate matters further, it distressed him to learn what *he* had missed when they compared notes and debriefed after their daily work. Even more perplexing were his colleagues' occasional comments that revealed a clear misunderstanding about aspects of the culture of these youngsters and their responses to life in schools. What was going on here? Three questions came to mind. First, could it be that the universal educational evaluator [one size fits all] was a wrong-headed idea? Second, could it be that the more highly trained evaluator needed more training? Third, could it be that cultural competence and/or incompetence lay at the heart of a successful or unsuccessful educational evaluation?

To bring the story up to date, we feel that the three questions can be answered yes, yes, and yes. Our collective experience now enables us to reject the notion that methodological training alone will suffice for evaluations of educational activities that serve children of the underclass. We have in hand preliminary training modules that show promise of bringing culturally incompetent evaluators up to speed. We have zero tolerance for continuing the current practice of assigning evaluators unaware of the cultural landscape to projects that serve the least-served children of our society (i.e., children of color and those in poverty). This is *not* a matter of race or one ethnic group having exclusive rights or insights because of their family of origin. It *is* a matter of acknowledging who is aware of what and how we can maximize our collective talent, skills and insight to make educational evaluation as effective as possible.

This volume gives the reader a broad view of many issues relating to culturally responsive evaluation. It reveals the contentiousness that underlies shifts in a field. There *is* disagreement. There are vague notions that need further clarification and there *is* unfinished business. Far more important, we feel are the commonalities and clear pictures of what needs to be done and how to do it.

One finds a consistent theme of the need for change in our traditional ways of practicing educational evaluation. One finds universal agreement that sensitivity to cultural context in the conduct of educational evaluation must be met. Our authors provide readers with philosophical justification, stories of practical experience, visions of alternative conceptualizations, and a sense of hope that we are finally ready to both address the issues and redress the shortcomings of evaluation theory and practice as it relates to culturally responsive evaluation.

In Chapter 2, Jennifer C. Greene argues that through the use of practice-centered examples, a conceptualization of evaluation as a public craft and of evaluators as stewards of the public good can enable and support an evaluation practice that serves explicitly inclusive and democratizing aims. Her chapter views such aims of evaluation—specifically the validation of the value and richness of our culturally diverse society—as deserving the highest priority.

In Chapter 3, Karen Kirkhart journeys through the broad arena of validity theory itself to scrutinize culturally bound assumptions and the influence of cultural context on the accuracy of theoretical understandings. The chapter concludes by highlighting the implications of these arguments for the professional training of evaluators and the responsible practice of evaluation.

Melvin Hall and Denice Ward-Hood, in Chapter 4, suggest that especially persuasive communication is a critical element of any culturally responsive evaluation and its relationship with decision making. They demonstrate how communication interacts with cultural issues, and, as a result, why cultural competence ultimately enhances the fidelity of communication for those involved.

Sharon Nelson-Barber, Elise Trumbull, Joan LaFrance, and Sofia Aburto, in Chapter 5, draw from their experiences in indigenous and other sociocultural contexts to provide examples of standards of good practice in the evaluation of culturally diverse communities. Indigenous evaluation experts decry the high level of discontinuity between the assumptions and expectations of many program evaluators and the operational norms of the communities they evaluate. How to resolve such antagonisms is explored.

In Chapter 6, Rodney Hopson and Stafford Hood both contribute and extend notions of culturally responsive evaluation from both a historical and contemporary perspective, giving voice and recognition to the influence of early evaluators of color as well as the implications for the field of evaluation. In their chapter, they also reflect on the current context of evaluation and the extent that it is meeting the needs of communities and persons of color. The chapter also provides another installment to the untold legacy of early African American evaluators, their contributions to evaluation history, theory, and practice.

Carolyne White and Mary Hermes use jazz as a metaphor, in Chapter 7, for understanding the creation and negotiation of a space in between the dualism of western scientific ways of knowing and valuing and traditional Hopi ways of knowing and valuing in their powerful exploration of a culturally responsive evaluation of the Hopi Teachers for Hopi Schools Project.

Gaetano Senese, in Chapter 8, takes the reader on a poignant journey to the Little Singer Navajo Wellness Center, situated in a rural reservation community school near Flagstaff, Arizona. The author worries about the evaluator "selling out" to the dominant culture, which he identifies as rampant capitalism, and the angst he experienced in his attempt to be culturally responsive in his 3-year evaluation efforts.

In Chapter 9, Nona Burney, Mary Weems, and Carolyne White emphasize collaboration and narrative telling in their documentation of an effort in urban school reform. Their innovative approach to cultural responsiveness embraces ethnographic and poetic epistemologies as they explore culturally responsive evaluation.

Katrina L. Bledsoe, in Chapter 10, challenges those who argue that theory-driven evaluations are inherently insensitive to the needs, unique perspectives, and circumstances of ethnic communities. She defends theory-driven approaches to evaluation and assessment as an effective approach to identify and explore the subtleties and nuances unique to communities of color, thus leading to more relevant and focused programming

Dedra Eatmon, Michelle Jay, and Henry Frierson, in Chapter 11, examine perceptions of African American doctoral students who were previous participants in a summer research education program at the University of North Carolina at Chapel Hill. The research program, directed and staffed by African Americans, is aimed primarily at underrepresented minority college students. This portion of the evaluation study examined how the shared cultural and racial background between participants and staff affected the perceptions and experiences as indicated by past participants who enrolled in PhD programs at the university.

In Chapter 12, Elmina Johnson offers an innovative framework for broadening participation in science as well as several evaluation strategies that focus on the use of culture in developing indicators and using nontraditional methods to assess progress and outcomes toward equitable achievement and parity in science disciplines.

Our chapter authors provide the reader with compelling arguments for the adoption of culturally responsive strategies. Equally important are the many practical examples they provide for the enhancement of current educational evaluative practice. The coeditors of this volume are throwing down their collective gauntlet at the educational evaluation community: If you don't know our territory, either work in your own territory or open your mind and heart to matters that heretofore have escaped you. We welcome all sentient human beings in our quest to enhance the power of educational evaluators to become more culturally competent in their practice of educational evaluation. The road ahead is a long one and we have already experienced defeat—but our quest is invincible. We particularly hold dear the interests of our students and junior colleagues who are now entering the profession. This volume is dedicated to them and to others who join our collaborative efforts to change the face of educational evaluation.

CHAPTER 2

EVALUATORS AS STEWARDS OF THE PUBLIC GOOD

Jennifer C. Greene
University of Illinois, Urbana–Champaign

The evaluation of educational and social programs is (nearly) consensually envisioned as a practice intended to contribute to societal improvement and social betterment, to social action and social change, to making the world a better place. Donald Campbell's (1984) vision of an "experimenting society," a society that uses experimentation as the engine of social progress, is anchored in the practical science of evaluation. Lee Cronbach (Cronbach & Associates, 1980) positions evaluation as a practice that can importantly enable society to meaningfully learn about its persistent social problems and how to effectively address them. Ernie House (House & Howe, 1999) locates evaluation as an influential player in inspiring public discourse to be more inclusive and thereby more democratic. And most other evaluators, ancestral and contemporary alike, aim to "do good" in their work—to improve the program or the organization being evaluated, to contribute to wise decision making, to provide enlightenment or illumination of the issues at hand, or to be of service of some other good kind.

So, amidst the diverse topography that characterizes program evaluation today, there is actually a common underlying commitment, shared by most, to doing good. We do not squabble over this shared self-understanding of our work as an important service to society. What we do squabble over is just how best to enact this shared commitment to societal improve-

The Role of Culture and Cultural Context in Evaluation, pages 7–20
Copyright © 2005 by Information Age Publishing

ment or social betterment, to social action or social change. That is, the
form of this commitment, or the character of evaluation's contribution to
societal improvement, is resolutely different in different evaluation
approaches. And at root, these differences are about (a) the political positioning of evaluation in society, or the kind and extent of evaluation's
engagement with the contestations and conflicts that characterize our
contexts, and, in turn, (b) the relational positioning of the evaluator
within the inquiry, or the kind and extent of the evaluator's relationships
with members of the context being studied. These two controversial
dimensions of evaluation practice—the political and the relational—are
the focus of the present discussion.

In particular, I wish to discuss these two dimensions within a vision of
evaluation conducted in the public interest, for the public good. The public interest in this discussion is not construed as a list of policy priorities,
but rather as an emphasis on the quality of public reason and the inclusiveness of public discourse. Adapting Willinsky's (2001) plea for the public
value of educational research to evaluation (substituting evaluation for
educational research in this plea):

> If evaluation is to be a greater part of a thoughtful and informed discussion
> of educational [and social] issues, then it should offer an alternative source
> of public information to the increasing corporate concentration within the
> media and the commercialization of information economies. It should play a
> more dynamic role in leveling the informational playing field of an educa-
> tional [and social policy] politics that is increasingly swayed by interest
> groups.... It should provide touchstones for current debates over...the
> impact of high-stakes testing [the merits of universal health insurance, and
> other critical social issues]. It should fairly serve [to help] redress inequities
> in the availability of educational [and other social] services.... Democratic
> evaluation is about increasing people's ability to participate in their own
> governance...[and] people benefit from the process, it can be said, not just
> in knowledge, but in rights, recognition, justice, and dignity. (p. 9)

That is, evaluation in this vision does not yield to the simplistic demands
of the new public management for unidimensional "scores" on designated
performance indicators, but rather insists upon the complexity and con-
textuality of social phenomena and offers opportunities for engagement
with this complexity—across contexts, value perspectives, and cultural
experiences. Evaluation conducted for the public good, that is, aims to
enlighten the relevant policy conversation and *especially* to include therein
diverse voices, perspectives, and experiences. For it is inarguably in the
public interest in contemporary American society, and indeed in the
broader global society, to engage with our diversity, to learn how to live
with, appreciate, and accept our differences. Isn't a root meaning of

democracy that of understanding and toleration of difference? Doesn't the public good of our society at this moment in history rest crucially on a deep and profound acceptance of difference, differences of all kinds? How many more people need to live wasted lives or die young before we can come to some meaningful and serious acceptance of the "other" as a fellow human being, with equal rights to respect, dignity, and justice?

In this context, a serious engagement with difference requires the rejection of old myths, stereotyped images, and racialized code words like "urban" and "inner city" (Lee, 2003). It also requires rejection of race, ethnicity, culture, social class, and other markers of historical disadvantage as fixed or essentialized categories rather than as multifaceted, situated, dynamic, and socially constructed dimensions of experience and identity (Orellana & Bowman, 2003). Again, extending a discussion of the need to rethink race and ethnicity in educational research to the field of evaluation:

> [We need to] resist simplistic assumptions about the meaning of group membership and develop more nuanced and complex research agendas [and evaluation questions] that work from a basic assumption that human beings always have agency, always have resources, and make meaning of their experience in varied ways.... [We need to disrupt and challenge persistent] folk theories about groups in the human family that are inextricably tied to relationships of power and dominance.... [We need to use] a dynamic view of culture as located in history, in belief systems, and as carried forward through institutional practices [to better understand, respect, and accept the Other]. (Lee, 2003, pp. 3, 4)

Moreover, in the present discussion, what I mean by difference includes both the historical markers of "disadvantage" in our contemporary society—notably, race, ethnicity, class, gender, sexual orientation, able-bodiedness, and cultural traditions—*and* the infinitely astonishing other ways in which human beings are different from one another. As discussed later in the chapter, this broad conceptualization of difference is specifically intended to resist fixed and presumably known or familiar meanings of difference and thereby to strengthen the insistence that the difference be contextually understood and culturally engaged.

In short, I believe that engagement with diversity and difference in evaluation is both a substantive and a moral commitment. It is enacted in what issues we address, what methods we used, what kinds of reports we craft—that is, where we locate our work in society—*and* in who we are as evaluators, where we position ourselves in our work, what kinds of relationships we forge with others, and what we attend to and what matters in those relationships. In this discussion, I elaborate on this vision of evaluation as a public craft in service of the public good. I focus on the two key dimensions of this value-engaged evaluative stance identified above—how evaluation is positioned in society and how the evaluator is positioned in her work. Throughout, I attend to contemporary challenges of diversity and difference, as present in the richly varied cultural and contextual dimensions of our work, for these are of fundamental relevance to the public good in today's troubled world.

COMMITTING EVALUATION TO THE PUBLIC GOOD

There is already a starting point for a vision of evaluation centrally committed to the public good, and that is the evaluation community's "Guiding Principles" for professional, ethical evaluation practice, adopted in 1994 by the American Evaluation Association (http://www.eval.org/Evaluation-Documents/aeaprin6.html). One of these five Guiding Principles states that evaluators have some responsibility for the "general and public welfare." More specifically, "evaluators have obligations that encompass the public interest and good. These obligations are especially important when evaluators are supported by publicly generated funds; but clear threats to the public good should never be ignored in any evaluation. Because the public interest and good are rarely the same as the interests of any particular group (including those of the client or funding agency), evaluators will usually have to go beyond an analysis of particular stakeholder interests when considering the welfare of society as a whole."

Evaluation as a "Public Craft"

In this discussion, I wish to locate our responsibilities to the public good as central to our work, through a positioning of evaluation as a *public craft* and evaluators as *stewards of the public good.* A public craft, from Harry Boyte of the Center for Democracy and Citizenship (2000), is "work that is undertaken for public purposes and in public ways... [it is work that] adds public judgment or wisdom to knowledge... [work that invokes the technical canons of science *and* is] attentive to the local setting ...and to the civic implications of practices" (p. 1). As a public craft, evaluation is not only scientific knowledge and technical skills. It is not only methodological expertise in the service of program administrators or funders or other identified evaluation clients. It does not naively assume that technical rationality alone can answer important human questions or solve important social problems. Rather, evaluation as a public *craft* includes, in addition to a valuing of scientific knowledge, a respect for practitioner knowledge, for folk traditions and the wisdom born of everyday experiences, for the local and practical, for the aesthetic and the humanitarian. Evaluation as a public craft rests on an ethical, professional commitment to a public purpose, a common good. Says Harry Boyte:

> A singular celebration of the scientifically educated expert as the actor or initiator in public affairs marginalizes the amateur, while it produces mainly information and knowledge—neither wisdom nor public judgment. We need a very different and far more civic craft model of professional practice if we are to see any widespread democratic renewal in our time. (p. 3)

Just such a vision of professional practice has been advanced by William Sullivan in his book *Work and Integrity* (1995). This vision emphasizes the civic and public responsibilities of professions as *public* crafts. Sullivan aspires to recover a tradition of civic-mindedness in contemporary American professions, of using our scientific expertise and the power and privilege of our status for the common good, not just for self-interested gain. Sullivan bemoans the technocratic takeover of many professions in the United States during the past century, whereby utilitarian and individualistic ideals stripped professionals of their public responsibilities, leaving only decontextualized, self-interested technical expertise. He presents an eloquent and persuasive argument that by reclaiming their civic and moral agenda, professionals can importantly help to reverse the current unraveling of the social fabric, the decline of social trust, and the fraying of civic bonds. Professionals need to be a part of the democratic civic order, argues Sullivan. They need to recover their commitment to the public good, a commitment that extends beyond technical competence to moral and social issues of trust, equity, and civic cooperation. Genuine professionalism requires engagement with moral and civic aims, as well as technical means to reach those aims.

This argument complements that of Ernie House and Ken Howe (1999), who assert—also convincingly—that evaluation is an intrinsic part of the institutional fabric of public discourse and decision making about public issues. We are among the weavers of this fabric, not just observers or admirers of the weaving.

So, what kind of cloth do we wish to help weave? What kind of weavers do we as educational and social evaluators aspire to be? I agree with Harry Boyte and William Sullivan that we need to think of evaluation as a public craft; we need to endorse a model of civic professionalism for evaluation. This model recognizes and values our technical expertise and our craft knowledge but also locates that expertise as not detached from but rather interwoven into the fabric of our political and civil society, our democratic civic order. This model thereby accords to evaluators, as with other professionals, responsibilities to help constitute our democratic civic order as consonant with our noblest ideals of equity, justice, and freedom—responsibilities, in other words, for the public good.

Evaluation as Engagement with Difference[1]

So, evaluation as a public craft is fully engaged with public issues of contemporary importance because these are vital to our democratic civic order. Among the most critical of contemporary issues in American society are our persistent inequities in economic opportunity and social privilege and the unwillingness or inability of many in our society to seriously redress these inequities—either in the hallways of legislatures or in the pathways of our everyday lives. It is fully recognized in the United States today that most inequities in our society today arise from historical tragedies and exploitations. And it is fully recognized that people with dark skin, a native language other than English, an income below a livable wage, a culture that is not Anglo or western European, a religion that is not Judeo-Christian are "different" from mainstream (white, middle-class) American culture. What is less well recognized is that such differences are themselves historically and culturally situated, and the meaning of difference itself is thus dynamic, evolving, and contextually constructed. To attend to difference and diversity in evaluation is thereby to attend to context in all of its varied cultural richness, to be respectful of and responsive to the unique features of the particular contexts in which our work is located.

Broadly speaking, context refers to the setting within which the program being evaluated, and thus the evaluation, are situated. Context is the site, location, environment, or milieu for a given program. And it is an enormously complex phenomenon. Many programs are implemented in multiple contexts, or in multiple sites, which always differ in some important ways. Most contexts have multiple layers or levels, as in classrooms within schools within districts within communities within states. And, perhaps most challengingly, contexts have multiple strands or dimensions, all of which can be importantly intertwined with the character and quality of a program. These dimensions include (1) the descriptive and demographic character of a setting, in terms of the numbers, characteristics, and diversity of people who inhabit it; (2) the material and economic features of a setting, in terms of the quantity and quality of its physical features (buildings, gathering spaces, resources like books and technology), along with other indicators of material wealth or scarcity; (3) the institutional and organizational climate in a setting, in terms of the character of the organization (agency, public institution, private business) that is administering or implementing the program—its norms, decision-making structures, climate features, and so forth; (4) the interpersonal dimensions of a setting, in terms of the nature of interactions that take place and the norms that frame and guide relationships; (5) the political dynamics of a setting, particularly in terms of contested issues and interests, and in terms of power, influence, and privilege; and certainly (6) the physical, geographic location of a setting, its place.

Sensitivity and responsiveness to context understood this way is of fundamental importance in evaluation that aspires to meaningfully engage with difference, in service of the public good, for two main reasons. First, the very meaning and quality of a given program is embedded in and constituted by its context. Decontextualized questions like "How good is this educational program?" make no sense. Instead, evaluators need to ask questions like "How good is this program for these children in this school and this community at this time?" Definitions of goodness themselves become contextualized; that is, critical features of the context become embedded in or intertwined with meanings of quality and thus with standards or criteria for judgment. And so the program gets judged by how well it responds to these children in this place, rather than asking how well these children succeed in the program. This is a profound reversal of figure and ground (Kushner, 2000).

Second, emphasizing evaluative attention to the cultural, racial, ethnic, linguistic, geographic, gendered, political (and other) dimensions of a program context brings them to the forefront of our work, makes them important and worthy of our collective attention, signals the urgency of their place in public debate. Contextually responsive and engaged evaluation, that is, insists that educational and social programs be judged, at least in part, by how well they respect and advance the well-being of children, youth, and families who are traditionally ill-served by our educational and social systems. Definitions of goodness acknowledge the political inherency of evaluative judgments, and evaluation becomes accountable to social justice and equity; evaluations get judged by how well they advance these democratic ideals (Greene, Millett, & Hopson, 2004).

In short, evaluation conducted in service of the public good is evaluation that is fully engaged with difference and diversity, that privileges attention to what differences are manifest in a given context and how those differences matter to effective pedagogy, to quality health care, to meaningful employment, to fairness in court, and so on. This engagement is enacted in (1) the ways in which program quality is judged and (2) the ways in which evaluation itself is judged—ways that centrally highlight and legitimize diversity in context, which again refers to both historical conditions of advantage and disadvantage in our society, as well as the abundantly magnificent other ways in which humans are different from one another. (These multiple meanings of diversity will be further discussed in the next section.)

THE RELATIONAL RESPONSIBILITIES OF EVALUATORS

It is not enough, however, for evaluators committed to the public good to strive to heighten the quality of public debate about important public issues, notably by insisting upon attention to persistent injustices in our society and by ensuring that multiple, diverse understandings, experiences, stances, and claims are centrally legitimized and featured in the debate. For this is but the political face of evaluation, positioned on the big stage with concerns framed in macro terms of justice, equality, and democracy. Of equal if not even more importance is the relational character of evaluation—how we as evaluators are present in the contexts in which we work, the social, moral, and interactive dimensions of our work. For it is in these relationships that the political and value commitments of our work are importantly practiced and therefore realized, or not. Our work as evaluators is conducted in specific contexts with specific people, in places and spaces we share with them, even if just temporarily; so our "outrage for injustice must be balanced with renewing relationships of care for others— human and non-human [namely, ecological]" in the places that we share (Gruenewald, 2003, p. 10).

In this way of thinking, the character of the actual practice of evaluation—of what we do in the places in which we work—helps to constitute relational norms, values, and ideals in that place, notably about status, power, and privilege; trust, reciprocity, and caring; respect, tolerance, and acceptance. This relational enactment of evaluation refers to the relationships, roles, and interactions that take place as the evaluation is conducted—who speaks and who doesn't, how self and other are negotiated and constructed (Fine, 1994; Fine et al., 2000), where power and privilege are located, and so forth. More profoundly, in this relational view of the practice of evaluation, the very knowledge that is generated in evaluation—our results, our findings, our judgments of program quality—are understood to be generated *within and by* a particular set of evaluative relationships and interactions, and thus, to a significant degree, are actually constituted by these relationships and interactions. What we do and how we interact in a setting matters to what we learn. These relationships become constitutive of our evaluation findings.

So meaningfully engaging with difference in evaluation, in service of the public good, critically involves how we position ourselves in our work and the relational dimensions of that positioning. I am not speaking here about being respectful of interview respondents simply because that is a good way to get good data. That is but an instrumentalist view of evaluative relationships. What I am striving to probe and articulate is much deeper. It's about being respectful of interview respondents because I can learn important things from such a relationship, because a mutually respectful relationship generates different kinds of knowing than one that is not, because it is the right thing to do (Schwandt, 2002), because I wish to live in a society where such relationships are the norm.

Next, I offer some initial ideas about this relational dimension of evaluation, as germane to evaluation practice that is engaged with difference, in service of the public good. These ideas pertain first to the positioning of the evaluator and then to the meanings of difference.

"Visiting" and "Listening Well" in Our Evaluation Practice

This first set of ideas probes what it means to engage with difference in evaluation on the ground. The ideas come from the influential 20th-century Jewish philosopher Hannah Arendt, particularly her ideas about the intersections of political plurality or diversity and collective action for the common good.[2] A key question posed in her work is, How can we act collectively in the face of plurality without erasing it? How is common action even possible, given "the simultaneous presence of innumerable perspectives and aspects in which the common world presents itself and for which no common measurement or denominator can ever be devised"? For "though the common world is the common meeting ground of all, those who are present have different locations in it, and the location of one can no more coincide with the location of another than the location of two objects" (Arendt, 1958, p. 57, cited in Biesta, 2001, p. 395).

In response to this challenge, Arendt attends to the interconnections between action and political judgment, for common action requires good judgment. Arendt's views on what constitutes good judgment strongly affirm the importance of diversity.

> One judges as a member of a community. . . . Good judgment for Arendt is not a matter of objective knowledge or of subjective opinion, but a result of intersubjectivity; becoming a good judge depends largely on one's capacity to consider other viewpoints of the same experience, "to look upon the same world from another's standpoint, to see the same in very different and frequently opposing aspects." (Arendt, 1968, p. 51, cited Coulter & Wiens, 2002, p. 17)

For Arendt, a respect for plurality is thus a necessary attribute of good judgment. Arendt rejects both pluralism-without-judgment, or unfettered diversity, and judgment-without-pluralism, or judgments made outside the web of human diversity (Biesta, 2001).

And so, to develop good judgment, to develop an appreciation for and understanding of the viewpoints of others, Arendt advocates "visiting" and "listening well" to others. These concepts offer inspiration for evaluative engagement with difference.

> Visiting involves constructing stories of an event from each of the plurality of perspectives that might have an interest in telling it and imagining how I would respond as a character in a story very different from my own. (Disch, 1994, p. 158, cited in Biesta, 2001, p. 397)

> Visiting involves carefully listening to the perspectives of others because "the more people's standpoints I have present in my mind while I am pondering a given issue,...the better I can [judge]." (Arendt, 1968, p. 241, cited in Coulter & Wiens, 2002, p. 18)

> Visiting is not the same as *parochialism*, which is not to visit at all but to stay home. Visiting is also different from *tourism*, which is "to ensure that you will have all the comforts of home even as you travel." And further, visiting should also be distinguished from *empathy*, which, as a form of "assimilation-ism," is "forcibly to make yourself at home in a place that is not your home by appropriating its customs." (Disch, 1994, p. 159, cited in Biesta, 2002, p. 397, emphasis in original)

> ...Empathy, that is, denies both the situatedness of one's own seeing and thinking and that of the other. (Biesta, 2002, 398)

> Visiting, in contrast, involves respecting diverse standpoints through dialogue with other people, listening to their stories, and relating to their uniqueness without collapsing these divergent views into a generalized amalgam...[without essentializing them, *and* without losing your own unique standpoint].(Coulter & Wiens, 2002, p. 18)

> Visiting is therefore *not* to see through the eyes of someone else, but to see *with your own eyes* from a position that is not your own...in a story very different from [your] own. (Biesta, 2001, p. 398, emphasis in original)

In sum, for Arendt, good judgment rests on visiting with diverse others, listening well to them, and learning about their lived experiences from your own eyes but within their stories in their spaces and places. Good judgment, in turn, enables meaningful collective action for the common good, without either erasing or devaluing diversity. For evaluators who wish to engage with diversity and difference, as an enactment of their commitment to the public good, these ideas of Arendt are both inspirational and practical. They offer a vision of the kinds of relationships we can forge in our evaluation practice and the relational values and commitments we can thereby advance. And they provide tangible metaphors as starting points for our practical work.

Beyond Categorical Definitions of Difference

If we engage with difference in our evaluative work by visiting and listening well, in the spaces and places experienced by those we are evaluating, I believe we will hear the full symphony of timbres and tones, melodies and rhythms that comprise the human family. And if our ears are wide open and we are truly listening, we will hear not just the expected songs and sounds, not just the violins singing like angels or the tambourines dancing with joy. We will also hear the infinite interpretations and improvisations made by this orchestra or this band or this singer in this place at this time. We will not rely on understanding difference only through existing concepts and categories, thereby contributing to their continued reification and essentializing. We will experience and come to appreciate the particular character of human (musical) diversity in this particular place, in this unique context. And we will come to know that such diversity is fundamentally created anew in context.

So, the meanings of difference and diversity in this vision of evaluation conducted in service of the public good are at root multiplistic and contextual. They are defined in ways that both acknowledge and honor, as well as challenge and disrupt existing social categories that mark historical disadvantage. Clearly the process of social categorization—sorting and labeling people by race, ethnicity, class, gender, age, able-bodiedness, and so forth—distorts the meanings of diversity and often converts good intentions into prejudicial actions. And it is naive to think that a history of exclusion can be overcome simply by identifying and labeling those who have been excluded and giving them "voice" (Schick, 2002). Yet, to simply erase or ignore such meanings of diversity is also politically naive, and, moreover, it devalues the profound injustices suffered by those whose rights have been seized in the past. So, some of the meanings of difference to be engaged are these social categories—yet, as noted above, not as essentialized ways of being in the world, but rather as multifaceted, situated, dynamic, and socially constructed dimensions of experience and identity. To illustrate, *the* African American experience in the United States today is anchored in the shared ancestry of slavery and the continuing racism of our society, but is otherwise differentially mediated by all aspects of context and by the interaction of context with the unique characteristics of each black American today. So, there are as many African American experiences as there are African Americans. To meaningfully engage with difference then is to listen well to the story of each African American and to listen for its own contextualized particularities.

Moreover, in this vision of evaluation conducted in the service of the public good, it is fully recognized that there are other important dimensions of difference in human experience, dimensions that extend well beyond these social categories into the infinite constellations of character-istics, abilities, and aspirations that make each human unique. To meaning-fully engage with difference, therefore, is to see beyond, within, and through social categories to that person's shyness, wit, spirituality, creativ-ity, kindness, and the next person's and the next and the next.

In short, by intentionally conceptualizing difference as socially con-structed markers of experience and identity *and* as the infinite and won-drous other ways that people are different from one another, these markers of historical disadvantage can be both honored and challenged. And by visiting with others in their own places and listening well to their own stories, evaluators can convey substantial respect for these stories, car-ing about their significance to the teller, and acceptance of the dignity and worthiness of the teller. And these are surely among the most important and powerful of the evaluator's relational possibilities.

ASSUMING EVALUATIVE STEWARDSHIP
FOR THE PUBLIC GOOD

The public good, specifically the quality and inclusiveness of public debate about important public issues, is precious enough to compel the caretaking of all citizens. In a strong participatory democracy, the public good is indeed constituted by the collective actions of the caretakers (Bar-ber, 1984).

This discussion identifies the public good as central to the public craft of program evaluation, particularly the evaluation of publicly funded edu-cational and social programs. And in the discussion, I highlight the urgency of engaging meaningfully with difference as of priority impor-tance in evaluators' advancement of the public good. I further underscore the importance of enacting these commitments in the micropolitics of our work on the ground, in the relational dimensions of our evaluation activi-ties. We are just as responsible for the character of the relationships we establish as for the purposes and interests served by our work; these rela-tionships in fact importantly contribute to such purposes and interests. And finally, I offer some initial thinking about establishing evaluative rela-tionships that meaningfully engage with difference in service of the public good, namely, Hannah Arendt's notions of visiting and listening well to the wondrous diversity that is the human family—a diversity marked indelibly by social categories but categories with vastly different hues in different contexts and places, a diversity enriched by all of the other ways each of our life journeys through this world is unique.

NOTES

1. Many of these ideas were inspired by the culturally and contextually respon-
    sive evaluation model featured in the Howard University Evaluation Train-
    ing Institute, launched in June 2003 with support from the National Science
    Foundation.
2. Hannah Arendt fled Nazi Germany in 1933 and went first to France and
    then to the United States. Arendt's post-war work can be viewed as an effort
    to understand how and why the Holocaust could have happened. Much of
    this discussion rests on the interpretive work of Coulter and Wiens (2002)
    and Biesta (2001).

REFERENCES

Arendt, H. (1958). *The human condition.* Chicago: University of Chicago Press.

Arendt, H. (1968). *Between past and future: Eight exercises in political thought.* New
York: Penguin Books.

Barber, B. (1984). *Strong democracy: Participatory politics for a new age.* Berkeley: University of California Press.

Biesta, G. J. J. (2001). How difficult should education be? *Educational Theory, 51*(4),
385–400.

Boyte, H. C. (2000). *Professions as public crafts.* A background paper prepared for the
working conference on New Information Commons, Racine, WI.

Campbell, D. T. (1984). Can we be scientific in applied social science? In R. F. Con-
ner, D. G. Altman, & C. Jackson (Eds.), *Evaluation studies review annual* (Vol. 9,
pp. 26–48). Thousand Oaks, CA: Sage.

Coulter, D., & Wiens, J. R. (2002). Educational judgment: Linking the actor and
the spectator. *Educational Researcher, 31*(4), 15–25.

Cronbach, L. J., & Associates. (1980). *Toward reform of program evaluation.* San Francisco: Jossey-Bass.

Disch, L. J. (1994). *Hannah Arendt and the limits of philosophy.* Ithaca, NY: Cornell
Univiersity Press.

Fine, M. (1994). Working the hyphens: Reinventing self and other in qualitative
research. In N. K. Denzin & Y. S. Lincoln (Eds.), *Handbook of qualitative research.*
Thousand Oaks, CA: Sage.

Fine, M., et al. (2000). For whom? Qualitative research, representations, and social
responsibilities. In N. K. Denzin & Y. S. Lincoln (Eds.), *Handbook of qualitative
research* (2nd ed.). Thousand Oaks, CA: Sage.

Greene, J. C., Millet, R., & Hopson, R. (in press). Evaluation as a democratizing
practice. In M. T. Braverman, N. A. Constantine, & J. K. Slater (Eds.), *Foundations and evaluation: Contexts and practices for effective philanthropy* (pp. 96–118).
San Francisco: Jossey-Bass.

Gruenewald, D.A. (2003). The best of both worlds: A critical pedagogy of place.
Educational Researcher, 32(4), 3–12.

House, E. R., & Howe, K. R. (1999). *Values in evaluation and social research.* Thousand
Oaks, CA: Sage.

Kushner, S. (2000). *Personalizing evaluation*. London: Sage.

Lee, C. D. (2003). Why we need to re-think race and ethnicity in educational research. *Educational Researcher, 32*(5), 3–5.

Orellena, M. F., & Bowman, P. (2003). Cultural diversity research on learning and development: Conceptual, methodological, and strategic considerations. *Educational Researcher, 32*(5), 26–32.

Schick, N. (2002). When the subject is difference: Conditions of voice in policy-oriented qualitative research. *Qualitative Inquiry, 8*(5), 632–651.

Schwandt, T. A. (2002). *Evaluation practice reconsidered*. New York: Peter Lang.

Sullivan, W. M. (1995). *Work and integrity: The crisis and promise of professionalism in America*. New York: HarperBusiness.

Willinsky, J. (2001). The Strategic Education Research Program and the public value of research. *Educational Researcher, 30*(1), 5–14.

CHAPTER 3

THROUGH A CULTURAL LENS

Reflections on Validity and Theory in Evaluation

Karen E. Kirkhart
Syracuse University

Cultural diversity has become a critical issue for program evaluation in the United States due to population demographics in general and to the nature of the target populations of many educational and social programs in particular. Marked differences among the personal characteristics, backgrounds, and belief systems of the *consumers* of human service programs, the *providers* of human service programs, and the *evaluators* of human service programs make understanding the impact of culture a priority concern. Culture impacts all aspects of evaluation—from the formation of evaluation questions to the selection of data sources; from data gathering methods and data analysis techniques to strategies for communicating findings. As with all knowledge, evaluative understandings and judgments are culturally contextualized. To establish the validity of such understandings and judgments, cultural diversity must be explicitly addressed. Appreciations of diverse cultural perspectives strengthen validity; they must be expanded and deepened. Biases embedded in cultural diversity threaten validity; they must be exposed and interrupted (Fine & Powell, 1997).

The Role of Culture and Cultural Context in Evaluation, pages 21–39
Copyright © 2005 by Information Age Publishing

In evaluation as in measurement, validity is *the* most important construct (Linn, 1997). It references the accuracy and limits of understandings; it guides what can and cannot appropriately be concluded from evaluative inquiry. Validity addresses the fundamental correctness of evaluation. A key dimension of validity involves appreciating the culturally bound nature of understandings and judgments. Valid evaluation presumes an understanding of culture and culturally based discrimination as well as the ability to identify appropriate and inappropriate considerations of cultural context in evaluation's epistemological, methodological, and theoretical foundations, professional practices, and standards and guiding principles.

VALIDITY THROUGH A CULTURAL LENS

Though culture belongs at the center of any conversation about validity, in practice it has often been excluded. Kirkhart (1995b) introduced the term *multicultural validity* to move considerations of culture to the center of validity arguments. Multicultural validity refers to the correctness or authenticity of understandings across multiple, intersecting cultural contexts (Kirkhart, 1995b). It focuses attention on how well evaluation captures meaning across dimensions of cultural diversity, and it scrutinizes the accuracy or trustworthiness of the ensuing judgments of merit and worth. Like validity in general, it is a multifaceted construct, permitting one to explore the many ways in which culture impacts meaning and understanding. Multicultural validity may be argued and understood in terms of methodology, consequences, interpersonal relationships, lived experience, and theory (Kirkhart, 2004). Figure 3.1 summarizes the five justifications. Each justificatory perspective directs attention to a different type of evidence to support or challenge validity. Methodological justifications of multicultural validity direct attention to the validity of measurement and design elements; consequential justifications examine the impacts or sequelae of evaluation to reflect on validity; interpersonal justifications scrutinize relationships among the researcher(s) and the researched; experiential justifications examine validity in terms of the lived experience of program participants; theoretical justifications of multicultural validity scrutinize theoretical foundations. This chapter explores the relationships among culture, validity, and theory and examines how culture may support or threaten theoretical justifications of multicultural validity of program evaluation.

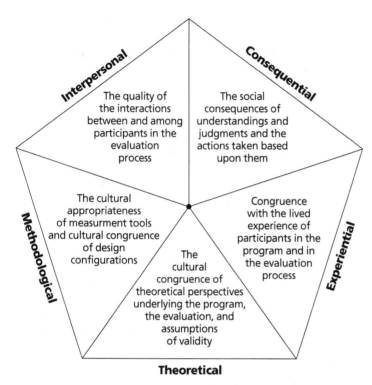

Figure 3.1.   Five justifications of multicultural validity.

THINKING MULTICULTURALLY ABOUT THEORY

Theory is a powerful source of influence on evaluation practice (Lipsey & Pollard, 1989; Weiss, 1995). Theory guides method. Before developing "culturally anchored methodology" (Hughes, Seidman, & Williams, 1993), one needs to pause to articulate and examine the foundational theory or theories in which methods are grounded. Similarly, to appreciate cultural influences on validity, one must scrutinize the theory that guides the practice. While absence of theory may weaken multicultural validity, the presence of theory is no assurance of multicultural validity, because the theory itself may be culturally biased. Bias in theory is less frequently examined than bias in method, yet both are tied explicitly to evaluation practice.

The importance of theory stems from its ability to guide evaluators, to steer program developers and providers, and to set the standards of scientific credibility. Accordingly, this chapter addresses three domains of theory: evaluation theory, program theory, and validity theory. The interactions of culture and validity within these three domains are presented as three propositions, each of which is justified and discussed. The propositions are grounded in the central argument that understanding how theory engages culture is a prerequisite to strengthening theoretical justifications of multicultural validity. The chapter closes with nine recommendations for scrutinizing theory through a cultural lens.

CULTURE, VALIDITY, AND EVALUATION THEORY

Evaluation theory guides epistemological, methodological, and practical choices; therefore, it is critical to question how well evaluation theory addresses dimensions of cultural context and conversely to reflect on how culturally biased assumptions may enter evaluation theory. Good theory suggests epistemological options. Good theory suggests the circumstances in which certain methods should be chosen over others, ways in which methods should be sequenced or combined, and costs and benefits of different methods, including the types of questions that are best addressed via a particular strategy. Good theory suggests who participates in evaluation via what roles. Simply put, it lays the foundation for evaluation practice. In evaluation theory, it is important to scrutinize how culture is framed and incorporated, if, in fact, it is addressed at all. Major sources in the field note the connection of theory to the background and worldviews of the various authors and proponents; however, none explicitly addresses cultural context (e.g., Alkin, 2004; Fitzpatrick, Sanders & Worthen, 2004; Shadish, Cook & Leviton, 1991; Stufflebeam, 2001). This is an omission that needs to be addressed.

> **Proposition 1:** *Validity is enhanced to the extent that evaluation theory guides practitioners in selecting epistemologies, methods, and procedures appropriate to a well-informed consideration of cultural diversity and thoughtful reflection on potential culturally bound biases. Validity is threatened to the extent that culture is ignored or diversity variables are included as simplistic, atheoretical stereotypes.*

In their classic text on evaluation theory, Shadish and colleagues (1991) define *theory* as "a body of knowledge that organizes, categorizes, describes, predicts, explains, and otherwise aids in understanding and controlling a topic" (p. 30). Evaluation theory provides a logical framework for the evaluation enterprise, defining what is included and excluded as necessary and legitimate components, controlling what is left in or out of a definition of evaluation. The key issue here is how the boundaries of the topic are defined and legitimated and how the nature of the enterprise is understood. There is no single, universal evaluation theory; rather, multiple theoretical perspectives are available for evaluators' reflection and guidance. Each casts its own worldview on program evaluation. Shadish and colleagues see evaluation in terms of causal processes, Scriven (1991) in terms of logic and values, Schwandt (1997) in terms of practical hermeneutics, House (1980, 1993) in terms of social justice, Fetterman (1994a, 1994b; Fetterman, Kaftarian, & Wandersman, 1996) as empowerment, Mertens (1998) as emancipation, Smith (1987) in terms of justification of claims, Greene (1995) in terms of social advocacy, Preskill and Torres (2000) as transformational learning, Hood (2001) and Thomas and Stevens (2004) in terms of culture and context, and Patton (1997) in terms of managerial support, to illustrate from among current theorists. How the nature of evaluation is understood—the language, metaphors, symbols, images, and arguments—sets the context for defining and operationalizing constructs such as race, culture, and power and gender (Hopson, 2000). Some theories "presuppose fairness" (Thomas, 1997) and do not elaborate on it, while others explicitly address issues of power, privilege, and social justice. But these constructs themselves are not ones about which there is universal agreement.

The influence of evaluation theory and culture is bidirectional; culture both impacts and is impacted by evaluation theory. First, culture shapes theory in evaluation through the historical and cultural contexts of theory development, including the theorists themselves. Evaluators' personal characteristics, orientations and identifications, life histories, academic training, and cultural experiences are inescapably woven into the theoretical understandings they put forth for consideration. Issues of culture and evaluator voice are visible at the level of individual theorists (Alkin, 2004), and in the ways in which entire societies have been theorized (Smith, 1999). For example, Scheurich and Young (1997) trace racial bias affecting research from the individual level through a hierarchy that progresses through institutional racism, societal racism, and civilizational racism. They argue that *epistemological racism,* a construct relevant to thoughtful reflection on evaluation theory, is grounded in the broadest, civilizational level and must be understood in those terms to be productively addressed.[1] No evaluation theory is context-free, but among current evaluation theory the dominance of white social history must be acknowledged and understood as a source of cultural bias (Hood, 2001).

Second, theory shapes cultural understanding. Evaluation theory offers a framework for addressing cultural context in the evaluation of social programs. With each theoretical perspective comes a potential window on cultural influence. For example, Shadish and colleagues' (1991) version of evaluation theory is primarily interested in describing causal processes that mediate a relationship. In their worldview, the ideal (never achievable) evaluation theory would describe and justify why certain evaluation practices lead to particular kinds of results across situations that evaluators confront. It would (a) clarify the activities, processes, and goals of evaluation; (b) explicate relationships among evaluative activities and the processes and goals they facilitate; and (c) empirically test propositions to identify and address those that conflict with research or other critically appraised knowledge about evaluation. (pp. 30–31)

Consistent with their view of the fundamental purpose of program evaluation theory, they define the scope of evaluation theory in terms of five theoretical bases: social programming, knowledge construction, valuing, knowledge use, and evaluation practice. Each of these theory bases can then be scrutinized for how it may support valid treatment of cultural diversity in evaluation or how it may constrain understandings and contribute to bias and discrimination. For example, under the value component of evaluation theory, Shadish and colleagues address the need to "make value problems explicit, deal with them openly, and produce a sensitive analysis of the value implications of programs" (p. 47). They open a window to discussions of power and privilege, although the culturally bound nature of values is only touched upon, and no dimensions of diversity are illustrated or explored. In their discussion of values, they privilege descriptive theory (theory that describes values without advocating one as best) over prescriptive theory (theory that advocates the primacy of particular values), defending descriptive theories as "more consistent than prescriptive theories with the social and political organization of the United States, which is based upon fostering a pluralism of values that compete against each other in social and political arenas" (p. 47). One can then trace the implications of this position for the multicultural validity of their evaluation theory. If values are to be sorted out in the social and political arena, then those arenas themselves must be scrutinized with respect to cultural bias. The other components of their theoretical model may be similarly examined (Kirkhart, 1995a).

The central point of this argument is that within any theoretical framework, one must scrutinize implications for multicultural validity. If the theoretical basis of an evaluation were changed, then the parameters of the enterprise, the types of cultural bias perceived, the relationship of diversity to evaluative judgments of social programs, and the methods deemed appropriate would all shift. Evaluation theory provides powerful lenses, magnifying certain aspects of evaluation, minimizing or even filtering out others. Contrast the role of utilization of results, for example, in the theories of Patton (1997), who views it as integral to the enterprise, and Scriven (1991), who views it as optional to undesirable, depending on context.

In summary, evaluation theory is impacted by culturally bound bias ranging from individual to civilizational levels. Theory also defines frameworks within which evaluation can address cultural diversity and reflect on issues of power and privilege. Evaluation theory is the first domain in which culture and validity interact. The second domain is program theory.

CULTURE, VALIDITY, AND PROGRAM THEORY

Program theory describes causal linkages presumed to exist between program activities and intended outcomes. It guides program design and implementation as well as program evaluation. Program theory can illuminate program operations and hidden assumptions, potentially including assumptions about culture. Two major sources of program theory are social science and practice wisdom, each of which is subject to cultural bias. Therefore, program theory raises two distinct validity issues.

Proposition 2A: *Validity is strengthened to the extent that program theory is guided by empirical social science research that itself addressed cultural diversity in a valid manner. Conversely, validity is undermined by the adoption of social science models as frameworks for practice or evaluation despite inappropriate or inadequate attention to culture.*

First, program theory may originate in social science (i.e., the logic underlying a social program or its intervention components may come from discipline-based, empirically tested social science theory). It is appropriate to strive to build upon prior knowledge; if relevant social science theory exists, it can form a solid groundwork for program intervention. However, three potential threats to multicultural validity emerge from this strategy. First, the original research may have been conducted from a majority perspective that at best severely limits and at worst severely distorts the conclusions. Here, the desire to ground program theory in "proven" social science knowledge bases opens up a wealth of challenges to the multicultural validity of those understandings. The uncritical use of social science theory proliferates majority viewpoints that may systematically exclude cultural standpoints. Evaluators must be trained to examine the assumptions underlying social science theory and the methods previously used to develop and test that theory before relying upon the social sciences as a firm foundation for program theory. The first potential threat to the validity of social-science-based program theory lies within the research itself.

The second potential validity threat lies in the translation of social science to social programs and the fact that social science theory does not lend itself to being used "off the shelf," as Chen and Rossi (1983, p. 285) acknowledge. This threat includes, but extends beyond, traditional concerns with the generalizability of social science theory to persons different from the populations studied. It also addresses the adaptations that are inherent in the translation of theory to practice. The modifications may involve subtle shifts of emphasis or operationalization, or major recasting or selective use of theory components. The application contexts of concern may be the social problems themselves or the programs that are designed to address them. In the first instance, the translation of social science theory into program policy and procedures must be scrutinized with respect to assumptions underlying the definition of the social problem and plausible programmatic solutions. To what extent, for example, do middle-class Anglocentric understandings of a social problem lead to selective use of social science theory? How do medical models of aging relate to the life experiences of octogenarians? How does a plausible solution or intervention strategy make the leap from controlled environment to culturally contextualized service delivery setting, replete with resource constraints and implementation challenges? As social science theory is translated into program theory, what is lost or gained in the translation? This is the second point at which cultural diversity may influence social-science-based program theory.

The third point of influence relates specifically to the use of social science theory in the practice of *evaluation*. The best use of social science in developing program theory is identified early and used to guide the program itself. However, it is sometimes the case that evaluators peruse social science literature to design a theory-based evaluation of an essentially atheoretical program. In addition to the validity threats identified above, this runs the additional risk of creating a "straw" program theory for purposes of evaluation that bears no connection to either the intention or the reality of the program providers. Potential bias inherent in this translation may either go unexamined and unrecognized or be recognized and superficially acknowledged yet fail to influence evaluation practice. Either way, cultural bias has entered the evaluation process via the use of social-science-based program theory, undermining the multicultural validity of the evaluation.

An alternate source of program theory is program providers and other stakeholders. Local theory has the advantage of intimate knowledge of program realities and operations and can potentially offer greater attention to the program's cultural context. These advantages notwithstanding, cultural bias may enter program microtheory through either the content of local knowledge or through the process of theory construction itself.

Proposition 2B: *To the extent that program theory is guided by practice wisdom grounded in the cultural traditions and beliefs of program participants, validity is supported. However, when practice wisdom itself is prejudicial, validity is threatened.*

There are two distinct paths through which culture shapes local theory. First, culture enters program microtheory through the *content* of what key players bring to the table. Second, culture enters theory development through the *process* of development itself. In the first case, local theory reflects the knowledge and understanding of persons close to the programs—designers, administrators, providers—regarding how the program operates or is intended to operate. Many models of evaluation in fact privilege this source of program theory over others (Fetterman, 1994a; Guba & Lincoln, 1989; Patton, 1997). There is an implicit—and sometimes explicit—assumption that grounding theory in the understandings of local stakeholders is necessarily more genuine, more multiculturally valid and less biased. But there is a danger here that often goes unaddressed. What happens to program theory when "common knowledge" is based on ignorance, misunderstanding, or lack of historical context of cultural standpoints? For example, validity of program theory is threatened when "local wisdom" is racist or otherwise prejudicial (Stanfield, 1993). How this is addressed (or not addressed) leads to a second way in which culture shapes local theory, and that is through the development process itself.

Examining how culture affects the process of developing local theory shifts attention to the broader arenas of participation and group dynamics. At least two issues can be highlighted here. First, one must consider who is invited or included in the conversations surrounding program theory. This includes personal characteristics, but it also includes issues of stakeholder role and privilege. Most discussions of program theory development recognize the need to include a diverse cross-section of providers (e.g., program designers, administrators, middle managers, and direct service providers); however, consumers are rarely represented in the dialog. Madison's (1992) advocacy for primary inclusion of consumers in the evaluation process applies equally to the development of local program theory. Second, one must reflect carefully on how the interaction is orchestrated or managed. The extent to which the interactions are structured, and by whom, are key parameters of the formal process. Mathie and Greene (1997) mark an important distinction between creating opportunities for meaningful engagement and treating diversity as token representation. But issues of power and privilege also influence the interactions and communications informally in terms of who is heard. For example, Bell (1997) asserts that Blacks are often listened to but not believed unless speaking White scripts.

In applying program theory to the development of comprehensive community initiatives for children and families, Weiss (1995) discusses the process through which local theory may be developed.

> An important step will be to discuss the theories that practitioners and residents engaged in community-building activities actually have in mind as they

go about their practice. Often their theories will be implicit rather than explicit and it may take time for them to think through their assumptions about how their work will lead to the effects they seek. Nevertheless, *the feasibility of theory-based evaluation rests on their ability to articulate their assumptions (or assent to someone else's formulation)*, and it is important to see how well this phase of the task can be done. (p. 82, emphasis added)

Issues of power and privilege imbedded in the development of local theory are clearly visible in this passage. There is a vast difference between articulating one's own assumptions and assenting to someone else's formulation, and the validity of the resulting theory hangs in the balance.

In summary, program theory provides a window for viewing the logic and assumptions that undergrid human service programs. What it reveals must be scrutinized to identify and challenge cultural bias. This demands an attitude of vigilance that is equally critical of social-science-based theory and local theory. Cultural bias may be present in either program theory content or the process of theory development. These are complex, difficult issues that merit the evaluation profession's most thoughtful attention; inattention leaves program theory vulnerable to bias and distortion, undermining multicultural validity.

CULTURE, VALIDITY, AND VALIDITY THEORY

Finally, validity theory itself must be examined reflexively. Validity theory provides rules for judging the accuracy of knowledge claims and data-based inferences as well as judging the worth of their applications. Validity theory sets the parameters of what is to be included and excluded under the rubric of validity and how the multiple dimensions or facets of validity fit together. The scope of what should be included under the umbrella of validity or validation has been much debated. Consistent with the argument that follows, this chapter adopts an inclusive definition of validity, as *an overall judgment of the adequacy and appropriateness of evaluation-based inferences and actions and their respective consequences.*

Proposition 3:   *Validity is strengthened to the extent that validity theory provides a broad framework for examining the accuracy of understandings across cultural differences, and promotes reflection on bias, misunderstandings and assumptions born of majority privilege. The validity of evaluation is threatened to the extent that validity theory is narrowly construed, excluding dialogues about social consequences.*

Proposition 3 is supported by two related arguments. The first argument refers to the inclusiveness of the definition of validity, while the second concerns the culturally bound nature of validity itself as a social construction. First, consider culture in relation to the scope of the definition of validity itself. Validity occupies a privileged status as "the most fundamental consideration in developing and evaluating tests" (American Educational Research Association, American Psychological Association, & National Council on Measurement in Education, 1999, p. 9). To retain that position, it must continue to evolve to incorporate the considerations essential to determining the correctness of our understandings and actions. Nowhere is the need for an inclusive definition of validity more apparent than in the practice of program evaluation. Consider three illustrations of such inclusion: inclusion of alternate epistemologies, of actions and their consequences, and of social justice.

First, validity theory must be inclusive in its attention to alternate epistemologies. Epistemological racism and other bias imbedded within traditional methods of inquiry has led to calls for alternate epistemologies (Gordon, Miller, & Rollock, 1990; Scheurich & Young, 1997; Stanfield, 1993). These calls have been answered both within and outside of the evaluation community by the creation of alternative epistemologies, including but not limited to epistemology grounded in race and ethnic standpoints, feminist theory and queer theory (see, e.g., Alcoff & Potter, 1993; Fetterman, et al., 1996; Guba & Lincoln, 1989; Harding, 1998; Jagose, 1996; Kershaw, 1992; Ladner, 1973; LaFrance, 2003; Parker, 2004; Seigart & Brisolara, 2002; Smith, 1999; Sullivan, 2003). The validity of these new epistemologies must then be examined in its own right. To do so requires an expanded definition of validity, however, since the alternative epistemologies are based on arguments that fall outside of (and in some cases explicitly oppose) traditional definitions. In this sense, considerations of culture open up the construct of validity. Addressing culture within validity requires a construct capacious enough to honor and build upon traditional concepts plus embrace alternative paradigms, including those previously marginalized (Rosaldo, 1993).

Second, validity theory must be inclusive in terms of attention to actions and the consequences of those actions. Invalid, prejudicial inferences drawn from data are certainly a concern, but one must also consider the actions taken based upon inferences and the consequences of those actions, both of which may have profound implications for underrepresented populations. Cronbach (1971) explicitly included within the scope of validity decisions and actions based on test scores as well as descriptive interpretations, noting that a decision is a choice between courses of action. Similarly, Messick (1981) explicitly included actions as the object of validation, defining test validity as "an overall evaluative judgment of both the adequacy and the appropriateness of both inferences and actions derived from test scores," a definition reiterated in subsequent work (Messick, 1988, 1989a, 1989b, 1995). Applied to validity of program evaluation, this means that in considering how cultural diversity interacts with validity, one must examine not only the interpretations made and the evaluative conclusions reached, but also the actions taken based on evaluation results.

The second half of the argument for inclusion addressed by point two refers to the consequences of the actions taken based upon evaluation. As Shepard (1997) points out, these two arguments are related, since once the definition of validity expands beyond descriptions or interpretations without actions to include the soundness of test-based decisions, one must necessarily think about the consequences of those decisions. Messick and his supporters argue that the consequences of drawing certain test-based inferences or taking certain test-based actions must be scrutinized as part of the validation process.[2] In parallel, judging the validity of evaluation requires attention to the social consequences of the judgments made and the evaluation-based actions taken. The focus on consequences is especially necessary in examining issues of fairness and equity across individual, institutional, and societal levels. Shifting focus to societal consequences leads to the third aspect of the argument for an inclusive definition of validity, social justice.

Inclusion of social justice comes from broad concerns about the ways in which power and privilege are distributed and controlled in our society and the role of evaluation within that system. House (1980) first cast social justice as a validity concern for evaluators. His broad definition of validity as "worthiness of being recognized" (p. 249) includes but extends beyond the truth claims of measurement validity and experimental method to include credibility (of the evaluator and of the evaluation) and normative correctness or justice.[3] The following quote captures the argument well:

> Evaluation is by nature a political activity. It serves decision-makers, results in reallocations of resources, and legitimizes who gets what. It is intimately implicated in the distribution of basic goods in society. It is more than a statement of ideas; it is a social mechanism for distribution, one which aspires to institutional status. Evaluation should not only be true; it should also be just. Current evaluation schemes, independently of their truth value, reflect justice in quite varying degrees. And justice provides an important standard by which evaluation should be judged. (House, 1980, p. 121)

In effect, validity becomes a point of intersection of justice with social program evaluation because of the focal issue of power. Support for the connection between validity and issues of power is contributed from perspectives as diverse as psychometrics (Cronbach, 1988) and dialectical materialism (Enerstvedt, 1989). To evaluate social programs with validity means expressly addressing issues of power and privilege—whose interests are served and not served—and how those interests are registered and understood. In matters of validity, as in matters of social justice, evaluators are not value-neutral (Cronbach, 1980; House, 1993). An ethic of public responsibility underlies and connects these arguments.

In sum, three arguments have been advanced to support the need for an inclusive definition of validity as a construct. First, validity needs to be defined broadly enough to address alternate epistemologies, many of which have been developed to give greater voice to historically underrepresented groups. Second, validity must include more than evidence-based inference; it must address decisions made and actions taken based on those understandings as well as the consequences of those actions. Third, a broad definition is needed to address the social justice implications of understandings, actions, and consequences. Granted the necessary scope, validity has the power to interrupt dynamics of prejudice, while a narrow, tightly constrained definition of validity works to restrict dialog and maintain the hegemony of the status quo.

The second argument of Proposition 3 examines the cultural implications of the construct of validity itself. This reflection on the validity of the validity question itself has been well articulated by Kvale (1995, p. 36) who asks, "Is the question of validity in social science a valid and legitimate question?" What are the cultural boundaries of validity as a social construction? Neither the term itself nor the concept of seeking validation carries the same meaning across cultural contexts. It follows that scrutinizing validity may not always be a productive avenue for improving practice. What if attention to validity in fact hinders or impairs practice or distracts us from more important ways of considering culture? For example, concern for control and legitimation might potentially overshadow and suppress creativity and production of new insights (Kvale, 1995).

Whether validity and creativity work to complement or to oppose one another is a matter of empirical examination, but Kvale's point concerning issues of control surrounding definitions of validity in the scientific community is well worth noting. As argued above, validity acts in important ways as gatekeeper to what is seen as legitimate contributions to the knowledge base of practice. To the extent that this gatekeeping function suppresses nonmajority viewpoints, supports the status quo, and restricts conversations that challenge power distributions, validity may itself become oppressive or discriminatory in its consequences. This interacts with the scope of the definition of validity accepted as legitimate, the first argument advanced under Proposition 3.

This section has advanced two related arguments to support Proposition 3. The first is the need for an inclusive definition of validity to create a construct of sufficient breadth to scrutinize the many ramifications of culture and cultural bias. The second is a need to be critically reflective about the validity of validity itself and the ways in which it dispenses legitimacy and influence within the academy in general and the evaluation profession in particular.

CONCLUDING THOUGHTS AND DIRECTIONS

This chapter has argued that culture is relevant to all aspects of evaluation and that it must be appropriately addressed to establish the fundamental validity of evaluative inferences and actions. Multicultural validity marks the centrality of culture in reflections on validity. Theory can support or undermine multicultural validity of evaluation, an argument advanced by considering three dimensions of theory: evaluation theory, program theory, and validity theory itself.

Multicultural validity of evaluation can be strengthened by theory that approaches culture in knowledgeable, thoughtful, and respectful ways; yet no theory ensures perfect understanding across cultural differences and none can be above scrutiny. Evaluators must continue to remain vigilant. To support necessary critical reflection, the chapter closes with nine recommendations for examining theory through a cultural lens.

1. Notice who the authors are and explore their background, location, training, experience, and personal characteristics. Theories are not "value-free" and understanding the persons behind the theory will give greater insight into the cultural context of the authors' ideas. Notice also how the conventions of format and style of professional publications shape the author information available for inspection.

2. Consider the time period in which the theory was developed and/or came to prominence. What is the historical context of civil rights, economic trends, and political issues of that period? Pay particular attention to how the public good was defined and understood.

3. Notice whether the theory assumes an implicit strengths or deficit model of the phenomenon of interest. Theories are not neutral in their relationship to their subject matter.

4. Notice when multiculturally valid practice requires a shift in theory base. Absolute commitment to a single theory of practice may hamper cultural responsiveness.

5. Consider how the theory positions the evaluator in relation to those who are evaluated—either as program providers or consumers. Look past the rhetoric of intent to notice the power dynamics implicit or explicit in the parameters of theory. Theories named with language of empowerment or emancipation should not be exempt from scrutiny for colonizing or paternalistic stances (Smith, 1999).

6. Notice the theorist's use of language and metaphor. Language is a manifestation of power (Patton, 2000). The language of evaluation shapes wider evaluation agendas, defining the issues we consider and the answers that we seek (Kaminsky, 2000). Metaphors may be used to enrich communication and generate fresh ways of thinking about evaluation or to frame arguments, justify inclusion or exclusion of key elements, and restrict options (Smith, 1981).

7. Consider both heterogeneity within cultural domains and similarities across domains. To what extent are these taken up in this theory? Is the theory sufficiently nuanced to capture the complexity of similarities and differences, disrupting simplistic, dichotomous representation?

8. Work both within and across cultural standpoints to explore the relevance of diverse theoretical perspectives. Evaluators must listen carefully, reflect deeply, and challenge articulately the prejudice that infuses theory viewed from a particular standpoint. However, one must also avoid reducing the complexities of culture and power to a simplistic univariate model in which any single standpoint is the only consideration.

9. Consider both what's included in a particular theory and what is *not* addressed. Gordon and colleagues (1990) express this in the words of Burke (1935), who noted, "a way of seeing is also a way of not seeing." Theory must be examined for what it reveals and what it conceals.

As we evaluators hone our ability to scrutinize theory, we will gain a fuller understanding of the many ways in which culture intersects theory. Deeper appreciation of the influence of culture will in turn support theory development as well as more thoughtful selection of culturally congruent theories in the practice of evaluation. These advances in theory and practice stand to improve the multicultural validity of evaluation throughout the profession.

NOTES

1. Scheurich and Young (1997, p. 8) offer the following definition of their term: "Epistemological racism means that our current range of research epistemologies—positivism to postmodernisms/poststructuralisms—arise out of the social history and culture of the dominant race, that these epistemologies logically reflect and reinforce that social history and that racial group (while excluding the epistemologies of other races/cultures), and that this has negative results for people of color in general and scholars of color in particular."

2. Though consequential justifications of validity are most frequently identified with the work of Messick (1989b), the roots of the idea also appear in

earlier measurement literature. Moss (1992) and, most recently, Shepard (1993, 1997) have traced the historical role of social consequences of assessment use as a component of validity, noting useful comparisons among the perspectives.

3. House (1980, p. 249) grounds his broad definition of the construct in the *Oxford English Dictionary* definition of validity as "the quality of being well-founded on fact, or established on sound principles, and thoroughly applicable to the case or circumstances; soundness and strength (of argument, proof, authority, etc.)."

4. Portions of this chapter were presented as part of the panel entitled "Racism, Validity, and Program Evaluation" (Karen E. Kirkhart, Chair), Public Interest Directorate Mini-convention on Psychology and Racism: The Colors of Privilege and Power, 105th Annual Convention of the American Psychological Association, August 15–19, 1997, Chicago.

REFERENCES

Alcoff, L., & Potter, E. (Ed.) (1993). *Feminist epistemologies.* New York: Routledge.

Alkin, M. C. (Ed.) (2004). *Evaluation Roots: Tracing theorists' views and influences.* Thousand Oaks, CA: Sage.

American Educational Research Association, American Psychological Association, & National Council on Measurement in Education (1999). *Standards for educational and psychological testing.* Washington, DC: American Educational Research Association.

Bell, D. (1997, August). *What President Clinton should tell whites about racism and how blacks should respond.* Paper presented at the annual meeting of the American Psychological Association, Chicago.

Burke, K. (1935). *Permanence and change.* New York: New Republic.

Chen, H-T., & Rossi, P. H. (1983). Evaluating with sense: The theory-driven approach. *Evaluation Review, 7,* 283–302.

Cronbach, L. J. (1971). Test validation. In R. L. Thorndike (Ed.), *Educational measurement* (2nd ed., pp. 443–507). Washington, DC: American Council on Education.

Cronbach, L. J. (1980). Validity on parole: How can we go straight? In W. B. Schrader (Ed.), *Measuring achievement: Progress over a decade. New Directions for Testing and Measurement,* No. 5, 99–108.

Cronbach, L. J. (1988). Five perspectives on validity argument. In H. Wainer & H. I. Braun (Eds.), *Test validity* (pp. 3–17). Hillsdale, NJ: Erlbaum.

Enerstvedt, R. T. (1989). The problem of validity in social science. In S. Kvale (Ed.), *Issues of validity in qualitative research* (pp. 135–173). Lund, Sweden: Studentlitteratur.

Fetterman, D. M. (1994a). Empowerment evaluation. *Evaluation Practice, 15*(1), 1–15.

Fetterman, D. M. (1994b). Steps of empowerment evaluation: From California to Cape Town. *Evaluation and Program Planning, 17,* 305–313.

Fetterman, D. M., Kaftarian, S., & Wandersman, A. (1996). *Empowerment evaluation: Knowledge and tools for self-assessment and accountability.* Thousand Oaks, CA: Sage.

Fine, M., & Powell, L. (1997, August). *White-out: Reflections on the study of racism in psychology.* Paper presented at the annual meeting of the American Psychological Association, Chicago.

Fitzpatrick, J. L., Sanders, J. R., & Worthen, B. R. (2004). *Program evaluation: Alternative approaches and practical guidelines* (3rd ed.). Boston: Allyn & Bacon.

Gordon, E. W., Miller, F., & Rollock, D. (1990). Coping with communicentric bias in knowledge production in the social sciences. *Educational Researcher, 19*(3), 14–19.

Greene, J. (1995, November). *Evaluators as advocates.* Paper presented at the annual meeting of the American Evaluation Association, Vancouver, BC, Canada.

Guba, E. G., & Lincoln, Y. S. (1989). *Fourth generation evaluation.* Newbury Park, CA: Sage.

Harding, S. (1998). *Is science multicultural? Postcolonialisms, feminisms, and epistemologies.* Bloomington, IN: Indiana University Press.

Hood, S. (2001). Nobody knows my name: In praise of African American evaluators who were responsive. In J. C. Greene & T. A. Abma (Eds.), *Responsive evaluation, New Directions for Evaluation,* No. 92 (pp. 31–43). San Francisco: Jossey-Bass.

Hopson, R. K. (Ed.). (2000). *How and why language matters in evaluation, New Directions for Evaluation,* No. 86. San Francisco: Jossey-Bass.

House, E. R. (1980). *Evaluating with validity.* Beverly Hills, CA: Sage.

House, E. R. (1993). *Professional evaluation: Social impact and political consequences.* Newbury Park, CA: Sage.

Hughes, D., Seidman, E., & Williams, N. (1993). Cultural phenomena and the research enterprise: Toward a culturally anchored methodology. *American Journal of Community Psychology, 21,* 687–703.

Jagose, A. (1996). *Queer theory: An introduction.* New York: New York University Press.

Kaminsky, A. (2000). Beyond the literal: Metaphors and why they matter. In R. K. Hopson (Ed.) *How and why language matters in evaluation. New Directions for Evaluation,* No. 86 (pp. 69–80). San Francisco: Jossey-Bass.

Kershaw, T. (1992). Afrocentrism and the afrocentric method. *Western Journal of Black Studies, 16*(3), 160–168.

Kirkhart, K. E. (1995a). Multiculturalism, validity and evaluation theory. *Evaluation Theories, 2*(2), 1–3, 5–6.

Kirkhart, K. E. (1995b). Seeking multicultural validity: A postcard from the road. *Evaluation Practice, 16*(1), 1–12.

Kirkhart, K. E. (2004, February). *Multicultural competence: A question of validity in evaluation.* Keynote address presented at the conference, RACE 2004: Relevance of Assessment and Culture in Evaluation, Arizona State University, College of Education, Tempe, AZ.

Kvale, S. (1995). The social construction of validity. *Qualitative Inquiry, 1,* 19–40.

Ladner, J. A. (Ed.). (1973). *The death of white sociology.* New York: Random House.

LaFrance, J. (2003, November). *Creating an indigenous evaluation framework: Methodological implications for evaluation.* Paper presented at the annual meeting of the American Evaluation Association, Reno, NV.

Linn, R. L. (1997). Evaluating the validity of assessments: The consequences of use. *Educational Measurement, 16*(2), 14–16.

Lipsey, M. W., & Pollard, J. A. (1989). Driving toward theory in program evaluation: More models to choose from. *Evaluation and Program Planning, 12,* 317–328.

Madison, A. (Ed.). (1992). *Minority issues in program evaluation. New Directions for Program Evaluation,* No. 53. San Francisco: Jossey-Bass.

Mathie, A., & Greene, J. C. (1997). Stakeholder participation in evaluation: How important is diversity? *Evaluation and Program Planning, 20,* 279–285.

Mertens, D. M. (1998). *Research methods in education and psychology: Integrating diversity with quantitative and qualitative approaches.* Thousand Oaks, CA: Sage.

Messick, S. (1981). Evidence and ethics in the evaluation of tests. *Educational Researcher, 10*(9), 9–20.

Messick, S. (1988). The once and future issues of validity: Assessing the meaning and consequences of measurement. In H. Wainer & H. I. Braun (Eds.), *Test validity* (pp. 33–45). Hillsdale, NJ: Erlbaum.

Messick, S. (1989a). Meaning and values in test validation: The science and ethics of assessment. *Educational Researcher, 18*(2), 5–11.

Messick, S. (1989b). Validity. In R. L. Linn (Ed.), *Educational measurement* (3rd ed., pp. 13–103). New York: Macmillan.

Messick, S. (1995). Validity of psychological assessment: Validation of inferences from persons' responses and performance as scientific inquiry into score meaning. *American Psychologist, 50,* 741–749.

Moss, P. A. (1992). Shifting concepts of validity in educational measurement: Implications for performance assessment. *Review of Educational Research, 62*(3), 229–258.

Parker, L. (2004). Can critical theories of or on race be used in evaluation research in education? In V. G. Thomas & F. I. Stevens (Eds.), *Co-constructing a contextually responsive evaluation framework: The Talent Development Model of School Reform. New Directions for Evaluation,* No. 101 (pp. 85–93). San Francisco: Jossey-Bass.

Patton, M. Q. (1997). *Utilization-focused evaluation: The new century text* (3rd ed.) Thousand Oaks, CA: Sage.

Patton, M. Q. (2000). Overview: Language matters. In R. K. Hopson (Ed.) *How and why language matters in evaluation. New Directions for Evaluation,* No. 86 (pp. 5–16). San Francisco: Jossey-Bass.

Preskill, H., & Torres, R. T. (2000). The learning dimension of evaluation use. In V. Caracelli & H. Preskill (Eds.), *The expanding scope of evaluation use. New Directions for evaluation,* No. 88 (pp. 25–37). San Francisco: Jossey-Bass.

Rosaldo, R. (1993). *Culture and truth: The remaking of social analysis.* Boston: Beacon Press.

Scheurich, J. J., & Young, M. D. (1997). Coloring epistemologies: Are our research epistemologies racially biased? *Educational Research, 26*(4), 4–16.

Schwandt, T. A. (1997). Evaluation as practical hermeneutics. *Evaluation, 3*(1), 69–83.

Scriven, M. (1991). *The evaluation thesaurus* (4th ed.). Newbury Park: Sage.

Seigart, D., & Brisolara, S. (Eds.) (2002). *Feminist evaluation: Explorations and experiences. New Directions for Evaluation,* No. 96. San Francisco: Jossey-Bass.

Shadish, W. R., Jr., Cook, T. D., & Leviton, L. C. (1991). *Foundations of program evaluation: Theories of practice*. Newbury Park, CA: Sage.

Shepard, L. A. (1993). Evaluating test validity. *Review of Research in Education, 19*, 405–450.

Shepard, L. A. (1997). The centrality of test use and consequences for test validity. *Education Measurement, 16*(2), 5–8, 13, 24.

Smith, L. T. (1999). *Decolonizing methodologies: Research and indigenous peoples*. New York: Zed Books, Ltd.

Smith, N. L. (Ed.) (1981). *Metaphors for evaluation: Sources of new methods: New perspectives in evaluation* (Vol. 1). Beverly Hills, CA: Sage.

Smith, N. L. (1987). Toward the justification of claims in evaluation research. *Evaluation and Program Planning, 10*, 309–314.

Stanfield, J. H., II (1993). Epistemological considerations. In J. H. Stanfield II & R. M. Dennis (Eds.), *Race and ethnicity in research methods* (pp. 16–36). Newbury Park: Sage.

Stufflebeam, D. L. (2001). *Evaluation models. New Directions for Evaluation*, No. 89. San Francisco: Jossey-Bass.

Sullivan, N. (2003). *A critical introduction to queer theory*. New York: New York University Press.

Thomas, C. L. (1997, August). Social justice and evaluative research: Implications for validity, design, and method. In K. E. Kirkhart (Chair), *Racism, validity, and program evaluation*. Symposium conducted at the annual meeting of the American Psychological Association, Chicago.

Thomas, V. G., & Stevens, F. I. (Eds.) (2004). *Co-constructing a contextually responsive evaluation framework: The Talent Development Model of School Reform. New Directions for Evaluation*, No. 101. San Francisco: Jossey-Bass.

Weiss, C. H. (1995). Nothing as practical as good theory: Exploring theory-based evaluation for comprehensive community initiatives for children and families. In J. P. Connell, A. C. Kubisch, L. B. Schorr, & C. H. Weiss (Eds.), *New approaches to evaluating community initiatives: Concepts, methods, and contexts* (pp. 65–92). Washington, DC: The Aspen Institute.

CHAPTER 4

PERSUASIVE LANGUAGE, RESPONSIVE DESIGN

A Framework for Interculturally Responsive Evaluation

Melvin Hall and Denice Ward Hood
Northern Arizona University

The authors of scientific reports and similar papers often think that if they merely report certain experiments, mention certain facts, or enunciate a certain number of truths, this is enough of itself to automatically arouse the interest of their hearers or readers. This attitude rests on the illusion, widespread in certain rationalistic and scientific circles, that facts speak for themselves and make such an indelible imprint on any human mind that the latter is forced to give its adherence regardless of its inclination. (Perelman & Olbrechts-Tyeca, 1969)

Regardless of strategy, purpose, or who is involved, evaluations are done to support decision making. Whether a decision to continue or terminate a program or activity, determine quality or merit in current practice, alter program design and implementation, or simply confirm and support the way the object is perceived, evaluation supports action that is facilitated by a better understanding of the object of the evaluation (evaluand). Some-

The Role of Culture and Cultural Context in Evaluation, pages 41–60
Copyright © 2005 by Information Age Publishing
41

times the evaluation seeks to impact decisions to be made by program participants and staff; more often the intended decision-making groups are sponsors or others external to day-to-day program operations. Despite evaluator recognition of a responsibility to serve the interests of decision-makers and other stakeholders, the field has yet to develop a corresponding sense of responsibility for how the design of the evaluation and communication of findings, issues, and recommendations unequally empower various stakeholder groups and may completely disenfranchise others. This differential impact comes both from the manner in which evidence is identified and collected, as well as results communicated. The operating assumption implicit in evaluation practice is that through use of scientifically tinged methodology, evaluations stand on their own merit as useful tools to decision-makers regardless of which stakeholder groups are involved. With this "scientific" orientation and faith in the universal appeal of rigorous methodology, evaluation succumbs to the double fallacy that facts speak for themselves, and they speak with equal clarity, utility, credibility, and urgency to all who encounter them. From this perspective an inability to find meaning in evaluation outcomes is often assumed to be the result of a problem within the stakeholder group, rather than acknowledged as an issue for the evaluation.

EVALUATION AS AN ACT OF COMMUNICATION

Because of its service to decision making, evaluation is an act of communication in which the evaluator seeks to provide a persuasive presentation, prompting the intended audience(s) to see and interpret the program as the evaluator has come to conceptualize or operationalize it. Even in evaluations where description is the central objective and judgment of the evaluand is withheld, the final product is communication of evaluator representation of the evaluand. In situations where different cultural, language, or social status issues are present, the fidelity of this communication becomes more suspect, impacting the credibility and centrality of stakeholder interests and ultimately stakeholder group enfranchisement.

House (1977) invited evaluators to think about the underlying logic of evaluation. In a monograph titled "The Logic of Evaluative Argument," he focused on key aspects of the logic of evaluation discourse and provided a critical metaphor in "evaluation as argumentation." Within this discussion, House introduced the idea of evaluation as an act of persuasive communication by:

- Acknowledging that rarely if ever are we able to design evaluation studies that compel people to action.

- Suggesting that more typically we are in a position to persuade the audience by presenting an argument aimed at this goal.
- Asserting that experimental designs, which attempt to win support for outcomes by demonstrating significant results and rejecting the proposition that outcomes are merely random, hope to compel through demonstration but rarely are evaluators in a position to provide this level of certainty in their results.
- Concluding that as a result of the limits of our techniques, evaluators build arguments that focus on the plausible, the probable, and the credible.

House summarizes these points in his assertion that, "Evaluations themselves, I would contend, can be no more than acts of persuasion" (1977, p 5). This requirement of persuasiveness is central to the evaluation's potential impact, utility, and use. Where the audience to be persuaded is multifaceted and multicultural, issues of communicating with fidelity across these group boundaries are placed in sharp relief against the backdrop of other evaluation concerns.

Because evaluation representations and findings are established and presented through a composite lens unique to the evaluation, the audience to be persuaded by the evaluation must be envisioned during the process. Evaluations support decision making through persuasively describing, valuing, or analyzing the evaluand. Success in this effort requires understanding the disparate meanings associated with the evaluand held by various stakeholder groups. Without advance recognition of the audiences and the subsequent tailoring of the arguments posed, evaluation results are seldom influential and generally uneven in empowering various audiences. When evaluation is viewed as an act of persuasive communication, considering audience needs and desires is no longer viewed as pandering, but rather an important aspect of being responsive to the purposes for which the evaluation was commissioned. In traditional evaluation practice this "responsiveness" begins during the design stages of the evaluation as issues are identified and the scope of the review determined. It is our contention that during these activities the evaluator is necessarily, though often tacitly, recognizing the audience's interests and working iteratively between those needs and options for evaluation design strategies. In determining whether the review will be more formative or summative, qualitative or quantitative, focused on inputs or outcomes, and which questions or perspectives to privilege in the design, the evaluator is meshing methodological options with the anticipated priorities of the client. This meshing process is further impacted by the evaluator's personal/professional biases and skill set. An evaluator can only select among methodological solutions he or she knows well enough to consider, opening the question of the degree of match between evaluator skills and biases and what is required to respond to the multiple audiences to be addressed.

In comparison with traditional evaluation practice, an interculturally responsive evaluation focuses more consciously on aspects of design decisions that interact with culture, power, language, and related issues—or that should entertain these issues yet traditionally fail to do so. The challenge of an interculturally responsive evaluator is to be overt in entertaining factors traditionally more covert in their influence, recognizing that the degree of attention to and congruence with various stakeholder perspectives will determine limits on evaluation quality and persuasiveness. Whether stakeholders are constantly present and engaged in the evaluation or more distant, interculturally responsive evaluators realize that they are not alone in their enterprise. Evaluation practice must always be conditioned by an adequate conceptualization of those who must be persuaded, if the evaluation is to avoid being discredited or ignored.

PERSUASION IN AN INTERCULTURAL COMMUNICATION FRAME AND ITS CHALLENGES

Within the larger discussion of evaluation context, some attention to the significance of evaluation as an act of persuasive communication is critical. Furthermore, this must be accomplished with recognition of persuasion as a distinct communication style/expectation that places extra burden upon both the audience and the evaluator. It is this search for a full, persuasive, and high-fidelity translation of the evaluand that occasions interest in evaluations that focus on contextually responsive, culturally responsive, culturally competent, and interculturally responsive strategies. Our preference for the concept of interculturally responsive evaluation honors the centrality of culture and adds the importance of communicating across multiple boundaries if an evaluation is truly to represent a multicultural evaluand.

The underlying logic of evaluation acknowledges the importance of context. Little imagination is required to see culture, wealth, privilege, social tradition, and politics as elements of context. With this recognition also comes acknowledgment of the differential status of various stakeholders along these dimensions and a realization that this element of context is not the same for everyone involved with the evaluand. Resistance continues, however, to the follow-on expectation that evaluators be conversant in the ramifications of these contextual elements when seeking work in environments where they are salient features. To be contextually responsive and interculturally competent, evaluators must effectively develop knowledge of the multiple important audiences to the evaluation and actively posture the evaluation to be informative, if not persuasive, to each of these constituents.

Fidelity of communication across stakeholder group boundaries engages the evaluator in understanding the differences present in perspectives of the evaluand, but equally requires increased understanding of areas of overlap in values or perspectives held. Locating and assessing differences is more consistent with the focus of traditional evaluation methods, rendering the evaluator more challenged to cogently identify and describe areas of overlap—features often taken for granted or interpreted as inconsequential because of the apparent agreement. In viewing evaluation as an act of persuasive communication it becomes clearer that these areas of commonality, if identified, can be used to bridge stakeholder perspectives and perhaps provide the most useful foundation for decision making about the evaluand.

In addition, where multiple groups are involved, an analysis of what appear to be common perceptions may reveal insights into how stakeholders derive very different but similarly valued meanings from the activities associated with the evaluand. Failure to probe the underlying meanings upon which individual or group perceptions are based overlooks the reality that groups often support the same program action but for very different reasons or based upon very different assumptions and understandings; adopting a combined intercultural communication and persuasion frame results in questions of meaning-making becoming more central to the evaluation enterprise. The issues associated with intercultural communication, both as they relate to meaning-making and the communication of these ideas, serve to direct the evaluation in a more democratic and inclusive direction. Evaluations of this type add value by foregrounding important issues associated with each stakeholder group, although this effort places significant demands on evaluator skills to identify and assess nuances in the understandings held by various groups.

In interculturally responsive evaluation, communication and especially persuasive communication must be viewed as a central element; the evaluator seeks to understand how communication interacts with cultural issues in the context of the evaluand and as a result, how the fidelity of communication between those involved can be enhanced, promoting more balance in empowerment. When there is recognition of the omnipresent impact of culture, class, and related perspectives, culturally responsive evaluation and traditional discussion of quality evaluation become synonymous—a condition that exists more often than is acknowledged. Recognizing that culture, power, language, class, and so on, are almost universally present in the evaluand broadens the applicability of interculturally responsive evaluation strategies and demonstrates the frequency of important omissions when these issues have not been identified despite their influence upon the evaluation and communication of results.

EVALUATION AND THE FALLACY OF UNIVERSAL CULTURE

> Without any kind of supposition or hypothesis about the cultural differences we may encounter in an intercultural situation, we may fall prey to naïve individualism, where we assume that every person is acting in some completely unique way. Or we may rely inordinately on "common sense" to direct our communication behavior. Common sense is, of course, common only to a particular culture. Its application outside of one's own culture is usually ethnocentric. (Bennett, 1998, p. 6)

Too often the methodological predisposition of evaluation models and approaches have an embedded assumption that those engaged in the evaluand can be treated as "individuals" without the necessity to factor in culturally based assumptions or understandings. Failure to acknowledge and provide for the impact of culture weakens evaluation theory and approaches, unleashing powerful forces without a theory-based means of identifying potential impacts. Because the role of theory is to assist in interpreting what is observed, failure to recognize when observations have a cultural link creates an opportunity for making interpretations far removed from what is actually occurring. Without the interpretive lens of cultural understanding, the powerful products of culture have their usual impact, yet we are without the tools for accurate identification and interpretation. This is an issue whether culture is completely ignored or vaguely and broadly attributed as "common or universal" across truly diverse groups of stakeholders. Very typical of this phenomenon is the notion of a broadly subscribed set of "American" values unique to the citizens of the United States. Growing out of the melting pot metaphor, this notion presumes commonality not in evidence when either values or behaviors are considered. The reality of American life is that:

> We flee to the suburbs or behind walls to avoid cultural difference, and if we are forced to confront it, there often is a fight ... Of course one doesn't need to physically terminate the existence of others to effectively eliminate them. When we make their lives miserable in our organizations and neighborhoods, we also "kill" them—they cannot flourish, and often they do not survive." (Bennett 1998, p. 2)

One potent mechanism of this intolerance is simply to make difference disappear by ignoring it or dismissing its importance. Such is the case when monocultural communication strategies are employed in a multicultural evaluand. Where an evaluation proceeds with the assumption of universal cultural identification or that people function "just as individuals," it masks the impact of cultural understandings and contributes to differential empowerment, disadvantaging stakeholders with less cultural capital in common with other stakeholders. When culture is assumed to be universal and therefore not a factor, the stand-in for culture is the norms of the dominant group. Where differences are acknowledged but individuals treated as separate from any cultural norms, the weight of their differences becomes an individual rather than group burden. Relative to the power of evaluation, a stakeholder group rendered invisible through lack of attention or misinterpreted through biased or misinformed analysis has its influence on the evaluand effectively neutralized or negatively valued.

Honoring the participation of significant players in an evaluation setting involves acknowledging their existence and distinct relationship with the evaluand; full engagement goes further by incorporating an understanding of how to influence these significant players. Both require understanding how to interpret what groups are saying about their experiences. Much of any group's understanding of the evaluand comes directly from culture as it creates the lenses through which experiences and the language that describes these experiences is produced. To seek to persuade these audiences without access to the culturally based understandings that define them as an audience is certain to reduce the power and perhaps credibility of the evaluation report.

LANGUAGE AS CULTURALLY BASED EXPRESSION

Sensitivity to and skillful use of language are core evaluation competencies. The language we use, both among ourselves and with stakeholders, necessarily and inherently shapes perceptions, defines "reality," and affects mutual understanding. Whatever we seek to understand or do, a full analysis will lead us to consider the words and concepts that undergrid our understandings and actions—because language matters. (Patton, 2000)

Interculturally responsive evaluators recognize that language serves as more than a tool of communication. It additionally is a system of representation for perception and thinking. This function of language provides verbal categories and prototypes that guide formation of concepts and categorization of objects; it directs how "reality" is experienced (Stewart & Bennett, 1991).

For evaluation, attention has been given to the importance of metaphors and other language constructions as they convey important meaning to audiences. However, the value of language forms is conditioned by the degree to which underlying meanings are shared. Inability to unlock the meaning of a metaphor, technical language, or illustration renders the underlying information inaccessible. Where this is the case with a central stakeholder group or audience, the evaluation has failed. Where the use of evaluation language alters perceptions of the evaluand and changes perceptions of stakeholder or audience groups, the evaluation has effectively changed the evaluand and its utility for these groups.

In addition to a failure to attend to cultural diversity implications, many evaluations suffer from reliance upon characterizations of the impact of culture that do not support the intercultural communication and persuasion requirements of evaluation. In these instances the role of culture is acknowledged, but the mode of addressing implications is too anemic to attend fully to the dynamics of cultural influence. Often the result of inadequate conceptualization is the use of metaphors and terms that do not provide a basis for looking at the culture's influence on communication both in the saying and the hearing of evaluation findings. The use of these concepts provides a portrayal of culturally linked attitudes and perceptions that play down impact, suggest less significance and permanence than may be the case, and obscures the centrality of communicating these attitudes and perceptions.

While it is useful to discuss interculturally responsive evaluation treating cultural groups as relatively homogeneous, when compared to those outside the group, the range of variability in communication within groups is significant and should not be ignored. Determining how far to take this analysis is an important aspect of evaluating with multicultural validity, and hence central to this chapter. In evaluation terms, the depth of pursuit of inter- and intra-group communication differences should be determined by the purpose of the evaluation and where it must be persuasive.

The juxtaposition of within-group and between-group variability in multicultural evaluation settings highlights the complexity of choices facing the interculturally responsive evaluator and is effectively portrayed by the metaphor of the statistical procedure, analysis of variance. In analysis of variance the important underlying concept is a comparison of the amount of variation with a group to the variation present between several such groups. In assessing this ratio of "within-group" to "between-group" variance, we gain an appreciation of the significance or homogeneity of group membership when compared to the significance of the group identity relative to other groups. This is analogous to the issue of cultural or other subgroup identification. As each participant holds multiple "memberships" that affect relationships with the evaluand, matters of class, gender, race, ethnicity, and so on, will potentially have overlapping influence forming distinct groups in relation to the evaluand. Rather than suffering from an inappropriate assumption that one factor or another defines the cultural component directing participant experiences with the evaluand, the evaluation must seek to understand these relative influences, and how each colors perceptions and meaning-making. "These identities are woven together and impossible to examine as purely separate entities. The lived reality of those identities defines who we are and informs how we engage and interpret the world around us" (Hood & Cassaro 2002, p. 27). Treating those with noticeable characteristics defining difference, such as language or race, as a monolithic minority masks the important and sometimes subtle realities of their lives. Evaluators must come to understand the nature of group affiliation influence if it is to be weighed appropriately.

Giving these issues the importance associated with allocation of evaluation resources is central to interculturally responsive evaluation and should be seen as synonymous with democratic orientations as well. In many power-based relationships the allocation of resources directed at promoting understanding is reflective of honoring the perspective and the participation involved. Evaluations that fail to appropriate resources to promote understanding of a stakeholder group effectively disenfranchise the group and operationalize power relationships that promote a sense of their lack of importance. There is more than irony involved when decision makers decry the inability of stakeholder groups to accept the results of an evaluation that has systematically ignored or undermined their perceptions of and participation in the evaluand. For many groups whose perspectives have been ignored, evaluation findings reflect but a shadow of the evaluand that has been a significant part of their reality.

PERSUASION AND KNOWLEDGE OF STAKEHOLDER GROUP CULTURE

The need for culture-based insights into behavior affirms intercultural communication as a very relevant discipline for evaluators and other professionals involved in the world of human affairs, for it is in deciphering communications about the evaluand that the evaluator comes to understand these varied and important relationships and perspectives. Effective intercultural communication is not simply an esoteric skill for overseas travelers, but a constructive approach to managing diversity in domestic settings (Bennett, 1998). Evaluators promoting their skill and ability to capture value oversell to the extent that they are unable or unwilling to delve into the multiple culturally based understandings that inevitably coexist within the evaluand.

Making sense of language and communication within the often-diverse cultural contexts of program beneficiaries, staff, and policymakers further connects issues of language to contemporary discussions on democratization in evaluation. By definition, efforts at more democratic evaluation that use a monocultural perspective in a multicultural setting increase rather than reduce cultural hegemony, producing an impact exactly opposite of the intent.

In evaluations that seek to be interculturally responsive, representations of reality are proposed on the evaluation stage so that stakeholders and audiences have an opportunity to work with these representations to form the basis for ultimate judgment and valuation. Of issue then is the extent to which all stakeholders internal to the evaluand have access to influence these portrayals. Our central theme is the evaluator's responsibility and options for fully and adequately integrating and considering the various perspectives of stakeholders on the evaluand, as well as the challenges of the other side of this consideration—the fidelity with which stakeholder views are heard and incorporated.

Despite significant attention to matters of cultural competence in other fields of human affairs, evaluation has lagged behind in codifying expectations relative to handling culture and related variables (SenGupta et al, 2004). Other disciplines have suggested several key components related to culturally competent practice that may inform the development of an evaluation framework. Among these concepts are:

- An awareness of one's own cultural limitations;
- An openness, respect, and appreciation for cultural differences;
- Regard for intercultural diversity as a source of learning opportunities;
- Ability to use cultural resources in interventions;
- An acknowledgment of the integrity and value of all cultures (Le Roux, 2002).

Cultural competence does not imply knowing everything about all cultures engaged with the evaluand, it does, however, require demonstration of respect for differences, eagerness to learn about other cultures, acceptance of different epistemologies, and a flexibility and willingness to adjust, change, and reorient where required (Le Roux, 2002). For an evaluation to have validity and utility, cultural perspectives must be skillfully addressed. Evaluators must understand their personal points of view and how these interact with the vantage points from which they observe and interact with the evaluand. Evaluation guidelines encourage the evaluator to reveal those elements of practice that impact vantage point (design, methodology, source of commission, or funding), yet ask less of the practitioner relative to identifying their point of view. Left unexamined, a point of view challenges validity and credibility in ways at least as significant as vantage point.

With competent attention to the issues of cultures present in the evaluand, the evaluation must tackle the follow-on issues of intercultural communication of these culturally based understandings. As complex as cultural understandings can be, mastering them does not complete the cultural competence requirement because these understandings must be effectively communicated to have full value. Knowing about culture is a necessary but not sufficient prerequisite for effectively communicating its impact. Being persuasive requires effectiveness in both the knowing and the telling of the informants' stories.

Typical evaluation situations involve multiple identifiable communities that share some cultural elements but differ in many other meaningful ways. Evaluation contexts are additionally complicated by role-based power differentials, especially when power is also aligned with cultural membership. In either case, communication within the evaluation activities and of the evaluation findings presents the challenge of remaining responsive to evaluation purposes while effectively communicating within and between diverse participating groups.

Standards for program evaluation developed by the Joint Committee on Standards for Educational Evaluation acknowledge the importance of culture and its expression through language in evaluation, especially as stated in Propriety Standard P4 Human Interactions (The Joint Committee on Standards for Educational Evaluation, 1994). This standard encourages evaluators to be ever mindful of the power of language and therefore the significance of words chosen and images invoked in evaluation. The guidelines associated with this standard advises evaluators to "Make every effort to understand the culture, social values, and language differences of the participants" (p. 99). In this standard we are reminded of the power and importance of metaphors as a way to convey rich meaning, but also of the importance of understanding that to be useful, the metaphor must be accessible and convey the intended meaning to all audiences of the report. Just as we acknowledge the prevalence of multiple audiences to evaluation reports, we must recognize that often what distinguishes audiences to an evaluand are boundaries corresponding to culture, language, and similar variables.

The existence of this standard alongside a reluctance to accept the importance of culturally responsive evaluation reveals the gap between our theoretical perspectives, which attempt to recognize the significance of culture, and evaluation practice perspectives, which tend to ignore the importance of using cultural frames as a key element of evaluation practice. We argue that it is the combination of culture and context that provide the bridge between language and the underlying meaning or intent of the message. The accepted goal of evaluation, as expressed in the Human Interactions standard (P4), is to promote the understanding of language in context. In this endeavor, Hymes (1972) appropriately admonishes that understanding language in context requires starting with an understanding of context not language. The failure of evaluation to make context a central design issue makes language the powerful but undisciplined factor that has often led to the differential empowerment and enfranchisement issues of concern here.

Clearly evaluation resources can only stretch in so many directions; delving deeply into nuances of intra- and inter-group communication styles could totally consume limited resources at the expense of other evaluation activities. The argument of this chapter is that evaluators must find appropriate balance and not avoid the challenge by demoting the importance of cultural factors. Efforts to argue that objectivity requires ignoring subgroup differences in understanding must logically be coupled with caveats that the evaluation will have limited credibility, utility, and validity for those perspectives that have been ignored.[1]

INTERCULTURALLY RESPONSIVE EVALUATION BY DESIGN

Evaluation design has significant influence on evaluator vantage point in observing and interacting with the evaluand, and vantage point significantly impacts how observations are judged and communicated. Focusing on the importance of persuasive communication brings further clarity to the centrality of design and vantage point, illustrating the importance of both to validity and utility concerns. Evaluation that fails to meet the test of multicultural validity, as defined by Kirkhart (2000), cannot offer utility in settings where culture is a salient feature. With the intent to provide persuasive communication across multiple groups, evaluation must be based on a design that facilitates or enhances these features; design issues are central to validity.

As a communication-intense professional activity, the skill and perspective involved in crafting evaluation matters. The extent to which culture and other factors are salient features of the evaluation context suggests that these factors also contribute to the validity of any representations of this context. A framework for interculturally responsive evaluation must address the vantage point provided by methodology and design strategies, and their success in creating a foundation for persuasive communication. Beginning with competent assessment of context, the interculturally responsive evaluation builds a solid foundation for understanding language and the structures used to express experiences with the evaluand. This broader foundation of understanding each group, combined with the related increase in understanding of language and meaning, provide evaluation with elements basic to cultural competence and hence persuasion.

DESIGNING FOR PERSUASIVENESS

Intercultural persuasiveness places a dual challenge on evaluation design to avoid structurally biased methodology and select options that enhance multicultural validity. Combining the requirements for persuasive communication across multiple groups, with multicultural validity concerns growing out of the combination of methodology and design, provides a beginning outline of expectations for interculturally responsive evaluation. In summary, this framework should provide for effective identification of the various groups involved, development of an enlightened strategy for addressing the needs/expectations of each group based on knowledge of the group, and selection of evaluation design and methodology that supports these important goals. While it is consistent with traditional practice, appears efficient, and is often tempting, selecting design and methodology prior to fully defining the audiences to be engaged introduces significant risk of the evaluation moving down a path that inadvertently closes off options for meeting the needs of those who must be reached and persuaded if the evaluation is to be useful. Such preordinate evaluation planning and methods should have an explicit component to prompt reflection and modification during implementation, if this limitation is to be avoided.

In addition to concerns regarding flexible design options, once audiences have been identified, evaluation must avoid biases and limitations growing out of the cultural assumptions and underpinnings of the methodology utilized. Methodology can bias views of the evaluand, privilege some perspectives over others, and alter how stakeholder views are processed or evaluated. For example, an internal or self-evaluation effort, conducted within a community by its own members, can still infuse cultural conflict if it utilizes methodology that fails to allow for honoring community values. Consider faculty from a minority institution attempting to use standard accreditation guidelines in a self-study of an innovative program that grows out of their unique mission. Despite probable congruence of values and perspectives among those involved with the evaluand, the introduction of evaluation design issues from the accreditation guidelines presents an implicit set of values that also affect the evaluation process. Where the epistemological or methodological underpinning of the evaluation design imposes values on assessments of the evaluand, the evaluation becomes a vehicle of subjugation. These evaluations may fail to acknowledge or even impugn the value perceived by those who share a common sense of the program's purpose. When stakeholder understanding of the evaluand is not aligned with the values privileged by methodology, evaluation will be a frustrating and perhaps futile exercise.

An evaluation that seeks to persuade multiple stakeholder and audience groups must have options for adjusting data definitions, collection strategies, and participation so that the demands of persuasiveness can be met; balancing needs present in different groups becomes a central and overt activity. Given the complexity of these needs, a full appreciation of the design requirements may not evolve until the evaluation is underway. Evaluation approaches that accommodate in-progress augmentation or modification will inherently provide a more flexible platform for designs engaging a multicultural context. Only evaluation approaches that provide options for this customization and midcourse correction carry the potential for fully meeting the needs of a multicultural evaluand. Multimethod and mixed-method designs are particularly well adapted to meet this requirement.

FRAMING THE EVALUAND

Many evaluations begin with efforts to clarify just what is being evaluated. Seldom do we have adequate evaluation resources to look at every imaginable element of a program, so deciding what is to be included is an important activity. Are the entire program and all of its ramifications to be reviewed or simply the intended outcomes of selected purposeful activities and their direct impact? Is the evaluand limited to delivery of the program and its services or inclusive of participant experiences in utilizing those services?

In social programs or any effort involving people, delineation of what is included in the evaluand expresses a value perspective and position. Any effort to draw a boundary around what is to be reviewed in the evaluation includes the priorities of some groups and at least potentially excludes matters of interest or concern to others. In culturally responsive evaluation it is effective to identify the audiences and stakeholders early in the process and then confirm the boundaries of the evaluand as including a compilation of their collective sense of what it is. In this way the evaluation evolves somewhat slowly and in stages, with an opportunity to identify and respond to the information needs of various constituents in accordance with evaluation purposes.

Developing a clear conception of the boundaries of the evaluand is also an important place for identifying common perspectives as well as differences in views of the evaluand. A useful analogy for the evaluand is the intersection of Venn diagrams that relate to each groups assessment of the evaluand. By counteranalysis, reviewing those items outside the area of congruence provides the assessment of differences in views of the evaluand held by each group. The level of common definition represents one form of assessment of the evaluand, across the various groups involved. A well-articulated evaluand will create a clearer and more shared sense of its boundaries, especially when they are acknowledged to differ across involved groups.

It is here that the language of description and inclusion is key. The evaluation can't persuade those whose connection to the evaluand is defined outside the bounded case for review. This is a common place for expression of value differences between those who commission evaluations and those whose lives are impacted by the evaluand.

IDENTIFY STAKEHOLDERS AND AUDIENCES TO THE EVALUATION

Distinguishing among those who are stakeholders in the evaluand and those who are audiences to the evaluation is both an exercise in planning/organization and an expression of evaluation priorities, values, and strategy. An evaluation that fails to recognize the area of overlap including all groups could define the evaluand based upon the views of either group or a combination. More typically the evaluand could be defined by the plans or project design ignoring each of the specialized views held by groups participating in the evaluand.

In identifying participating groups we must understand them at least to the point of knowing how to access them and make the evaluation accessible to them. Anything short of identifying all key groups who are participants in the evaluand redefines the object of evaluation in significant and limiting ways. While sometimes unavoidable or of practical necessity, this redefinition of the evaluand must be a conscious and defensible action consistent with the evaluation purposes and recognized in interpretations of findings and recommendations. Identifying stakeholder groups is a key opportunity to express values in the evaluation as we weigh the often competing stakeholder and audience claims of connection and priority in the evaluation.

DETERMINE HOW TO MAXIMIZE VALIDITY, UTILITY, AND EFFECTIVENESS OF EVALUATION METHODS

As the evaluation design is completed and throughout implementation, mechanisms for keeping on track must be balanced against the opportunity costs in validity and utility, with evaluation purposes guiding decision making in these matters. Data collection methods are central to evaluation design and reveal an area of particular challenge for evaluators. One aspect of challenge is in appropriately recognizing nonverbal aspects of stakeholder participation. Lack of understanding, poor observation skills, and other evaluator performance limitations may result in prejudice toward people from cultures other than their own. In a review of the language of nonverbal communication, LeRoux provides a discussion of hair, dress, kinesics (body language), proxemics (social space), facial expressions, eye contact, paralanguage (sounds that are vocal but nonverbal), codes, and gestures, as important elements of this central dimension (Le Roux, 2002, pp 43–44). In an interesting review of communication style features in the African American community, Hecht and colleagues (1993) provide a detailed look at distinguishing factors that are significant and commonplace in both verbal and nonverbal communication and introduce the mediating variables of class and regional patterns. It is in this realm of both verbal and nonverbal communication that cultural competence presents the evaluation with a formidable challenge, but also an opportunity to strongly undergrid validity and utility by making evaluation more richly accessible and linked to familiar cultural cues.

- Validity requires a focus on all important contextual elements.
- Both subjective and objective cultures are important elements of context inasmuch as they provide the lens through which the evaluand is experienced and within which the evaluand operates.

As both possibilities and conflicts are encountered and acknowledged, choices must be driven by or relate to overall evaluation intents. Like methodology assists the evaluator in systematically addressing the purpose of the evaluation, design and methodology must guide decisions to maximize evaluation persuasiveness.

RESTORYING

Program participants share their behaviors, beliefs, attitudes, and expectations with evaluators who then summarize and analyze these data to form impressions and judgments about the larger program. But who certifies that they got it right? When the evaluator is conversant in the culture and circumstances surrounding the program, this is a legitimate question. When there is significant social distance between the evaluator and others, the question should be viewed as both legitimate and compulsory. Building an evaluation upon the stories of participants grounds the evaluation in these important facts; getting it right is a prerequisite for persuasiveness with those whose story is being told.

PACKAGING THE EVALUATION

Throughout the evaluation process it is clear that something will be produced and presented as evaluation activities draw to a close. Quantitative
methodology provides direction regarding at least the elements of this
final presentation; however, qualitative strategies provide a virtual open
field of options for this purpose. These choices are clearly value-laden and
impact subsequent formal and informal communication. What guides
these decisions?

We see the development of final reports and results as a critical element
of the evaluation process, one with implications for each of the other
stages of the evaluation process, and one that can illuminate many of the
biases and perspectives that have gone undetected in earlier phases of the
evaluation. Decisions about what will be included in the report; in what
voice the report will speak; what the relative emphasis of various sections
and issues will be; and choices regarding what raw data to include verba-
tim: are but a few of the critical acts associated with final report development that have clear connection to the issues associated with need for
cultural competency.

Style of presentation, content, timing, and so on, all impact accessibility.
Anticipation of evaluation audiences and use precondition the evaluator to
favor certain approaches and should be part of a conscious plan for impact
and persuasiveness.

CLOSING

The bridge-building metaphor fits evaluation because evaluation studies
are not done as mere compilations of facts and impressions; they are done
to influence action. And, just as in education or counseling settings, this
bridge will be more useful if it begins where current understandings of the
evaluand rest and move audiences to the expanded appreciation that
evolved during the review. An evaluation that ignores this important starting point can be thorough and accurate but still fail to be useful because it
lacks persuasiveness and ease of access for its audiences.

This analysis of the foundation upon which persuasive communication
is built relates directly to considerations of cultural competency and the
relevance of culture to the evaluation enterprise. As interculturally responsive evaluators attempt to provide a vicarious experience for report consumers, they are engaged in an act of persuasive communication designed
to influence the understanding and valuing of the evaluation object. For
responsive evaluators the goal is to establish this important connection to
the audience(s) and stakeholders by which their work is viewed as credible,

powerful, and a contribution to subsequent valuing and decision making. It is instructive to acknowledge that in this regard knowing the audience is a fundamental concern both in assembling data that may become persuasive and developing reporting strategies that can gain the "adherence of those to whom it is addressed."

To be responsive in evaluating a program where culture may be a salient feature, the evaluation must include strategies that incorporate an authentic representation of the views of participants. Without attention to authenticity, data going into evaluation is subject to inaccuracy and incompleteness and analysis coming out is subject to significant flaws. Interculturally responsive practices in evaluation are necessary components of quality evaluation practice, not optional or discretionary embellishments with utility limited to practitioners who hold a special evaluation orientation. Regardless of the basis upon which the conversation advocating interculturally responsive strategies continues, it is an important conversation. "How we think about the usefulness of our evaluation approaches, the applicability of our methods to communities and those who we wish to involve in the evaluation enterprise, and the validity of our claims all have cultural responsive implications, and potentially liberating and decolonizing ones as well" (Hopson, 2003).

A useful framework for evaluation in settings where culture, language, race, ethnicity, or social status are salient issues is one that integrates the intercultural communications frame, engages stakeholders through persuasive language, and incorporates cultural context through utilization of a responsive design. The role and purpose of this chapter was to assert the logical and necessary connection between these elements, as they apply to the process of evaluation, within the context of our discussion of the relevance of culture and the need for cultural competency this creates. Stated in the positive sense, this chapter is about cultural relevance—in the negative sense it is about constraining bias so that we can produce evaluations that bear more in common with the evaluand of interest. The expectation that a responsive evaluation will recognize the variety of stakeholders and interests present in the evaluand should not be separated from an understanding of how to provide this portrayal with fidelity. And furthermore, the evaluand cannot be effectively evaluated without attention to the audiences for the evaluation because this is a central and necessary step in providing an evaluation with persuasive potential. Persuasiveness lies as much in responsiveness to the reason the evaluation is read as why it was done (Denny, 1978).

NOTE

1. For a useful discussion of the objectivity/subjectivity issue in evaluation, see House (1977, pp. 39–43).

REFERENCES

Agar, M. (2000). Border lessons: Linguistic "rich points" and evaluative understanding. In *How and why language matters in evaluation* (New Directions for Evaluation, Vol. 86, pp. 93–110). San Francisco: Jossey-Bass.

Bennett, M. J. (1998). Intercultural communication: A current perspective. In M. Bennett (Ed.), *Basic concepts of intercultural communication: Selected readings.* Yarmouth, ME: Intercultural Press.

Bruner, J. (1990). *Acts of meaning.* Cambridge, MA: Harvard University Press.

Denny, T. (1978). *Story telling and educational understanding.* Occasional Paper Series, #12.

Greene, J. (2002). Telling tales. *Qualitative Social Work, 3,* 297–302.

Gudykunst, W. B. (1989). Cultural variability in ethnolinquistic identity. In *International and Intercultural Communications Annual* (Vol. 13). Newbury Park, CA: Sage.

Hall, E. T. (1998). The power of hidden differences. In M. Bennett (Ed.), *Basic concepts of intercultural communication: Selected readings.* Yarmouth, ME: Intercultural Press.

Hecht, M., Collier, M., and Ribeau, S. (1993). *African American communication: Ethnic identity and cultural interpretation.* Newbury Park, CA: Sage.

Hood, D. W., & Cassaro, D. A. (2002). Feminist evaluation and the inclusion of difference. (New Directions for Evaluation, Vol. 92, pp. 27–40). New York: Wiley Periodicals.

Hopson, R. (2003). Paper presented at the annual meeting of the American Educational Research Association.

House, E. (1977). *The logic of evaluative argument.* Los Angeles: UCLA Center for the Study of Evaluation.

Hymes, D. (1972). On communicative competence. In J. Price & J. Holmes (Eds.), *Sociolinguistics.* Penquin Books.

Joint Committee on Standards for Educational Evaluation (1994). *The program evaluation standards* (2nd ed.). Thousand Oaks, CA: Sage.

Kaminsky, A. (2000). Beyond the literal: Metaphors and why they matter. In *How and why language matters in evaluation* (New Directions for Evaluation, Vol. 86, pp. 69–80). San Francisco: Jossey-Bass.

Kirkhart, K. (2000). Reconceptualizing evaluation use: An integrated theory of influence. In *How and why language matters in evaluation* (New Directions for Evaluation, Vol. 86). San Francisco: Jossey-Bass.

Lakoff, G., & Johnson, M. (1980). *Metaphors we live by.* Chicago: University of Chicago Press.

Le Roux, J. (2002). Effective educators are culturally competent communicators. *Intercultural Education, 13*(1), 37–48.

Lincoln, Y. S. (2002). On the nature of qualitative evidence. In W. G. Tierney & L. S. Hagedorn (Eds.), *Verifying data: Papers prepared for the 27th annual meeting of the Association for the Study of Higher Education* (pp. 3–15). Los Angeles: USC Center for Higher Education Policy Analysis.

Madison, A. M. (2000). Language in defining social problems and in evaluating social programs. In *How and why language matters in evaluation* (New Directions for Evaluation, Vol. 86, pp. 17–28). San Francisco: Jossey-Bass.

Patton, M. Q. (2000). Overview: Language matters. In *How and why language matters in evaluation* (New Directions for Evaluation, Vol. 86, pp. 5–16). San Francisco: Jossey-Bass.

Perelman, C., & Olbrechts-Tyteca, L. (1969). *The new rhetoric: A treatise on argumentation* (J. Wilkinson &P. Weaver. Trans.). Notre Dame, IN: University of Notre Dame Press.

Stake, R. E. (2004). *Standards based and responsive evaluation.* Thousand Oaks: Sage.

Stewart, E. C., & Bennett, M. J. (1991). *American cultural patterns: A cross-cultural perspective.* Yarmouth, ME: Intercultural Press.

Thomas, V., (2004). Building a contextually responsive evaluation framework: Lessons from working with urban school interventions. (New Directions for Evaluation, Vol. 101, pp. 3–23). San Francisco: Jossey-Bass.

CHAPTER 5

PROMOTING CULTURALLY RELIABLE AND VALID EVALUATION PRACTICE[1]

Sharon Nelson-Barber
WestEd

Joan LaFrance
Mekinak Consulting

Elise Trumbull
WestEd

Sofia Aburto
WestEd

Ensuring standards of good practice among evaluators working in culturally diverse communities is a high priority for the evaluation field in the 21st century. Given our nation's expanding societal diversity, it is essential that those who study the effectiveness of organizations, programs, policies, or personnel be mindful of ways in which evaluation theory and practices must account for cultural context. Failure to understand how cultural context interacts with program implementation and impact jeopardizes the validity of the evaluation. In the worst case, spurious conclusions may be drawn that unfairly affect access to resources. One can only conclude that

The Role of Culture and Cultural Context in Evaluation, pages 61–85
Copyright © 2005 by Information Age Publishing

61

there are both ethical and validity concerns that make it mandatory for all evaluators to learn about cultural context. Culture and cultural diversity influence every context, not only those that spring to mind, such as large urban settings. It is a matter of surfacing the culture-based assumptions of both those being evaluated and those doing the evaluation.

In the process of assessing strengths and weaknesses of a program, evaluators must have the competence to build on important aspects of cultural knowledge. Without specific understandings of the cultural context in which a program is being implemented, for example, evaluators are likely to miss important information that can shed light on *why* a program has particular outcomes or impact on a community. This point is relevant not only to the interpretation of data or evidence but also to evaluation design and data collection.

For example, when a school district mounts a program to promote parent involvement among Latino immigrants, evaluators need to find out *how* parents have wanted to be involved and why. Parents who have been educated elsewhere may have very different expectations for what counts as an appropriate way to interact with teachers, parent–teacher organizations, and administrators. They may not believe it is their role to make suggestions to the school on the educational program or to tutor their children at home (Goldenberg & Gallimore, 1995; Valdés, 1996). When they do approach the administration about a problem, as people likely to hold collectivistic values, they may prefer to do so as a group rather than individually—something the school may perceive as aggressive rather than the natural group-oriented thing to do (Trumbull, Rothstein-Fisch, Greenfield, & Quiroz, 2001).

Evaluators of a parent involvement effort would need to understand these culture-based issues and more if they were to understand the patterns of participation observed. They might surmise that allowing parents to determine the grouping for a focus group rather than planning for individual interviews or assigning people to groups would result in greater participation and response. They might interpret parents' failure to engage in academic tutoring not as resistance but as a natural response to an alien demand. In the process, they might be able to point to ways parents could be encouraged to shift roles (Goldenberg & Gallimore, 1995; Trumbull, Rothstein-Fisch, & Hernandez, 2003). With knowledge of the context, evaluators might be able to contribute positively to future outcomes. Of course, ideally, the district should have brought this knowledge to light, but if that is not the case, evaluators are in an excellent position to do so.

Evaluators need to be aware of diverse perspectives and knowledgeable about how variables represent themselves across various groups. They must understand factors that require special attention or that may be manifested in unique ways (e.g., the impact of second language acquisition in the case of English learners, the unique challenge of learning and teaching academic content in a second language, or in indigenous and Asian communities the power of tribal and filial influences). Certainly evaluators cannot know "everything" about all cultural contexts. However, developing understandings about local cultures and contexts, and the issues arising in those contexts, would better enable them to adopt strategies that are consistent with the settings under examination. Would a study designed for second language learners, but really "English" learners, hold for Native American students acquiring their heritage language and not English as a second language? "Second language learner" can mean different things depending on the context.

It is clear that evaluators must have increased awareness of both external and internal factors impacting program goals, and such knowledge would contribute to more valid assessment of a program's overall functioning. Continuing to rely on a universal approach to evaluation will likely fail to produce reliable and valid inferences about program implementation and outcomes, much as a universal approach to education leaves some students on the margins.

In this chapter, we explore how cultural competence contributes to the reliability and validity of program evaluation—using examples related to community-based programs in indigenous American communities and educational programs in multicultural/multiethnic urban settings. We hope that these examples from two vastly different sets of sociocultural settings stimulate evaluation professionals to consider how cultural competence may come into play in the communities in which they work.

THE PROBLEM OF GENERIC "GOOD" APPROACHES TO EVALUATION

Recently a number of educators of color attending national meetings of professional organizations[2] and invited meetings[3] were asked to speak to the concerns we have identified above. They reinforced the general need for evaluators to assess how current evaluation practices take into account the influences of cultural context on program implementation and outcomes and how evaluators gather data to determine and evaluate program outcomes. They would agree that some evaluation methods lend themselves more readily to cultural responsiveness than others. Among these are participatory evaluation and empowerment evaluation, both of which emphasize the role of stakeholders in the entire evaluation process. However, no method can ensure valid evaluation outcomes if deep understanding of the cultural (and historical and political) context is lacking on the part of the person or persons carrying out or facilitating the evaluation.

Even such fundamental questions as "What counts as data?", "How should key informants be identified?", "How should informants' knowledge and perspectives be tapped?", or "Who should have access to information generated by an evaluation?" cannot be answered without reference to the immediate context. For example, there may be more than one organizational hierarchy within a school district. It may not be only the superintendent, principals, and teachers who can offer insights into a program's functioning, but (as in the case of American Indian groups) also respected elders who hold no formal position within the district.

Numerous American Evaluation Association speakers from different cultural and ethnic groups attest that, for the most part, the conceptual foundations for what is accepted as "good" or "progressive" practice do not include the experiences, perspectives, and knowledge of populations that fall outside the American mainstream (Hood, 2002; Johnston, 2002; Nelson-Barber, 2003; Rai & Yang, 2002; Rodriguez, 2002; Symonette, 2002). Some of the American Indian evaluators add that they frequently observe a high degree of discontinuity between the assumptions and expectations of many program evaluators and the operational norms of the indigenous[4] communities under study (Carriere, 2003; Johnston, 2003; Jolly, 2002; LaFrance, 2002b).

These observations parallel those of leaders in indigenous education, who have identified the need for educators as well as program evaluators to become more knowledgeable about indigenous ways of knowing (e.g., What are the belief systems? How are teaching and learning defined?, What counts as problem solving?, etc.) so that these particulars can be utilized in analyses of their contexts. In the classroom, for example, teachers from the community may emphasize group-constructed knowledge, cooperative learning, and shared test preparation—or even completion; other teachers may emphasize dominant culture values such as individual mastery of knowledge, independent learning, and individual testing (Rothstein-Fisch, Trumbull, Isaac, Daley, & Pérez, 2002). What is an evaluator to make of such differences without understanding their cultural underpinnings?

Such fine-grained understandings depend upon knowledge of local language and culture, which evaluators may make attempts to discern. However, context and culture must also be understood within broader political and historical contexts (Rogoff, 2003). The evaluator, as well, must understand his or her own cultural perspective. "[P]eople are always functioning in a sociocultural context. One's interpretation of [any] situation is necessarily that of a person from a particular time and constellation of background experiences" (Rogoff, 2003, p. 28). Perhaps the most difficult task is to make explicit one's own culturally influenced assumptions (Spindler & Spindler, 1988).

Often when seeking "cultural understanding" of different ethnic and minority groups, there is a tendency to overgeneralize a set of histories, attributes, and behaviors to a particular group. For instance, in the educational arena, evaluators may unconsciously accept a pattern of poorer performance by nonwhite students as natural, rather than looking for reasons in the implementation of a program to explain such a pattern. Gutiérrez and Rogoff (2003) describe a "reductive" tendency in the social sciences to seek singular effects to explain social and cognitive phenomena. When group membership alone is accepted as an explanation for a pattern of performance, the truth is deeply distorted.

Sometimes efforts at cultural understanding are superficial and can get in the way of more important learning. American Indians and Alaskan Natives encounter this tendency when they are asked, "Which name do you prefer—American Indian or Native American?" The implication is that a particular label will capture the correct (or currently agreed upon) identifier, and that once specified, ethnicity will be honored. In reality, such questions reflect a lack of awareness of the wide-ranging variation among indigenous Americans. There is no single answer even to such a seemingly simple and well-meaning question as this one. Distinctive linguistic and cultural traditions as well as histories of contact with European Americans have contributed to vast differences in the experiences and current realities of various tribes. These dissimilarities in background may be evidenced in differences in reserved land bases (reservations, rancherìas, land claims), economic resources, religious influences, and—ultimately—access to health, social, and educational programs. An evaluator would do better to listen carefully to how group members speak of themselves and refer to others in their group. The label can wait and is trivial compared to what may lie beneath it.

Likewise, the "Hispanic community," though it ostensibly shares a common home language, is extremely diverse. Spanish speakers (or those whose parents are/were Spanish speakers) in the United States may have ancestry that goes back generations within the geographical boundaries of what is now the U.S. or that began in any number of other countries—each group having its own cultural, social, and economic history. Thus there can be vast differences among immigrant and U.S.-born "Hispanics" regarding their proficiency in Spanish, as well as their knowledge of English as a second language. Other differences can include socioeconomic well-being, issues affecting the community, religious beliefs, and general ties to a common national or cultural group. While organizations such as schools often consider "Hispanics" a single, unified group, they in fact represent a diverse body along a continuum of acculturation that can differ even among members of the same family. Evaluators must assume responsibility for capturing and correctly interpreting within-group variability for all sub-groups under study.[5]

ILLUSTRATING THE IMPORTANCE OF CONTEXT

To address many of the challenges to authentic evaluation, we have chosen indigenous examples to illustrate the importance of sociocultural and historical context. We draw from these examples in part because we have experience in working within indigenous communities and in part because of the rich diversity of settings represented by such communities. American Indians, Alaska Natives, and Pacific Islanders represent a wide spectrum of tribes and settings within the United States and its territories. At the same time, although these groups have distinct cultures and traditions, there are many commonalities among them. For one thing, unlike other groups in the nation, indigenous peoples have special political relationships with the federal government that allow different treatment within the law (i.e., nation–nation status in the case of federally recognized Indian tribes, land entitlements for Alaska Natives, or various trust relationships as in the north Pacific). Whether they live in intact homogeneous communities or as part of the diaspora of peoples forcibly removed from their homelands or pushed out by a variety of social pressures, most remain strongly connected to tribal traditions and languages and are significantly affected by the ways of thinking and communicating of their ancestral communities.

The examples of evaluation practice in indigenous communities described in this article are drawn from experience working with programs run by tribal organizations within the mainland United States. In such cases, it is important for the evaluator to understand the cultural and political context of the tribe. However, this same understanding is just as important when evaluating public schools and other nontribal institutions' programs that serve reservation populations. More often than not, these types of programs, along with the evaluation approaches used to assess them, have been developed and implemented by outsiders and are at odds with the pulse of their communities.

A second context—large, heterogeneous (and sometimes ethnically homogeneous), chronically underperforming schools—poses additional dilemmas. Some of these have been alluded to earlier, in our discussion of parent involvement. Heavily populated with low-income and minority children, these resource-poor schools struggle (and often fail) to provide high-quality schooling. Program evaluators must be sensitive to the widely divergent educational experiences, backgrounds, and cultures of these students and explore the ways in which those factors interact with the cultures of teaching, learning, and assessment (Hughes, 2000). We will discuss how community ways of knowing can affect the authenticity (validity) and use-fulness of evaluation in each of these settings.

PROMISING APPROACHES TO PROGRAM EVALUATION

Some approaches to program evaluation lend themselves more readily to accounting for context than others. Traditional objectivist evaluation, by definition, is distanced from communities, evaluator-controlled, and non-participatory. In recent years, alternatives to the traditional objectivist forms of evaluation have become increasingly acceptable to the "main-stream" (Fetterman, 2001), something that bodes well for those who wish to see evaluation move more toward internal accountability and serve the needs of communities. Preskill and Caracelli (1997) conducted a survey of evaluators and practitioners (program implementers) and reported, "The greatest change from ten years ago . . . is in the importance placed on organizational learning, participatory, and practitioner-centered action research or empowerment approaches to evaluation. Respondents believe that evaluation can not only facilitate organizational learning, but that evaluation can be a powerful change strategy" (p. 221). This perspective is harmonious with that of American Indian evaluation leaders who participated in a Roundtable on evaluation in indigenous communities in San Francisco early in 2003. Participants stressed that evaluation should create knowledge useful to the community and contribute positively to people's personal lives.

Even when evaluation is driven by external demands, it should be organized in a way that allows it to remain owned in the internal environment and creates useful knowledge for the community. In any case, there should be some degree of reciprocity: Evaluators ask for a community's time and information and should give something in return (Weiss, 1998). When a community believes it is getting something from an evaluation, it is more likely to act on its findings to improve a program.

Recent trends in federal legislation (e.g., the No Child Left Behind Act), calling for improvements for underperforming schools, demand that evaluation approaches facilitate organizational learning that will lead to long-term, systemic change. Evaluation in educational settings is no longer simply carried out for evaluation's sake (i.e., identifying strengths and needs), but rather to facilitate and implement change that will lead to improved services and academic outcomes. More and more, evaluators are being asked not only to know general evaluation methodology, but also to deeply understand the contexts and populations they are studying so they can build organizational capacity and supports. This expectation may imply sustaining schools with a long history of underachievement, schools that serve unique populations (e.g., schools with nearly 100% English learner enrollments, all-white rural schools), or schools that face unique challenges (e.g., secondary schools with thousands of students, schools with 100% poverty rates).

PARTICIPATORY EVALUATION APPROACHES

Weiss (1998) includes "empowerment," "collaborative," and "stakeholder" forms of evaluation under the general heading of "participatory evaluation." We use the terms "empowerment," "participatory," "collaborative," and "stakeholder" evaluation to distinguish a decreasing role of control on the part of the community. The community retains the greatest control in *empowerment* evaluation. In an empowerment evaluation, the external evaluator takes on the role of facilitator or, sometimes, consultant. Primary goals of empowerment evaluation are to foster self-determination within a community and to build the community's capacity to conduct its own evaluation and improve its own programs. As such, empowerment evaluation is situated within the tradition of emancipatory research (Patton, 1997)—research dedicated to improving the lives of members of communities, in terms meaningful to themselves. Of the three major purposes for evaluation (*development, accountability,* and *knowledge generation*; Chelimsky, 1997), empowerment evaluation is best suited to development (capacity building) and knowledge generation (cf. LaFrance, 2002a; Weiss, 1998).

If external accountability is required, *participatory* evaluation may be more appropriate or acceptable to an external stakeholder. Participatory evaluation is characterized as balancing control between outside evaluators and members of a community for whom a program is implemented (Brunner & Guzman, 1989). In the case of participatory evaluation, the evaluator takes charge of the evaluation at first and gradually cedes power to participants, until they take charge. In both empowerment and participatory evaluation, the external evaluator helps build local capacity. According to Patton (1990), "One of the negative connotations often associated with evaluation is that it is something done to people. One is evaluated. Participatory evaluation, in contrast, is a process controlled by the people in the program or community. It is something they undertake as a formal, reflective process for their own development and empowerment" (p. 129).

In a *collaborative* evaluation, the evaluator and practioner(s) are involved in a joint inquiry. The evaluator takes charge of the research end of the endeavor, relying on the practitioners for knowledge about the program and its clients. Rather than render judgments of the processes or outcomes, the evaluator helps gather and organize the data that practitioners will then reflect on in order to improve their program. In a *stakeholder* evaluation, the evaluator is in charge but relies heavily on stakeholders (practitioners, clients, others who may be identified) for advice about what they want out of the evaluation. Stakeholders will also be engaged in interpreting the findings of the evaluation and how they will be used.

A rosy scenario of fruitful and harmonious participation by community members in a program evaluation is appealing but not guaranteed, of course. As Smith (1999) notes, "Idealistic ideas about community collaboration and active participation need to be tempered with realistic assessments of a community's resources and capabilities, even if there is enthusiasm and goodwill. Similarly, the involvement of community resource people also needs to be considered before putting an additional responsibility on individuals already carrying heavy burdens of duty" (p. 140).

An important element of any form of participatory evaluation (in Weiss's broader sense) is engaging participants in identifying their theory of change—that is, their set of assumptions about what actions will lead to what changes and why (Ashton, 1998; Weiss, 1998). Identifying these assumptions will help in building a map of the relationships among program components, their implementation, and outcomes. Simultaneously, the evaluator or facilitator can attempt to be aware of her own assumptions behind her own theory of change. Not incidentally, groups' maps will differ in the ways they represent relationships; and many will find that a linear logic model of change is not the best fit for them. One American Indian evaluator, who has worked with many Indian communities over the years, notes the value of "an intuitive process versus just a strictly logical, linear process [through which one would] perhaps get to more complex interrelationships" (Roundtable, 2003). Of course change is not merely an end in itself. Planning for change and implementing change are very important aspects of the work, and the process itself may have unexpected benefits in terms of learning and building community cohesion.

A CALIFORNIA EXAMPLE OF COMMUNITY PARTICIPATION

Recent California efforts to support underperforming schools (e.g., the Immediate Intervention/Underperforming Schools Program [II/USP] under the Public Schools Accountability Act) share characteristics of empowerment and participatory evaluation to varying degrees. In the case of II/USP, "external evaluators" supported schools through intensive, guided planning focused on developing action plans that would lead to improved student achievement. These external evaluators worked with school site and community member action planning teams to conduct a review of school and district conditions, identify current educational challenges and barriers, and identify strategies for removing barriers and improving student achievement.

Action plans were data-driven, with whole-school and disaggregated data on subgroups (e.g., English language learners, pupils with exceptional needs, Title I/low income) serving as the basis for identifying key goals and setting achievement growth targets. Staff, parents, and the community at large were involved in reviewing, offering feedback, and approving the final action plan throughout the development process. Ensuring implementation of the action plan and creating true systemic change were greatly enhanced when external evaluators strengthened the capacity of school community members to analyze data on an ongoing basis, review and adopt research-based programs and strategies, and locally monitor and evaluate plan implementation. The core purpose for "evaluation" within an II/USP context was to effect change and improve student achievement for all students.

A NORTHWEST EXAMPLE OF COMMUNITY INPUT TO PROGRAM CHANGE

In an evaluation of a child abuse prevention program, a small tribe in the Pacific Northwest defined their assumptions regarding family health. In their change model, they made it clear that they could not limit their services to training parents in positive parenting techniques. They believed that the tribal community as a whole has to participate in the healing of distressed families. If the tribe is not well, families facing Children Protective Service referrals cannot find strength to heal. After articulating these assumptions in their program's theory of change, the program staff effectively argued for a change in program priorities during a troubling year when the community faced a number of crises. An unusually large number of cherished elders died during the year, a tragic murder and suicide rocked the tribe, and political turmoil lead to a recall election.

Responding to these crises, the staff abandoned its training program and focused on helping families through grief and loss, provided cultural leadership for funeral activities, and assisted in preparing community meals. The program staff researched suicide response and prevention programs and put energy into supporting community-wide breakfasts and programs for children and youth. Since community health was an important component of their theory of change, they were able to justify these activities to their funder. As the community is healing and becoming healthier, the staff turned its attention to providing the positive parenting program that is central to the goals of the program's funding organization.

DEALING WITH POWER DIFFERENCES

One obstacle to participation of members of nondominant communities in school-based interventions as well as evaluation processes is the unequal distribution of power, resources, and knowledge within U.S. society (Young, 1999). Inherent in all of the participatory approaches to evaluation is the desire to reduce or eliminate the power differential between evaluator and practitioner (Weiss, 1998). In communities with histories of power issues vis-à-vis the dominant society, if an evaluation process is to not only do no harm but also engender positive outcomes such as capacity building, the power issue needs to be consciously addressed. Simply inviting everyone to the table does not ensure that the power differential recedes. "To mitigate such distinctions [among people of different role types and social backgrounds], evaluators have recommended such things as training for participants in the basics of evaluation, involving stakeholders through work in small groups that cross-cut the positions of participants, and cultivation of openness and sensitivity on the part of the evaluator to the expressed and unexpressed concerns of different groups" (Weiss, 1998, p. 106). In addition, flexible scheduling to accommodate participants' job demands (it tends to be only the professional class that can leave work early or come in late) is a must (Trumbull et al., 2003).

When working in diverse educational settings, this means ensuring that the voices of all stakeholders are included and their participation facilitated through deliberate evaluation designs and data collection methods. For example, it may mean interviewing teachers and parents of students from racial/ethnic/linguistic/special needs subgroups as well as representative students; conducting focus groups representative of all teaching clusters in the school; holding open community meetings at times convenient for parents; offering translators as needed; and integrating parents representative of various groups into planning and decision-making committees (cf. Trumbull et al., 2003).

MOVING TOWARD STANDARDS OF EXEMPLARY EVALUATION PRACTICE

We have argued that exemplary evaluation practice necessarily entails attention to sociocultural and historical contextual factors in a given community. Teasing apart the components of cultural competence in evaluation, we arrive at the following four broad areas:

1. Ability and willingness to take into account the influences of cultural context on program goals, implementation, and outcomes (how to understand the interaction of context with the program).

2. Ability and willingness to honor community-based values, traditions, and customs and capitalize on opportunities to draw from cultural understandings (how to be responsive to the values of the community).

3. Ability and willingness to engage knowledgeable community members in developing focused interventions, communications, and other supports to help ensure that strategies make sense and deliver valid results (how to engage community members).

4. Ability and willingness to create mutuality with community members (how to recognize that others have knowledge; how to distinguish between interpretation and ownership).

Development of competence in these areas requires *first* an awareness that one needs to learn as much as possible about a community and *second* a disposition to identify one's own values and assumptions and set aside judgments associated with them (cf. Fetterman, 1988; Rogoff, 2003; and others regarding anthropological research). Of course, what is also needed is the skill to connect with community members in meaningful ways in order to learn from them. Negotiating how the evaluation will proceed, who will participate, and how information is to be interpreted and shared will follow.

UNDERSTANDING THE CONTEXT

Evaluators can feel confident that their practices are reliable and valid when they know that the evaluative knowledge produced is not counterintuitive to their stakeholders from nondominant communities and, in the end, contributes understanding of those cultures and the program intended to serve them (Hood, 2000). In general, evaluators must be clear about the practical uses of the work in which they engage and be able to define terms (e.g., "student achievement") according to the language and culture of the community.[6] In the case of "student achievement," community members may have a broader definition than that embraced by school personnel. They may consider their children's moral and ethical development as a piece in concert with their grades and test scores and, accordingly, may look to outcomes relevant to their own definition rather than what the district defines (cf. Trumbull, Nelson-Barber, & Mitchell, 2002).

Evaluators must also understand the social and political forces affecting their client communities and make use of that information as they design and conduct the evaluation. Culturally sensitive designs acknowledge differences and capitalize on opportunities to include culturally specific factors and demographic variables that may require special attention or represent themselves in unique ways (e.g., racial treatment historically; immigrant experience; language(s) spoken; living and working conditions—as of migrant, inner-city, or indigenous families). The understanding of the complexity of community context supports the trustworthiness of the data gathered and of their interpretation (cf. Lincoln & Guba, 1983).

Potential threats to validity that are magnified in situations where evaluators are not members of the community they are working with are evaluator bias, insufficient data, and inaccurate data. Some of the activities suggested by Lincoln and Guba (1983) to increase the trustworthiness of an inquiry are particularly applicable to culturally responsive evaluation: (1) ensure that the evaluator spends enough time on site (prolonged engagement); (2) use multiple sources for the same type of information (triangulation); and (3) involve those from whom data has been gathered in reviewing it; verify their statements given in interviews (member checks).

Elements such as these are key when conducting evaluations in Indian communities where understanding the influence of tribal culture and context is critical. For example, here the goals of social services and educational programs are often twofold: to help the individual student or client and to strengthen the community's health and well-being. Given this dual set of goals, indicators of success might not correspond to the dominant society's narrow focus on individual achievement, for example, as mentioned earlier. School administrator Clayton Long (2003) emphasized this blending of boundaries when he noted that evaluators who come to study his schools need to understand that from the community perspective, "School is life and vice versa." These same values influence how tribal people view the role of researchers. Crazy Bull (1997) described these values in her advice to researchers who come into Indian Country:

> We, as tribal people, want research and scholarship that preserves, maintains, and restores our traditions and cultural practices. We want to restore our homelands; revitalize our traditional religious practices; regain our health; and cultivate our economic, social, and governing systems. Our research can help us maintain our economic, social, and governing systems. Our research can help us maintain our sovereignty and preserve our nationhood. (p. 17)

In Indian country, the important concept of "sovereignty" means the recognition of and respect for tribal governance and nationhood. Programs operating on Indian reservations operate within a civil structure unfamiliar to most Americans. Tribes are governmental units separate from state and local governments. Many tribes run their own educational, health, and welfare programs through funding relationships with the federal government. Since tribal governments are much smaller than local and state governments, programs operating under tribal authority are much more closely connected to local political structures than most other publicly funded programs. As a result, programs operating under the tribal governing structures tend to be more susceptible to social and political forces at work in a community. As such, they have a greater obligation to be responsive to community priorities and concerns.

To ground the evaluation in the community, evaluators should learn as much as possible about its history, resources, governance, and composition. If possible, evaluators should engage in community activities such as graduation ceremonies and dinners for the elders in the tribe, or funerals for honored tribal members. Engagement can also involve attending special events such as Treaty Day celebrations, powwows or tribal dances, rodeos, or canoe journeys. This participation can help the evaluator understand the context in which he or she is working. It also allows Indians in the community to build relationships with evaluators that are based on friendliness and respectful interest, rather than relationships that are defined by strict roles and outsider "expertise."

In fact, "expertise" in the form of education, degrees of higher learning, or professional reputation is of little value in Indian Country, if the community does not see the evaluator as a respectful individual capable of understanding an indigenous perspective. This value of *respect* is a primary one in many nondominant cultures, in comparison to the dominant culture, where self-expression can tend to be valued more strongly (e.g., Greenfield, Quiroz, & Raeff, 2000). One of the authors recalls sitting in a day-long meeting of a group collaborating on a complex project. A superior who was evaluating the progress of the group came in to offer her assessment. She minced no words in the process of giving the message that what the group had accomplished was short of her mark: More needed to be done, and it needed to be done better and faster. Her delivery was stern and direct. Everyone was somewhat stunned and uncomfortable, but the three Latin American women in the group all communicated to the superior (in respectful but firm terms) that they could accept criticism but not the lack of respect that was shown them. Not long after, one of these women quit the group, and another announced her intention to leave within a few months.

Govina (2003) described the importance of relationship building when working with her Maori culture. She noted in doing evaluation within the Maori culture that Maori values required that evidence be "trust-based" and grow out of mutual understanding and relationship. Likewise, another Maori researcher, Linda Tuhiwai Smith, emphasizes that indigenous communities tend to be persuaded not by the technical design of research but "by the open and 'good' intentions of the researchers" (1999, p. 140).

Similarly, the most critical dimension for evaluating programs that serve multicultural populations is a deep understanding of a program as it functions within the context of the culturally diverse groups it serves.

RESPONSIVENESS TO COMMUNITY VALUES

Certainly evaluators and clients need not share experiences and values. However, a lack of shared experience can lead to increased errors of definition, mutual comprehension, and interpretation of goals, processes, and outcomes. That is, evaluators and community members may operate on the basis of different assumptions and beliefs. When they succeed in surfacing those differences, evaluation can benefit. Both insider and outsider perspectives can shed light on what is going on within a community (Rogoff, 2003; Smith, 1999).

Culturally sensitive evaluation acknowledges the possibility of multiple frames of reference and different points of view regarding the program or project under review, including a possible mismatch between the program/project goals being promoted and their perceived cultural appropriateness by a given population. A lack of awareness and appreciation for cultural differences can result in erroneous assumptions about program implementation and program outcomes. Understanding "place" in this equation is crucial.

Indian people have a profound sense of place. Cajete (2000) describes how tribal people experience nature as part of themselves and themselves as part of nature, adding, "[t]his is the ultimate form of being 'indigenous' and forms the basis for a fully internalized bonding with that place" (p. 187). Although history of contact with Europeans has altered indigenous connections to their original lands, this sense of place is still a deeply held value. Reservations, which in the minds of some outsiders seem impoverished or limited in development, are cherished homelands. Tribes invest energy and resources to regain lost land and develop opportunities. For many programs operating on reservations, an important criterion of success is whether they in fact contribute to this larger tribal goal.

Indian tribes also possess a strong sense of community, as is evidenced in how tribes identify themselves: *Anishinabe* (the spontaneously created People); *Akimel O'odham* (the River People); *Tohono O'odham* (the Desert People); *Diné* (the People). The original tribal names distinguished the uniqueness of the groups in relation to the rest of the world (Deloria, 1994). The need to preserve and maintain each tribal community is another important criterion of successful programs and services.

In broader U.S. culture that values mobility, competitiveness, and progress, the Indian values of preservation and continuity seem somewhat out of place. Yet it is these more conservative values that undergird many of the programs and projects that are subject to outside evaluations. Failure to understand these values or imposition of more mainstream assumptions on the definitions of what successful program outcomes should be will result in evaluations that fail to contribute to tribal goals and program expectations. Tribal programs need to be evaluated within their own context and with consideration for these more conservative values. Key evaluation questions can become more tribe-specific, such as, "What have we learned from this program or project and how can we use the knowledge we have gained to improve our community?" Questions that imply comparison with populations outside the tribal community are less relevant to a community that is focused on its own identity and preservation. Rather, a group [tribe] may want to identify its own set of benchmarks of progress, which can be used as reference points for evaluating intermediate and long-term outcomes.

It is clear that having evaluators who are sensitive to a program's cultural context will aid in capturing and interpreting cultural nuances as part of the evaluation. This is particularly important for multicultural settings where various cultures may perceive the same scenario through different lenses. An example might involve evaluating the appropriateness of academic achievement and English language proficiency goals set for English learners, the type of services received, appropriateness of materials used, or the teachers' qualifications for serving second-language learners.

ENGAGING COMMUNITY MEMBERS

Gaining access to important information and knowing how to understand what has been gathered can be greatly enhanced through the identification and inclusion of stakeholders from within the populations and communities the evaluation will serve. Key stakeholders may be involved from the initial point of framing the evaluation questions to the end point of disseminating the evaluation results. It is critical that significant stakeholder questions be heard and addressed where appropriate. Discussions regarding what constitutes acceptable evidence should also be discussed with all significant stakeholders prior to data collection. Involving all significant groups in the evaluation's initial discussions will limit the possibility of data's being viewed as irrelevant or suspect by any particular group (Frierson, Hood, & Hughes, 2002).

One of us with extensive experience evaluating programs in Indian country has found that facilitating a workshop that includes program staff and stakeholders to design the evaluation provides an excellent opportunity to build a partnership between the evaluator and staff as well as develop capacity on the part of the group to monitor its own progress and outcomes. The first objective of the workshop is to explicate the underlying assumptions guiding the program. All of the workshop participants have an opportunity to discuss what they do in the program. Since everyone has tasks and activities, all are equally included in the discussion. Once activities are mapped out, the workshop participants are asked what will change as a result of the activities or what are the assumptions for change. This is a much deeper question and leads to a healthy discussion among program staff about their beliefs and values and hopes for the program. This discussion aids in building the program's theory of change (Weiss, 1998).

The second objective for the workshop participants is to identify the major information they will need in order to determine whether their assumptions are correct. The information from the workshop is used to design the evaluation plan that is responsive to the program's values and assumptions. This approach results in a conceptual model for the program that may or may not look like the traditional logic model. In fact, this evaluator never uses the words "logic model," as they connote an intellectualism that can come across as elitist and mysterious. This is not to argue that conceptualizing the program is not important. In fact, it is essential to good evaluation design. But the model should fit the program and the stakeholders' way of seeing the program. Traditional logic modeling formats may be too sequential and narrative-driven and, thus, not appropriate ways to capture the connections between program activities and underlying assumptions. Evaluators should feel creative in developing the pictures or models of the program's mechanisms for change.

Given the high value tribal communities place on their sovereignty and self-determination, it is recommended that external evaluators look for opportunities to build evaluation capacity whenever possible. Using the participatory workshop to build the program's conceptual model and evaluation plan demystifies the process of evaluation and builds ownership in the evaluation.

Many tribes sponsor their own community colleges. In one evaluation that involved a large community survey, one of the authors was able to work with college students who were interning with the tribal office during the summer. They assisted in recruiting focus group participants, developing questions for the survey, and fielding the survey at community events and meetings. Although opportunities like these may be rare, a culturally responsive evaluator should be aware that they are possible and try to incorporate as much training as possible in the evaluation plan.

In multicultural contexts the stakeholder group must be representative of the populations the project serves, specifically including the less powerful stakeholder groups or individuals, such as certain racial, cultural, or language groups. In many cultures, the age, race, gender, language skills, and credentials of the evaluators may have a significant impact on the evaluation process. Evaluation difficulties may arise due to cultural differences in language, values, expectations, and behavioral codes. Evaluators who are not knowledgeable of the cultural etiquette of the groups or context being evaluated could make serious errors in their interactions with evaluation participants. Imagine our chagrin when two of us presenting to a group of educators, administrators, and community leaders in an island setting were confronted by one participant who rose to say he would not be swayed by the perspectives of young women, much less one in a red dress.

In the case of educational evaluation, evaluators must have extensive knowledge of teaching and learning in classrooms and familiarity with what theory, research, and funding requirements are recommended for students receiving the type of program services under review (e.g., low-income students served through federally funded programs like Title I, English language learners, or students in the lowest performing quartile in literacy and mathematics).

INTERPRETATION AND OWNERSHIP

Just as with elements of evaluation already discussed, correctly interpreting data in settings where evaluators and program staff represent different cultural groups requires an understanding of the cultural context in which the data are gathered. Specifically, the meaning or purpose of behaviors may differ from culture to culture and the possibility of misinterpretation threatens the validity of an evaluation. Assistance in interpreting the data should be sought from evaluators who share a lived experience; community representatives who can bring an understanding of cultural norms, values, and behavioral codes; or review panels comprised primarily of members of stakeholder groups (Frierson et al., 2002; Grace, 1992).

The disaggregation of data by numerous variables (e.g., race/ethnicity, gender, socioeconomic status, and first- and second-language proficiency) is also highly recommended beyond the analysis of whole-group data. In regard to evaluating the academic achievement of children, evaluators need to consider the divergent educational experiences, backgrounds, and cultures of students and explore the ways in which those factors interact with teaching, learning, and assessment. To the extent that these factors are controllable or identifiable, they may be planned for in the research design. If they cannot actually be controlled, they can at least be measured and statistically controlled. Evaluations must recognize that a student's culture influences how he or she responds to assessments (Hughes, 2000). For instance, some cultures socialize their children to compete, while others socialize their children to cooperate. The implicit competitive frame of formal assessment thus privileges some students over others (cf., Rothstein-Fisch et al., 2002).

Students from minority backgrounds often populate schools and performance groups with the greatest needs. Given this common scenario, evaluators must pay special attention to school factors affecting the achievement of these students, including the quality of instruction; the opportunity to learn the material being assessed; and teacher characteristics such as efficacy, knowledge of content, teaching skills, years of experience, and attitudes and beliefs about students' capacity to learn and achieve to high standards. Student and family characteristics, including cultural orientation, use of the primary language, and socioeconomic status, can influence teacher expectations of students' academic performance (Hughes, 2000).

Culturally responsive evaluation makes heavy use of qualitative evaluation techniques, making it essential that the evaluators collect data directly from individuals (e.g., through interviews or classroom observations)—something that requires evaluators to be knowledgeable of the cultural context in which the program being evaluated exists. In particular, in data elicitation and interpretation among culturally diverse populations, team members need to understand the role nonverbal behaviors (e.g., body language and speech intonation) play. Oftentimes nonverbal behaviors are treated as "error variance" in the observation and ignored. Special care must also be taken when reviewing interview transcripts and observational protocol data that require the ability to interpret meaning based on the (largely) unwritten rules of cultural discourse (Frierson et al., 2002). Silence or sparseness of language, for example, may be wrongly viewed as resistance, lack of opinion or knowledge, or even rudeness. Yet in some cultures it is a sign of respect to consider one's words carefully and speak as little as possible (cf. Delpit, 1995; Dumont, 1979; Hinde, 1989; Scollon & Scollon, 1981).

ETHICS IN EVALUATION: CULTURAL FACTORS

In cases where a program has been designed without regard for variation in cultural settings, can the same expectations and standards be applied? This question has bearing on the ethical requirement to ensure that evaluation does not cause damage but brings about good for a community. In American Indian communities, the question, "Is the process healing for the group?" may be posed (HeavyRunner, 2003). As Ashton (1998) notes:

[One] problem is that many communities of color and groups who are labeled "minorities" have been evaluated to death. Deep mistrust of evaluation processes and of evaluators has developed over time because of perceived or actual misuse of the data gathered in such studies, and the often total disregard for the subjects in the process. Even the term "subjects" dehumanizes those whose behaviors and processes (their lives!) are being studied and evaluated. (p. 3)

Evaluation has a strong moral/ethical dimension in any case; yet this dimension looms larger in cases where a community has reason to withhold trust from outsiders. How should "bad news" be shared, interpreted, and used to improve a program? How can the evaluation process surface information about how the program interacts with community values and needs? Far too frequently causes of student underachievement are attributed to student or cultural characteristics rather than ineffective school strategies and programs for the population served. Such low expectations of children on the part of school staff are likely to negatively affect the amount of effort put forth to change practice and the school as a whole.

The ethics of evaluation require informed consent of those being interviewed. However, as LaFrance (2002a) notes, special care should be taken when interviewing across cultures. In her report of a conversation among Indian evaluators, she shares Christensen's concern that elders often think that everything they say will be reported, and do not understand that often in a final document only certain quotes will represent their interview. Christensen argues that informed consent is "making sure that the evaluators comprehend what you are saying, and that you understand and consent to how what you are saying will be used" (p. 67).

TOWARD A NEW PARADIGM FOR EVALUATORS

Partnership and Participation

Building a strong partnership between the stakeholders and the evaluator and being willing to relinquish some of the power embedded in being "the evaluator" challenges long-held assumptions that an evaluator is to be impartial and distant from the program's operations. These assumptions are based on the need for objectivity in research and evaluation. However, partnership with the program being evaluated or with the community members who are recipients of the program services does not imply that an evaluator loses the ability to remain "objective." There will always be some level of subjectivity influencing an evaluator's approach to her trade. This subjectivity is conditioned by the training and orientation (quantitative, qualitative, feminist, empiricist, critical, etc.) of the evaluator.

Responding to Community Values to Create Ownership

Evaluation methods that are responsive to community values and contexts are still "objective" in their application if the evaluator and the program's stakeholders value learning from the evaluation. The responsive evaluation practices described above should result in creating this sense of ownership. Once ownership is created, the stakeholders value the knowledge they can gain from the evaluation, and evaluation is all about creating knowledge. When the stakeholders own knowledge creation, the evaluator can discuss negative findings—failure to accomplish goals, assumptions that appear to be incorrect—as well as positive findings. The knowledge becomes empowering, and evaluation is not viewed as merely a judgmental activity that is imposed by funding agencies or other outsiders.

Defining New Roles for Evaluators

Participatory evaluation practices demand new roles for evaluators. Facilitation skills are needed when conducting workshops to define a conceptual model or theory of change or leading meetings that engage stakeholders in discussions regarding findings. Bens (1999) defines facilitation as "a way to provide leadership without taking the reins. A facilitator's job is to get others to assume responsibility and to take the lead" (p. 3). Evaluators need to balance the roles of directing an evaluation process and facilitating stakeholder involvement. As a facilitator, the evaluator provokes the program to think deeply about their assumptions, to explicate how cultural factors might come into play, and identify the questions critical to understanding process and outcomes. When the program stakeholders take responsibility for their own deeply held assumptions and cultural mores, then the evaluator can include these in the program model to be tested by the evaluation.

In the new paradigm, evaluators become change agents. By encouraging culturally relevant and reliable evaluation practice, stakeholders and program participants gain a voice in what is happening to them. As they develop the capacity to identify their own assumptions, they become more confident in questioning assumptions in the dominant society. They are better able to articulate their own goals for program success or demand that programs serving them become responsive to their needs.

Tolerating Uncertainty and Promoting Reflection

As evaluators apply their trade in communities that are not part of the dominant culture, they must be willing to become comfortable with feelings of uncertainty and confusion. Perhaps a final standard of good practice for culturally reliable and valid evaluation practice is valuing reflection. Responsive evaluators crossing into unfamiliar cultures will experience some levels of discomfort and confusion as they sort through new and changing roles for themselves as evaluators. There is no cookbook or clear set of instructions to follow. Becoming effective occurs as evaluators reflect on their own values and explore how they want to become responsive within their own practice. It happens through trial and error, and evaluators become better if they are open to learning from mistakes and willing to question some of their own assumptions regarding the place and role of evaluation when working with groups outside the mainstream. Such efforts will move us closer to ensuring culturally reliable and valid evaluation practice.

NOTES

1. The opinions expressed herein are those of the authors. Portions of this chapter were supported by the U.S. Department of Education, Institute of Education Sciences (formerly Office of Educational Research and Improvement) contract grant #ED-010CO-0012.
2. 2002 and 2003 annual meetings of the American Evaluation Association (AEA), American Educational Research Association (AERA), and Canadian Evaluation Society (CES).
3. The 2003 National Science Foundation–sponsored symposium, Cultural Context of Educational Evaluation: A Native American Perspective, and WestEd's 2003 Roundtable meeting of native evaluators.
4. The 2003 National Science Foundation–sponsored symposium, Cultural Context of Educational Evaluation: A Native American Perspective, and WestEd's 2003 Roundtable meeting of native evaluators.
5. The term "indigenous" refers to American Indian (or Native American), Alaska Native peoples, and to aboriginal peoples of Canada and the Pacific. We recognize that these cultural and ethnic groups are distinct, yet they can share many common values and practices. Furthermore, individuals from these groups do, on the whole, share similar experiences with evaluation today; and our concerns about appropriate evaluation practice extend to all of them.
6. As reported by Fadiman (1997), Asians, as a group are often characterized as "model" minorities who have a strong work ethic and excel academically. However, disaggregated data reveal differences between the children of highly educated first-wave Vietnamese immigrants, for example, and those of lesser-educated parents who followed. According to Walker-Moffat

(1995), more recent immigrants, the Hmong, achieve higher grade point averages than other Southeast Asian students as well as whites, blacks and Hispanics. But this statistic can be deceiving. In fact, many Hmong students are situated in low academic tracks.

7.   For instance, families from some cultural communities may have a more global notion of learning and achievement that includes a moral and ethical dimension (Goldenberg & Gallimore, 1995; Trumbull et al., 2002). Narrow standards of achievement may be less meaningful to them.

REFERENCES

Ashton, C. (1998). *Strategic considerations in facilitative evaluation approaches.* The Action Evaluation Research Institute. Retrieved on August 22, 2003, at www.aeprro.org/inprintconference/ashton.html

Bens, I. (1999). *Facilitation at a glance.* Cincinnati, OH: Association for Quality and Participation.

Brunner, I., & Guzman, A. (1989). Participatory evaluation: A tool to assess projects and empower people. In R. F. Connor & M. H. Hendricks (Eds.), *International innovations in evaluation methodology* (New Directions for Program Evaluation, Vol. 42, pp. 9–17). San Francisco: Jossey-Bass.

Cajete, G. (2000). *Native science: Natural laws of interdependence.* Santa Fe: Clear Light.

Carriere, J. (2003). *Program evaluation and the Cree medicine wheel: A work in progress.* Paper presented at the annual meeting of the Canadian Evaluation Society, Vancouver, BC, Canada.

Chelimsky, E. (1997). The coming transformations in evaluation. In E. Chelimsky & W. R. Shadish (Eds.), *Evaluation for the 21st century: A handbook* (pp. 1–26). Thousand Oaks, CA: Sage.

Crazy Bull, C. (1997). A Native conversation about research and scholarship. *Tribal College Journal. 9,* 17–23.

Deloria, V. (1994). *God is red: A Native view of religion.* Golden, CO: Fulcrum.

Delpit, L. (1995). *Other people's children.* New York: New Press.

Dumont, R. (1972). Learning English and how to be silent: Studies in Sioux and Cherokee classrooms. In C. Cazden, V. John, & D. Hymes (Eds.) *Functions of language in the vlassroom.* New York: Teachers College Press.

Fadiman, A. (1997). *The spirit catches you and you fall down.* New York: Farrar, Straus and Giroux.

Fetterman, D. M. (1988). *Ethnography step by step* (Applied Social Research Methods Series, Vol. 17). Newbury Park, CA: Sage.

Fetterman, D. M. (2001). *Foundations of Empowerment Evaluation.* Thousand Oaks, CA: Sage.

Frierson, H., Hood, S., & Hughes, G. (2002). Strategies that address culturally responsive evaluation. In J. Frechtling (Ed.), *The 2002 user-friendly handbook for project evaluation.* Arlington, VA: The National Science Foundation.

Goldenberg, C., & Gallimore, R. (1995). Immigrant Latino parents' values and beliefs about their children's education: Continuities and discontinuities across cultures and generations. In P. Pintrich & M. Maehr (Eds.), *Advances in achievement motivation* (Vol. 9, pp. 183–228). Greenwich, CT: JAI Press.

Govina, H. (2002). *Treaties and traditions: Cultural competencies in New Zealand evaluation design and practice.* Paper presented at the annual meeting of the American Evaluation Association, Washington, DC.

Grace, C. (1992). Practical considerations for program professionals and educators working with African-American communities. In *Cultural competence for evaluators: A guide for alcohol and other drug abuse prevention practitioners working with ethnic/racial communities.* Washington, DC: Office for Substance Abuse Prevention, U.S. Department of Health and Human Services.

Greenfield, P. M., Quiroz, B., & Raeff, C. (2000). Cross-cultural conflict and harmony in the social construction of the child. In S. Harkness, C. Raeff, & C. M. Super (Eds.), *Variability in the social construction of the child* (New Directions in Child Development, No. 87, pp. 93–108). San Francisco: Jossey-Bass.

Gutiérrez, K., & Rogoff, B. (2003). Cultural ways of learning: Individual traits or repertoires of practice, *Educational Researcher, 32*(5), 19–25.

HeavyRunner, I. (2003). *Comments at Roundtable.* San Francisco: WestEd.

Hinde, R. A. (Ed.). 1989. *Non-verbal communication.* Cambridge, UK: Cambridge University Press.

Hood, S. (2002). *Evaluation within a cultural context: An African American perspective.* Paper presented at the annual meeting of the American Evaluation Association, Washington, DC.

Hughes, G. (2000). *The cultural context of educational evaluation: The role of minority evaluation professionals.* Arlington, VA: National Science Foundation.

Johnston, A. (2002, November). *Building capacity: Ensuring evaluation findings contribute to program growth.* Paper presented at the annual meeting of the American Evaluation Association, Washington, DC.

Johnston, A. (2003). *A Canadian First Nations approach to evaluation.* Paper presented at the annual meeting of the Canadian Evaluation Society, Vancouver, BC, Canada.

Jolly, E. (2002, April). *On the quest for cultural context in evaluation: Non ceteris paribus.* Paper presented at the National Science Foundation workshop: The Cultural Context of Educational Evaluation: A Native American Perspective, Arlington, VA.

LaFrance, J. (2002a, April). *Networking: How to develop a line of communications.* Workshop Proceedings, The Cultural Context of Educational Evaluation: A Native American Perspective, National Science Foundation, Arlington, VA.

LaFrance, J. (2002b, November). *The role of an external evaluator at a small tribal college.* Paper presented at the annual meeting of the American Evaluation Association, Washington, DC.

Lincoln, Y. S., & Guba, E.G. (1983). *Naturalistic inquiry.* Beverly Hills, CA: Sage.

Long, C. (2003). *Comments at Roundtable.* San Francisco: WestEd.

Nelson-Barber, S. (2003). *Understanding the context: Cultural considerations for evaluation in Indian country.* Paper presented at the annual meeting of the Canadian Evaluation Society, Vancouver, BC, Canada.

Patton, M.Q. (1990). *Qualitative evaluation methods* (2nd ed.). Newbury Park, CA: Sage.

Patton, M.Q. (1997). Toward distinguishing empowerment evaluation and placing it in a larger context. *Evaluation Practice, 18*, 147–163.

Preskill, H., & Caracelli, V. (1997). Current and developing conceptions of use: Evaluation use TIG survey results. *Evaluation Practice, 18*(3), 209–225.

Rai, K., & Yang, N. (2002, November). *Neither this way nor that way: A "Mandala" approach to building evaluation capacity with the Hmong refugee community-based agencies in Wisconsin.* Paper presented at the annual meeting of the American Evaluation Association, Washington, DC.

Rodriguez, C. (2002). *Evaluation within a cultural context: A Latino perspective.* Paper presented at the annual meeting of the American Evaluation Association, Washington, DC.

Rogoff, B. (2003). *The cultural nature of human development.* Oxford, UK: Oxford University Press.

Rothstein-Fisch, C., Trumbull, E., Isaac, A., Daley, C., & Pérez, A. (2002). When "helping someone else" is the right answer: Teachers bridge cultures in assessment. *Journal of Latinos in Education, 2*(3), 123–140.

Roundtable on Native American Evaluation. (2003, March). San Francisco: WestEd.

Scollon, R., & Scollon, S. (1981). *Narrative, literacy and face in interethnic communication.* Norwood, NJ: Ablex.

Smith, L. T. (1999). *Decolonizing methodologies: Research and indigenous peoples.* London: Zed Books.

Spindler, G., & Spindler, L. (1988). Roger Harker and Schonhausen: From familiar to strange and back again. In G Spindler (Ed.), *Doing the ethnography of schooling: Educational anthropology in action* (pp. 21–43). Prospect Heights, IL: Waveland Press.

Symonette, H. (2002, November). *Boundaries, borderlands and border-crossers.* A workshop presented at the annual meeting of the American Evaluation Association, Washington, DC.

Trumbull, E., Nelson-Barber, S., & Mitchell, J. (2002). Enhancing mathematics instruction for indigenous American students. In J. Hankes (Ed.), *Changing the faces of mathematics: Perspectives on indigenous people of North America.* Reston, VA: National Council of Teachers of Mathematics.

Trumbull, E., Rothstein-Fisch, C., & Hernandez, E. (2003). Parent involvement—according to whose values? *School Community Journal, 13*(2), 45–72.

Walker-Moffat, W. (1995). *The other side of the Asian American success story.* San Francisco: Jossey-Bass.

Weiss, C. H. (1998). *Evaluation* (2nd ed.). Upper Saddle River, NJ: Prentice-Hall.

Young, M. D. (1999). Multifocal educational policy research: Toward a method for enhancing traditional educational policy studies. *American Educational Research Journal, 36*(4), 677–714.

CHAPTER 6

AN UNTOLD STORY IN EVALUATION ROOTS

Reid E. Jackson and His Contributions toward Culturally Responsive Evaluation at Three Quarters of a Century

Rodney Hopson
Duquesne University

Stafford Hood
Arizona State University

Recent scholarly attention to understanding culture, diversity, and social justice in education and the social sciences has far-reaching implications for the discipline and profession of evaluation. The evaluation community's recent attention to this matter suggests that either cultural context has been insufficiently addressed by most evaluation approaches or beneficial culturally appropriate approaches and explanations have been underdeveloped as they pertain to communities of color who remain on society's periphery. Omitting the centrality and relevance of culture in the context of evaluation leaves open the distinct possibility that too many variables are not understood and in many cases misunderstood. This may indeed be one of the important explanations about notions of difference, power rela-

The Role of Culture and Cultural Context in Evaluation, pages 87–104
Copyright © 2005 by Information Age Publishing

tions, and equity. Consequently, the rich intellectual history of the evaluation profession may be impoverished as a result of an overemphasis by
those who some have anointed as "fathers" (or "mothers," in recent history) of the field.

The need to reexamine conventional evaluation epistemologies, theories, methods, and history concerning communities and persons of color
cannot be overestimated. Gordon, Miller, and Rollock (1990) have portrayed the cultural and methodological hegemony that explain and affect
life experiences and groups of persons of color in the United States (and
the Americas). Gordon and colleagues view the result as "cultrocentric,
and ethnocentric chauvinism in Euro-American and male dominated production of social science knowledge" (p. 15). The authors describe this
chauvinism as "communicentric bias" and identify a number of problems
associated with the traditional/dominant culture paradigm that has served
as the primary lens for studying social phenomena. One deleterious aspect
of communicentric bias is failure to adequately understand groups with
unique cultural, ethnic, and gender experiences as well as their behavior,
perspective, and social systems. Another detrimental result is its assessment
of cultural and ethnic diversity. A third (particularly relevant to this chapter and emerging research) speaks to the unnerving attempts to silence or
ignore the developments and contributions of certain pioneers in the field
of educational research and evaluation.

Referring to knowledge about African Americans and treatment of this
group, Gordon and colleagues (1990) argue that communicentric hegemony has resulted in narrow cultrocentric perspectives, techniques, and
standards as well as incomplete and inadequate assessments of diversity. It
is apparent that the evaluation discipline and profession must seriously
engage in discourse that will inform our understanding of the implications
of cultural and methodological hegemony locally and globally. In mainstream evaluation theory and practice, notions of "minority issues" in evaluation still appear as an appendage, at best, to the foundations of
educational and program evaluation, more aligned with some historic and
static view of issues and perspectives about a marginalized community.
"Minority issues," like "diversity," may limit the manner in which we need
to engage and critique the hegemonic culture and science of evaluation as
well as those notions posited and accepted by the wider field. Persistent vigilance is required to redirect knowledge bases and traditions of educational evaluation away from narrow cultrocentric perspectives and
standards. This chapter seeks to challenge that narrow perspective.

Linda Tuhiwai Smith's (1999) work on the significance of indigenous
perspectives on research acknowledges the power of Western scholarship
and researchers who have perpetuated lingering effects of colonialism,
marginalization, and dominance. At a basic level, part of the damage lies in

broken protocols, failed tests, and in ignoring key people. But there were significantly more harmful consequences. Smith contends:

> The greater danger, however, was in the creeping policies that intruded into every aspect of our lives, legitimated by research, informed more often by ideology. The power of research was not in the visits made by researchers to our communities, nor in their fieldwork and the rude questions they often asked...At a common sense level research was talked about both in terms of its absolute worthlessness to us, the indigenous world, and its absolute usefulness to those who wielded it as an instrument. (p. 3)

Likewise, there has been a tendency to view indigenous and other marginalized communities, commonly assigned to the periphery in educational evaluation, nor were their life experiences perceived to be of value in the mainstream context of the field. Instead, increased gaps and tensions between communities of color or diverse cultural groups and evaluators (the evaluation establishment) portray a tenuous relationship (at best). It seems apparent to us (as well as a few others) that evaluation practice in such settings requires an additional perspective as well as a particular set of skills, competencies, and values that are more likely to make use of these communities' rich cultures, cultural contexts, and nuances (as opposed to documenting their bankruptcy and deficiencies) (Millett, 2002; Stanfield, 2001). To do so requires evaluation practitioners, methods, and approaches that are responsive, respectful, ethical, and beneficial to these communities. Asa Hilliard's plenary address at the 2002 American Educational Research Association directly calls attention to these very topics within the foundations of educational evaluation. His call for "beneficial" research in education speaks to the crux of the matter concerning responsive evaluation in general and culturally responsive evaluation in particular.

As a consequence of these noted efforts and discourse, an increasing number of education evaluators (but definitely not all) find it hard and even unacceptable to ignore the importance of a social agenda in evaluation and advocacy models for persons of color. While many in the evaluation community are familiar with recent efforts to promote a social agenda and advocacy models, few are aware of a legacy of similar efforts that were undertaken dating back to the late 1930s, 1940s, and 1950s (i.e., pre-*Brown v. Board of Education* I) by African American evaluators during the Jim Crow era. Hood's evolving work (2001) has reported on the overlooked work in educational evaluation by early African American scholars whose work clearly responded to a social agenda that addressed the intentional disenfranchisement and undereducation of African Americans during the period between *Plessy v. Ferguson* and *Brown v. Board.* In this chapter, we intend to define and claim our roots as African American evaluators through the untold legacy of one early African American evaluator, Reid E. Jackson.[1] We present the continued tracing of our roots as African American evaluators to demonstrate how these early evaluators both contributed to the literature on educational evaluation, its historical development and its utility, and also advanced a socially responsible agenda for the education of African Americans.

PURPOSE OF THIS CHAPTER

While the attention to evaluation models and approaches that validate non-Euro-American cultural hegemony is virtually absent, a number of social agenda and advocacy models in the field may serve as a necessary starting place for advancing more profound approaches that center on sociocultural perspectives and experiences of persons of color in this country. In taking this view, this chapter contributes and extends notions of culturally responsive evaluation from both a historical and contemporary perspective, giving voice and recognition to the influence of early evaluators of color as well as the implications for the field of evaluation.

An equally important purpose, though secondary to lifting and retelling contributions to evaluation roots, is to reflect upon the current context of evaluation and the extent to which it is meeting the needs of communities and persons of color. Ultimately, the chapter suggests ways in which culturally responsive evaluation has emerged and converged in evaluation, education, and larger social science, thereby shaping new possibilities for the discipline and communities it serves in this millennium. We take another step to provide another installment to the untold legacy of early African American evaluators, their contributions to evaluation history, theory, and practice, but equally as important their connectedness to social advocacy for African Americans. The first compelling story that must be told in this legacy is that of Reid E. Jackson.

REID E. JACKSON: THE FIRST BRIGHT LIGHT OF THE AFRICAN AMERICAN EVALUATION COMMUNITY

Unquestionably, the contributions of Ralph Tyler, Benjamin Bloom, Lee Cronbach, J. Thomas Hastings, and others to evaluation theory and practice during the early years of educational evaluation were exemplary and have been well documented. However, for us it has been enlightening and validating to discover the unrecognized and ignored important work by African American evaluators during the two decades prior to *Brown v. Board of Education I* (1954). This section of the current chapter specifically intends to give voice and recognition to the influences of early evaluators of color, their contributions to the field of evaluation, and the communities they were socially responsible to serve. The broader unfolding of this story, at least in regard to the early African American evaluators, cannot be fully told (nor should it be expected) in a single chapter. This is the second installment in the rediscovery of early African American evaluators that was begun in "Nobody Knows My Name" (Hood, 2001). Hood identified a group of African American scholars who studied, practiced, and published in the area of educational evaluation in the period of 1930–1951 and more importantly tapped into the genealogy of the field.

Hood (2001) reported that between 1935 and 1951, 25 African Americans had received their doctorates in education and conducted educational evaluations for their dissertations. Almost half published scholarly works on their large-scale evaluation studies, smaller evaluation studies, and essays on evaluation during the height of the Jim Crow era that followed *Plessy v. Ferguson*. The importance of their work to educational evaluation during this period is for the most part unrecognized in its social and educational significance for African American education. Hood argues that it would have been socially irresponsible for "African Americans, trained in evaluation techniques, to engage in evaluative efforts that did not address the unequal educational opportunities and resources that were implicit in many northern states and explicit in the southern ones" (p. 39). In essence, it was incumbent upon them to promote a "social agenda" model by using evaluation as their vehicle.

While Aaron Brown and Leander Boykin were most visible in this early work, it has become increasingly apparent that during this period there were other African American scholars who contributed to the evaluative inquiry of African American education but received their doctorate in disciplines and professional schools other than education. Their stories will further enrich and expand the subsequent work that underlies the story of African American evaluators. It is important to first note that evaluative inquiry of African American education, by African American scholars, dates back to 1900. Anderson (1988) reported that in 1900 and 1910 W.E. B DuBois made the "first attempts to evaluate and classify the black colleges" (p. 250). However, for the purpose of this chapter we focus on one African American evaluator, whose doctoral dissertation in education was an evaluation study and arguably the earliest, perhaps most prominent member of this group—Reid E. Jackson. Among the earliest scholarly work by an African American scholar that contributed to evaluation theory and methods to study African American education, the work of Reid E. Jackson stands tall. A snapshot of Jackson's experiences as an African American, teacher, administrator, scholar, and evaluator during the period of 1930–1940 will be used to illustrate the historical significance of his work to educational evaluation in general and the evaluation of African American education in particular.

Reid E. Jackson was born on December 8, 1908, in Paducah, Kentucky, where his father was a high school principal and later became the principal of a new elementary school for "Negroes" in Louisville prior to Reid reaching beginning school age, with his mother taking a position as a librarian at the "Negro Free Public Library" (Jackson, 1945). With a father as a principal and mother a librarian, it is not surprising that Reid would do well in school and pursue a college degree. As was typical in Southern states during the 1920s, if African Americans were to receive a college education they would be required to attend a "Negro" college. While there was a state normal school for Negroes in Frankfort, Kentucky, at the time, Reid was ready to enter college. He would pursue his college education at a prestigious private African American college in his neighboring state of Ohio (Wilberforce University), completing his BS in 1929. In order to contextualize the period from Jackson's birth to his graduation from Wilberforce, we must comment on the African American experience during this period.

CONTEXTUALIZING THE SIGNIFICANCE OF JACKSON'S ERA IN AFRICAN AMERICAN EDUCATION EVALUATION

We are reminded that the landmark case of *Plessy v. Ferguson* was decided in 1896 by the U.S. Supreme Court. Thurgood Marshall (1952) characterized the period of 1896–1930 as one where the "separate but equal doctrine became ingrained in our case law" (p. 317). This resulted in the legal sanctioning and institutionalization of "separate but equal" in the social, political, economic, and educational systems in America but particularly in southern states. Anderson (1988) reported that in 1900 for the 16 southern states, the African American teacher-to-student (ages 5–18) ratio was 93 to 1, while being 57 to 1 for whites. Thompson (1935) would also report that in 1900, the discrimination in per capita expenditure for white and Negro children was 60% in favor of the white children and increased to 253% by 1930; and while the academic preparation of Negro and white teachers was comparable, the discrimination in salaries of white and Negro teachers increased from 52.8% in 1900 to 113% in 1930.

Even in view of these major disparities, Anderson indicates that it was during the period of 1900 to 1935 that public elementary schools became available to the majority of southern black children—but was also accompanied by a major shortage of African American teachers to teach these students. Similarly there was the miniscule number of African Americans with PhDs to teach university-level students as well as to conduct research studies and evaluations focusing on the African American educational experience. It is important to note that two events of major significance in African American education occurred late in this period. The first was the awarding of the first PhD in Education to an American of African descent to Charles Thompson (1925, University of Chicago). Thompson would also be responsible for the second of these crucial events by founding the *Journal of Negro Education (JNE)*.

Unfortunately, Charles Thompson can be considered to be one of the lesser known icons of African American educational researchers and scholars. After completing his PhD in Education (3 years prior to Ralph Tyler receiving his doctorate from the University of Chicago), Thompson would join the faculty of Howard University. While students and scholars of African American education during this period have been aware of Thompson's numerous contributions, he is most renowned for his founding of the *JNE* in 1932 and his skillful editorship of the journal for nearly 31 years.

In 1932, Thompson articulated the critical importance for more meaningful research and evaluation focusing on African American education. He stated:

> ...there is a need for continuous, critical appraisal and discussion of the present and proposed practices relating to the education of Negroes. It is obvious that the mere collection of facts is only the first step in developing and understanding upon which to base the sane direction of any movement or institution. It can be truthfully said that proposals affecting the education of Negroes have not been subjected to an abundance of critical investigation and thinking. (pp. 1–2)

The purpose of *JNE* was clear and it would play a central role in scholarly discussions about African American education (and educational evaluation, more specifically) for the next 73 years, some of which were catapulted by Jackson's own scholarship.

Thompson viewed *JNE* as having a threefold purpose. The first and most obvious purpose grew out of a scholarly need: there was "no general means for collecting and disseminating facts about activities among Negroes" (1932, p. 1). It was true that in most cases there was very limited or no quantitative data available from any governmental or private entity that could provide any meaningful description of the condition of education for African Americans. Nor was there a vehicle to disseminate it, even if it were available. The second purpose was to address the need for "...continuous, critical appraisal and discussion of the present and proposed practices relating to the education of Negroes" (Thompson 1932, p. 2). It is in this second purpose of *JNE* that one sees how the journal would be a vehicle for disseminating evaluative inquiries about the education of African Americans for the purposes of judging the quality of educational curricula, pedagogy, and programs. The third purpose for founding the

JNE was that there was also a need for some entity to "stimulate and sponsor investigation of problems incident to the education of Negroes." This third reason clearly speaks to the need for the stimulation and sponsorship of empirical studies on the education of African Americans.

Thompson realized unequivocally that the preeminent white educational journals such as the *Journal of the National Education Association* or the *Journal of Educational Research* would be neither willing nor interested in serving as vehicles for the types of discussion necessary to address concerns facing the education of African Americans. Thompson made it clear that African American scholars should be the primary and central participants in this conversation when he stated that "leadership in the investigation of the problems incident to the education of Negroes should be assumed to a greater extent by Negro educators" (1932, p. 2). It would also have been unreasonable for African American educational researchers to expect that other journals for Negroes such as the civil rights journals *Crisis and Opportunity* or the *Journal of Negro History* could broaden their missions to meet their needs. The *JNE* issues of the 1930s would begin to fulfill the void in the education literature on educational research and evaluation pertaining to the education of African Americans but most significantly the literature was created by African American educational researchers and evaluators. Surely the news that African Americans were now receiving doctorates in education from northern elite institutions and that African American scholars were publishing important work in the new *Journal of Negro Education* that focused on the African American educational experience influenced Reid E. Jackson's professional ambitions during the 1930s.

JACKSON'S INFLUENCE TO EDUCATIONAL EVALUATION ROOTS

Upon graduating from Wilberforce University, Jackson taught for one year as a high school history teacher in Columbia, South Carolina, before returning to his home state of Kentucky to be a junior high school science and mathematics teacher in Louisville from 1930 to 1933. Following the completion of his master's degree in 1934 from Ohio State University, he accepted the position of Dean of Education at a small southern church college for Negroes (Edward Waters College, Jacksonville, Florida, from 1934 to 1936) where he made $25 less a month than before he started working on his PhD (Jackson, 1945, p. 289). It was during his tenure as Dean that he produced his first six scholarly publications, four published in 1935 alone, with two being published in the *Journal of Negro Education.*

Jackson's published work in 1935 included three studies that focused (not surprisingly) on secondary schooling for African Americans in his home state of Kentucky and in Florida where he was the Dean of Education at Edward Waters College. These studies were also attentive to one of the purposes of *JNE* to provide "...critical appraisal and discussion of the present and proposed practices relating to the education of Negroes" (Thompson 1932a, p. 1). An additional publication was an essay on the evaluation of reorganized secondary schools.

Thompson published Jackson's "The Development and Present Status of Secondary Education for Negroes in Kentucky" in the April 1935 issue of the *Journal of Negro Education*. In it, Jackson (1935a) relied on reports by the Kentucky Educational Commission and to a great extent another *JNE* publication by Myrtle Phillips (1932) on the "Origin, Development and Status of Public Secondary Education for Negroes in Kentucky." Jackson contextualized the Kentucky educational experiences of African Americans by first noting that Kentucky was one of two states that did not enact legislation forbidding the teaching of African Americans and consequently they had been openly taught in the state. Initially, the African American schools were financially supported solely on the taxation of the African American community, but by 1882 Kentucky had passed legislation for more financial equity in supporting the separate schools for African Americans—even though the state did not provide funds for building and maintaining these schools. By 1924, the Kentucky State Department of Education had established a Division of Negro Education and appointed a supervisor who appeared to be sensitive to the educational needs of African American children. Jackson further acknowledged that the year before his *JNE* publication, Kentucky had also passed a school code that provided for more equitable salaries for African American teachers and compulsory school attendance that would also contribute to the increased access to education for African Americans.

The more substantive findings of this study included: (1) the system of colored schools in Kentucky was established in 1874 but there was no real presence of secondary schools for African Americans until 1916; (2) most secondary schools for African Americans were in urban districts; (3) a large number of African American students were not in secondary schools, particularly in rural districts; and (4) African American secondary schools were held to a lesser standard by the State Board of Education.

Jackson's second 1935 publication was an essay on evaluation that appeared in *School and Society*. In the early 1930s public secondary education was embroiled in trying to recover from the Depression, influencing a call for the reorganization of the "people colleges" that should now place a higher emphasis on an industrial education curriculum than on a college preparation curriculum. These reorganized schools would be those that would be expected to include seventh and eighth grades with the traditional secondary grades. The expectation would be that there would be more continuity in the curriculum facilitating better articulation between the upper elementary school grades and the secondary grades. Jackson's (1935e) essay, "Some Criteria for Evaluation of the Reorganized Secondary School," provides an insight into the methods he would employ in his dissertation study and his later evaluations of African American reorganized schools. Jackson reported that a monograph entitled "Program of Studies," reported in the U.S. Office of Education's Bulletin in 1932, outlined 11 functions that should be present in reorganized schools. He asserted that that these functions would "present the best approach in evolving measures for their evaluation" (Jackson, 1935d, p. 772). However, Jackson was not fully impressed with the U.S. Office of Education's 11 stated functions because they had *not* been stated in a manner "to make them readily applicable as criteria" (p. 772). Therefore, Jackson reviewed these functions and condensed them to four criteria that could be used to evaluate reorganized schools. His evaluative questions, framed with a deliberate attention to a specific social agenda of the time and one of the earliest glimpses of culturally responsive evaluative judgments, were as follows:

1. Are there provisions for better articulation between the elementary and secondary levels of education?
2. Are more adequate provisions made for individual differences in the capacities, interests, and needs of the pupil?
3. Are there provisions for more adequate socialization?
4. Are there greater facilities and economy in administration?

His consideration of developing measures to evaluate reorganized schools that were congruent with the "functions" outlined in the U.S. Office of Education Bulletin may have partly been influenced by the early work on the Eight Year Study that was underway at Ohio State University under the direction of Ralph Tyler. It is also possible that Tyler's (1934) seminal work on constructing achievement tests based on the clear statement of objectives that could be used to design such measures may have also been considered by Jackson at this time. Let us now consider Jackson's first two publications in light of events that precipitated his conducting a third study that was published in *Opportunity*. Consider the following experience that may partially explain Jackson's pursuit of a socially responsible agenda by engaging in the evaluative inquiry of segregated education for African Americans.

Jackson's provides an informative biographical look into his experiences in the 1945 *The Crisis* publication, "Education in Black." This thoughtful piece confirms his numerous encounters with racism in the South. He faced major challenges of trying to prepare African teachers at Edward Waters College with nearly nonexistent financial resources that were further compounded by the College's informing the local community that it would open a demonstration school to use in the training of teacher trainees. Jackson was able to secure and install desks and blackboards that had been discarded by the county in addition to other repairs in order to convert the lower wing (the basement) of the girls' dormitory for the elementary school. After Jackson and his teacher preparation students had made substantial progress, they believed their efforts had resulted in their creating " . . . a worthwhile laboratory in the new progressive education movement then sweeping the country" (p. 290). All was well until they were visited by the state supervisor of Negro education, who stated:

> You are not training these prospective teachers in a practical manner. . . . Don't you know that it is a waste of time to try to teach Negroes science, history, mathematics, and the like? You should be preparing them for the kind of lives they must live. For example, they should be taught to use their hands in manual activities, such as repairing broken chair sets or putting in a new window pane. (p. 290)

Jackson reported that as a result of this experience he was determined to find out "the educational opportunities which the state was actually providing for its Negro citizens" (1945, p. 290). His study evaluated the extent to which Florida was "actually" providing educational opportunities to the African American community and was later published in 1935: "Educating Jacksonville's Tenth Child: A Close Up of Race Relations in Florida" (Jackson, 1935c). Jackson clearly undertook the evaluation in response to the visit by the Florida state supervisor of Negro education. Jackson's design primarily included an analysis of the data on Negro education in Duvall County, Florida, that had been collected for the Biennial Report of the State Superintendent of Public Instruction. Jackson reported that he had "politely" requested the necessary data from the Duvall County Board of Public Instruction's superintendent, but was denied. He would later report that after the superintendent had denied his request, he discovered that a "Negro menial worker could gain entry where the Negro professional was not allowed to go. The bribe of a box of cigars to the Negro janitor of the state office building procured for me those coveted figures which the county superintendent had surly denied me" (Jackson, 1945, p. 290). In this study, Jackson investigated the "status" of Negro schools in Duvall County, Florida (Jacksonville is in Duvall County). His evaluation of Duvall County's Negro schools primarily relied on the State Superintendent's Biennial Report, augmented by his personal visits to the Negro schools in Jacksonville. Jackson accurately understood that statistical data alone would be insufficient to this evaluative inquiry, particularly in the African American community. He understood the need for qualitative contextual description to enrich the meaning of the quantitative data. He reported:

An array of statistical data has great significance to the critically minded person, but a word picture of actual conditions can hardly escape the notice of all readers. To this end personal visits were made to the Negro schools of Jacksonville in order to procure information which might offset the limitations of statistical data. The school visits were made in order to procure information which might offset the limitations of statistical data. (Jackson 1935c, p. 213)

Many of his major findings were not surprising: Duvall County schools for Negroes were poorly supervised by the white Supervisor of Rural Schools; pupil-to-teacher ratio was 30.3 to 1 for white schools and 43 to 1 for Negro schools; only 13 Negroes were principals in the 41 county schools for Negroes; and salaries for Negro teachers ranged from $400 to $1,300 and for whites $500 to $3,000. However, the surprising finding was that 62.6% of the Negro teachers were college graduates compared to 47.8% for white teachers. Jackson's evaluation of Duvall County's schools for Negroes did provide sound evidence of the disproportionate educational opportunities for the African American community. However, his other work over the next 2 years, while in the doctoral program at Ohio State University, provides further valuable insights.

During the period of 1880 to 1935, there was a revolution in public secondary education as public high schools became more available to the masses, in addition to the white elite, with these schools becoming the "peoples' colleges." Anderson (1988) would report that there was a major expansion of southern white public high schools in rural areas of the South from which African American children were largely excluded. Northern philanthropic organizations such as the Rosenwald Fund and the General Education Board aggressively sought to support the development of a system of secondary industrial education that would prepare African Americans for "Negro jobs." Hence was the perspective of the white county supervisor that visited Jackson at Edward Waters College.

In his evaluation of "Reorganized Secondary Schools for Negroes in Kentucky" (Jackson, 1935d) that was also published in the *Journal of Negro Education,* he applied the criteria he had modified in his earlier publication, "Some Criteria for Evaluation of the Reorganized Secondary School." The purpose of this study was to evaluate the form of reorganization of secondary schools for African Americans in Kentucky. In this study, Jackson expanded his methods beyond the review of reports by the state department of education and made an unspecified number of personal visits to schools. For this study he selected five junior or senior high schools that had been determined to be "reorganized" and five determined to be "conventional" secondary schools. A questionnaire was developed for these 10 schools, with six completing the questionnaire (four reorganized and two conventional). Five reorganized schools and two conventional ones were visited and "inspected." A few of Jackson's major findings were: (1) the reorganization of Kentucky's secondary schools for African Americans was making minimal progress; (2) reorganized secondary schools for African Americans used a variety of measures to address the individual needs of their students; (3) teachers at these schools were inadequately prepared, underpaid, and lacked uniformity in standards; and (4) curricula in these schools had shifted from classical subjects to social studies. Some may wish to minimize the significance of Jackson's evaluation work in Florida and Kentucky because his methods only relied on reports by state departments of education, supplemented by his visits to a fairly small number of African American schools. However, the significance of his work lay in the reporting of the disaggregated state data to provide comparative analyses of educational indicators for African Americans and whites. These were data that the mainstream evaluation community chose not to respond to. Jackson's analyses were intended to "invoke realization on the part of public and school authorities alike, of the flagrant violations of the American ideal of equality of educational opportunity, insofar as the Negro is concerned" (Jackson, 1940b).

The following year he also published the "Status of Education of the Negro in Florida 1929–1934" (Jackson, 1936) where some of the findings in the two previous studies were reconfirmed, including a greater increase in the enrollment of African American students and schools for them during this period as well as an increase in the percentage of African American teachers but a decline in the number of white teachers. African Americans comprised 29.4% of Florida's population but the cost for the facilities and equipment for their schools was 6.4% of the state school budget; the per capita cost for African American students, based on teachers' salaries, was $9.10 compared to $25.04 for white students. In each of these three evaluations, his methods included an analysis of the Biennial Reports of the Superintendent of Public Instruction of the State of Florida, bulletins from the Florida State Department of Education, and personal visits to some of the schools. Similar methods would be noted in the evaluations he conducted and were published in 1935 on secondary schools in Kentucky.

After conducting his evaluations in Florida and Kentucky, prior to the completion of his doctorate, Jackson turned his attention to similar but more comprehensive evaluation efforts to the State of Alabama. It appears that Jackson's published evaluation of Alabama secondary schools (Jackson, 1939, 1940a, 1940b) was related to his dissertation study, "Critical Analysis of Curricula for Educating Secondary School Teachers in Negro Colleges of Alabama." Even though he did take the time to publish an essay on the "Evaluation of Institutions for Teacher Education in a Democracy" (Jackson, 1938), his seminal and most comprehensive evaluation work was

"An Evaluation of Educational Opportunities for the Negro Adolescent in Alabama I and II" (Jackson 1940a, 1940b).

Jackson furthermore accurately observed that the typical comparative analyses of quantitative educational indicators in previous studies of the "status" of education for African Americans were important to illustrate the disparities in the educational experiences of African Americans and whites in the South but these analyses were insufficient. In this regard, he had also been guilty in his evaluations in Florida and Kentucky. He stated:

> Certainly, any effort to stimulate an increase in educational facilities for an underprivileged group is laudable in itself; but there is no efficacy in the mere *numerical* increase in provisions for the education of a group. The point is that the educational opportunities of the Negro be enlarged in terms of the pressing demands of a democratic society; hence, the impersonal criterion offered in the computation of an arithmetical ratio deriving from population count does not suffice. The needs of the group, individually and collectively, must serve as a criterion if a true democracy is to be achieved. (1940a, p. 59)

Jackson's evaluation of secondary schools for African Americans in Alabama would employ a comprehensive evaluation design that incorporated comparative analyses based on state education data within a more refined qualitative approach. In this study, Jackson's design included:

1. A review of the Alabama State Superintendent of Education's annual report.
2. Responses to a 15-page questionnaire by 100 African American high schools in Alabama (60.3% response rate). These 60 schools employed 478 teachers for 7,776 students.
3. Review of current educational literature.
4. U.S. Census Reports
5. Personal interviews with a gender and racially mixed group of 150 adults (including college presidents, college teachers, high school administrators, classroom teachers, other professions, as well as skilled and semi-skilled laborers).
6. Questionnaires distributed to 275 students at teacher training institutions with follow-up interviews conducted when Jackson visited a particular institution or when a student had not received the questionnaire.

Analyses included the number of African American secondary schools that had been accredited between the period of 1929–30 (29.3%) to 1932–33 (46.9%), comparisons of African American and white student enrollment by grade levels 7–12, and the number of Negro schools by type of control.

Jackson's publications offer a glimpse into his work in evaluation. Between 1935 and 1940 Jackson would publish 14 scholarly articles that not only addressed the evaluation of secondary schools for African Americans but also the teacher training programs that he argued should both serve as vehicles to further democracy (Jackson, 1936, 1938) as well as the evaluation of educational objectives for African American adolescents (Jackson, 1940b).

Jackson's work sought to provide "critical appraisals" of African Americans' educational experiences in the states of Kentucky, Florida, and Alabama while focusing particularly on secondary schools and teacher training programs. Over the course of his career he would publish more articles while holding faculty and administrative appointments at Talladega College (Alabama), Dillard University (New Orleans, LA), Morgan College (Baltimore, MD), West Virginia State College, Langston University (Oklahoma), Southern University (Baton Rouge, LA), Arkansas State College, and his alma mater, Wilberforce University. He also was a member of numerous professional associations including the John Dewey Society and the American Educational Research Association. His work and contributions in evaluation have gone unrecognized. But as we are learning, he is only one of too many evaluators of color who have not been recognized by the American evaluation community.

Equally intriguing are the linkages that existed between the white male founders of the field of educational evaluation and African American PhDs in education. As we delved into the work of this one responsive evaluator, we noted that Jackson worked on his master's and doctorate degrees at Ohio State University during the same time that Ralph Tyler was doing his early groundbreaking work on the Eight Year Study with other notables such as Lee Cronbach and Benjamin Bloom. Even a casual reading of the above-noted publications on evaluation reveals echoes of Tyler's objective-oriented evaluation approach. Yet at the same time Jackson incorporated focused qualitative inquiry to address the shortcomings clearly seen to be of equal importance in his evaluative inquiries. Jackson understood that the collection and analysis of race-specific data (though often almost impossible to come by for an African American evaluator) could only partly tell the important stories regarding the African American educational experience. Three quarters of a century later there are those who will only begrudgingly accept this reality. Reid E. Jackson was an unsung leader in the early stages of educational evaluation. He made considerable achievements with little to no monetary or professional support from the evaluation community. He had a social agenda and acted on it.

He was responsive to his culture and acted as an advocate for the least served in his society.

IMPLICATIONS AND CONCLUSIONS

The significance of Jackson's seminal work gives good reason for recognizing his responsive evaluations as clear antecedents to Stake's (1973) defining work in the early 1970s. Rather than emphasize a discussion of who begat whom, these discoveries place social agenda and advocacy models of evaluation at the core of pioneers of evaluation in the African American educational experience more than three quarters of a century ago. Culturally responsive evaluation deserves its own branch of the evaluation tree and Reid E. Jackson's contributions deserve recognition as an early pioneer in the field. Not surprisingly, mainstream and conventional evaluative inquiry do not recognize culturally responsive evaluation nor Reid E. Jackson's input in the development of the field. The efforts of Jackson and others signal an important lesson for evaluators of color in the 21st century who look to develop beneficial, culturally appropriate approaches and explanations that have remained on our field's periphery. Jackson's own contributions challenge the narrow cultrocentric perspectives of his time, lessons for us to do the same.

James Baldwin's bestseller, *Nobody Knows My Name: More Notes of a Native Son*, written and published in the era of *Brown*, is a fitting title and testament to the unearthing of early responsive evaluators who happened to be African American. In fact, Baldwin's essays too portray this profound and unique American tradition of not recognizing the sons (and daughters) of the enslaved in this country. His context is the literary world, in explaining the complexity of being African American and his self-imposed exile to claim his identity and freedom in his discovery of what it means to be an American. Baldwin wrote then in this rediscovery, "The time has come, God knows, for us to examine ourselves, but we can only do this if we are willing to free ourselves of the myth of America and try to find out what is really happening here" (1961, pp. 22–23). Hence, the discovery of the intellectual history and scholarship of African American evaluators has been also a profound sense of reclaiming identity and freedom, not just for us but for the field at large. It is up to us to reclaim and redefine legacies in educational evaluation to uncover a rich and untapped reservoir of evaluation epistemologies, theories, and methods.

NOTE

1. While this chapter focuses on the legacy of Reid E. Jackson, the work of others such as Aaron Brown, Leander Boykin, and others deserve to be lifted and recognized as important roots in the evaluation field.

REFERENCES

Anderson, J. D. (1988) *The education of blacks in the South, 1860–1935*. Chapel Hill: University of North Carolina Press.

Baldwin, J. (1961). *Nobody knows my name: more notes of a native son*. New York: Dial.

Gordon, E. W., Miller, F., & Rollock, D. (1990). Coping with communicentric bias in knowledge production in the social sciences. *Educational Researcher, 19*(3), 14–19.

Hilliard, A. (2002, April). *Beneficial educational research: Assumptions, paradigms, definitions*. Paper presented at the annual meeting of the American Educational Research Association, New Orleans.

Hood, S. (2001). Nobody knows my name: In praise of African American evaluators who were responsive. *New Directions for Evaluation, 92*, 31–43.

Jackson, R. E. (1935a). The development and present status of secondary education for Negroes in Kentucky. *Journal of Negro Education* 4(2), 185–191.

Jackson, R. E. (1935b). Editorial note. *Journal of Negro Education, 4*(3), 289–292.

Jackson, R. E. (1935c). Educating Jacksonville's tenth child. *Opportunity, 13*(7), 212–215.

Jackson, R. E. (1935d). Reorganized secondary schools for Negroes in Kentucky. *Journal of Negro Education, 4*(4), 505–513.

Jackson, R. E. (1935e). Some criteria for evaluation of the reorganized secondary school. *School and Society, 41*, 772–773.

Jackson, R. E. (1936) Status of education of the Negro in Florida, 1929–1934. *Opportunity, 14*(11), 336–339.

Jackson, R. E. (1938). Evaluating institutions for teacher-education in a democracy. *School and Society, 48*, 630–632.

Jackson, R. E. (1939) Alabama County Training Schools. *School Review, 47*, 683–694.

Jackson, R. E. (1940a). An evaluation of educational opportunities for the Negro adolescent in Alabama, I. *Journal of Negro Education, 9*(1), 59–72.

Jackson, R. E. (1940b). A evaluation of educational opportunities for the Negro adolescent in Alabama, II. *Journal of Negro Education, 9*(2), 200–207.

Jackson, R. E. (1945). Education in black. *Crisis, 52*(10), 288–290.

Marshall, T. (1952). An evaluation of recent efforts to achieve racial integration in education through resort to the courts. *Journal of Negro Education, 21*(3), 316–327.

Millett, R. A. (2002, June). Missing voices: A personal perspective on diversity in program evaluation. *Non-Profit Quarterly Newsletter*.

Phillips, M. R. (1932) Financial support. *Journal of Negro Education,* 1(2), 108–136.

Smith, L. T. (1999). *Decolonizing methodologies: Research and indigenous peoples*. London: Zed Books.

Stake, R. (Ed.). (1975). *Evaluating the arts in education: A responsive approach*. Columbus, OH: Merrill.

Stanfield, J. H. (1999). Slipping through the front door: Relevant social scientific evaluation in the people of color century. *American Journal of Evaluation, 20*(3), 415–431.

Thompson, C. H. (1932). Editorial comment: Why a *Journal of Negro Education? Journal of Negro Education,* 1(1), 1–4.

CHAPTER 7

LEARNING TO PLAY SCHOLARLY JAZZ

A Culturally Responsive Evaluation of the Hopi Teachers for Hopi Schools Project

Carolyne J. White
Rutgers University

Mary Hermes
University of Minnesota Duluth

From the vantage point of the colonized ... the term "research" is inextricably linked to European imperialism and colonialism ... probably one of the dirtiest words in the indigenous world's vocabulary.

—Linda Tuhiwai Smith (1999, p. 1)

The jazz metaphor creates a pathway for making explicit the tacit understandings that enable us to make our way as researchers without fully orchestrated scores.

—Penny Oldfather and Jane West (1994, p. 22)

This chapter explores the tensions involved in our planning for a culturally responsive evaluation study of the Hopi Teachers for Hopi Schools Project

The Role of Culture and Cultural Context in Evaluation, pages 105–128
Copyright © 2005 by Information Age Publishing

(HTHS).[1] As argued by Carlos Rodriguez (2002) at the National Science Foundation Workshop on the Cultural Context of Educational Evaluation: A Native American Perspective, "We need more descriptive information about how we are doing it [culturally responsive evaluation] now. We do not have enough information about how Native American evaluations are actually playing out" (p. 78). In this chapter we respond to this need as we plan for a culturally responsive-based evaluation of the Hopi Teachers for Hopi Schools Project.

Following Smith (1999), we are deeply concerned about how to approach an evaluation of HTHS with colonial research tools, what Audre Lorde (1981) termed the "master's tools," and how to write an evaluation report with what Adrienne Rich (1978) termed "the father's tongue." Like Rich, we acknowledge that "this is the oppressor's language, yet [we] need it to talk to you." Seeking to use the language and the tools that we have— language and tools that are by definition born out of a system of oppression—in new and decolonizing ways, we turn to jazz.

Jazz has shown me the ways of achieving artistic structures that are personal.

—Romare Bearden (1997, p. 67)

I have learned from jazz how to work with limits and opportunities, possibility and ambiguity, obstacles and challenges. I see in jazz a model of meaning, a model of responsiveness without progress or repetition, without self-abnegation or self-righteousness. Jazz is a profound metaphor for the dynamics of community building and social responsibility.

—Sharon Welch (1999, p. 1)}

With Rasula (1995) we learn from jazz "how to hear the world differently" (p. 152). The metaphor of jazz illuminates both the functioning of the program and our collaborative journey with this project evaluation. Like jazz, our processes require a negotiation of in-between spaces, spaces in between Western and indigenous ways of knowing and being.

Students [faculty and staff] in the *Hopi Teachers for Hopi Schools Project* face the dilemma described by Robert Allen Warrior (1995): "A death dance of dependence between, on the one hand, abandoning ourselves to the intellectual strategies and categories of white European thought and, on the other hand, declaring we need nothing outside of ourselves and our culture in order to understand the world and our place in it" (pp. 123–124). Jazz is our metaphor for understanding the creation and negotiation of a space in between this dualism. Just as we are constantly negotiating Western educational standards with the desire and directions for revitalizing Hopi teaching traditions in the teacher education program, the evaluation of such a program must also represent a continual improvisation of working between these two distinct traditions.

As the vast majority of outstanding jazz performances are collaborative, collaboration is central to the work of the *Hopi Teachers for Hopi Schools* Program. From designing the program, to writing the grant proposal to fund the program, to implementing the program, collaboration has been the core method. As explained by Oldfather and West (1994), "Jazz is adaptive and is shaped by the participants. Their improvisations are collaborative and interdependent; the quality of music depends on each musician's hearing, responding to, and appreciating the performances of the other players" (p. 22). Our writing, as co-principal investigator and outside evaluator, mirrors this commitment to collaboration. Collaboration also marks our rejection of dualistic ways of knowing as well as our desire for more holistic, indigenous ways of knowing.

Qualitative inquiry informs our approach to this evaluation. A "civic, participatory, collaborative project that joins the researcher with the researched in an on-going moral dialogue" (Denzin & Lincoln, 2000, p. ix), qualitative inquiry embraces interpretive and critical paradigms and multiple methods in an inherently political approach to educational research. Here we join "the large-scale social movement of anticolonialist discourses" (see Lopez, 1998, p. 226) and seek to honor indigenous ways of knowing (see Bishop, 1998; Brayboy, 2000; Grande, 2000a, 2000b; Graveline, 2000; Mihesuah & Wilson, 2002; Rains, Archibald, & Deyhle, 2000; Smith, 1999). We want our evaluation inquiry to mirror the collaborative methods engaged in this specialized teacher education program. We seek a model for culturally responsive evaluation that follows Denzin (2003) and "aligns the ethics of research with a politics of the oppressed, with a politics of resistance, hope, and freedom" (p. 258).

Yet, there are no politically innocent spaces for educational research. We must acknowledge our precarious roles in this project as scholars who have been educated by the "whitestream" (see Denis, 1997; Grande, 2000a) institutions within which this work is to intervene. As explained by Minh-ha (1989):

> He who lays stress on the professional aspect of his work and defines himself essentially as a member of an institutionalized body of specialists capable of developing "a system of scientific analysis" spends his time searching exclusively for the stereotype in the Other. At no time, while he sets out scientifically to interpret the natives as bearers of a stamp imprinted on them "by the institutions in which they live, by the influence of tradition and folk-lore, by the very vehicle of thought, that is, by language," does he feel the scientific urge to specify where he himself stands, as a stereotype of his community, in his interpretation. (p. 72)

It is, therefore, crucial that we reflect upon our sociocultural positionality and consciously acknowledge the personal, political, and moral commitments that inform our work in this program and our relationship to the evaluation team, the research, and the researched (see Neumann, Pallas, & Peterson, 1999; Siddle Walker, 1999). Following Young (2001), "we must ask how our academic and cultural experience, points of view, social commitments, traditional and nontraditional sources of knowledge improve learning and life chances for a diverse [American Indian] population" (p. 3).

As exquisitely expressed by Reuben Honhanie (Hopi), "We are under a microscope. A lot of people are interested in Indians, so they look at them and analyze them and analyze them again and say, 'These people are good at this, but they are not very good at this.' The reason they say that is because they have looked at them so much, whereas they haven't looked at themselves so much" (quoted in White, 1995).

OUR POSITIONALITY

Here we gaze inward onto ourselves and outward onto our work in the *Hopi Teachers for Hopi Schools* Project. For us, a statement of evaluator positionality ought to accompany every evaluation report that seeks to be culturally responsive. As first-generation college graduates, we understand from the inside many of the challenges faced by the HTHS student participants.

As a woman of mixed heritage (M. H.), my life and professional career have been shaped by the dualism between Western intellectual categories and the reintegration of Native ways into my life and family. In the past 10 years, while working as a teacher educator, I have lived in both the ivory tower and those islands of pristine beauty and destitution—reservations. During my 4-year (untenured) tenure at Carleton College, I had the sense that I was assimilating into a college culture that would preclude membership in other groups. Meanwhile, my educational research was ever more clearly pointing toward indigenous language as the next evolution of culture-based curriculum for Native education. Ironically, the more I became dedicated to my research on culture and language, the further I became distanced from that culture due to my college teaching position. Three years ago, we moved back to the reservation to help start an Ojibwe language immersion school. During this time I have been teaching at the University of Minnesota–Duluth. Part of my assignment was to teach for the Fon d u Lac Ojibwe teacher education program—Gikinoo'imagejig. What the teachers seemed to be most interested in was learning their language. What the state system demanded they know for licensure was anything but an indigenous language. We are only trapped in the "death dance of dependency" when we have only English to think in.

I am comfortable being an "outside insider" (an inside outsider?); as an adoptee this is a familiar position. I can contribute that to this team of Hopi educators. While the specifics of the contexts vary considerably, the general impression left on native communities from colonization are all too familiar.

As an inheritor of white privilege (see McIntosh, 1998) who chooses to act as a white traitor (see Heldke, 1998, p. 94), I (C. J. W.) am accustomed to being a cultural outsider in my antiracist educational practice. Thirty-six years ago I was hired as the secretary for an Upward Bound Program at Southern Utah State College. Blind to the "sacred hoop" (see Allen, 1986) I was joining, blind to the seeding of my personal change, each time I moved from this sacred hoop of connection, I was returned. Following 2 years in New Orleans and 5 years in Illinois, completion of bachelor's and master's degrees, I was asked to direct the same Upward Bound Program. Later, following 8 years in Illinois, I returned to conduct dissertation research in collaboration with 11 former Navajo and Hopi graduates of the same Upward Bound Program (White, 1991).

Six years ago I returned to the hoop again, this time to accept a position at Northern Arizona University. A cultural insider to the university environment, collaboration with American Indian nations in the preparation of culturally responsive teachers my most important work at this university.

Western mind advises distance, objectivity, and administrative power. Indigenous mind advises close relation, vulnerability, and trust in the spiritual. People who lack a spiritual center are ill-equipped for indigenous education work. White people who lack an understanding of the workings of white privilege (see McIntosh, 1988) are ill-equipped for indigenous work. Educational evaluators who lack methodological and epistemological humility (see Narayan, 1988) are ill-equipped for conducting culturally responsive evaluations.

PROJECT BACKGROUND

Two years ago, a Navajo colleague, Joe Martin, tells me (C. J. W.) about a funding opportunity through the Office of Indian Education in the U.S. Department of Education. With only one week to submit the proposal, the task appears impossible. We need a tribal partner. Knowing that the Navajo Tribe has partnered with a couple of Arizona universities, Joe suggests the Hopi Tribe. He telephones Harvey Paymella, Executive Director of the Hopi Department of Education. Within 3 hours Harvey and I meet in my office to create the program. Artwork from the Hopi artist, Fred Kabotie, graces the cover of our proposal. Titled "Germinator," this artistic design symbolizes the long-term goal of the project: to seed significant institutional change in the educational system on the Hopi reservation and the teacher education program at Northern Arizona University. Lofty goals, indeed, this evaluation will provide an opportunity for critical reflection about how effectively we are moving toward their realization.

Prior to Contact, prior to the invasion of Europeans ideologically grounded in "American racial Anglo Saxonism" (see Horseman, 1981), American Indian communities effectively engaged in culturally responsive practices and educated young people into their tribal history, language, literature, values, science, art, and all other forms of education necessary to maintain their way of life.

After Contact, everything changed. American schooling for American Indian students became a process of deculturalization (see Alvord & Van Pelt, 1999; Lomawaima, 1995, 2000; Spring, 1994; Swisher & Tippeconnic, 1999; Yazzie, 2000), a process of using schools to colonize the minds of conquered people by erasing their language (see Fordham, 1998), denigrating their culture (see Chavers & Locke, 1989), and teaching exclusive acceptance to the dominating white male Eurocentric culture. This legacy of colonial schooling for American Indian children (see Adams, 1979, 1988a, 1988b, 1995; Axtell, 1981; Deyhle & Swisher, 1997; Hoxie, 1984; Prucha, 1979; Senese, 1986, 1999; Szasz, 1999; Szasz & Ryan, 1988) is a legacy of institutional racism (see Knowles & Prewitt, 1969) and sexism (see Feagin & Feagin, 1978) that persists today, sustained by educational institutions at every level, kindergarten through graduate education. And, it is often unwittingly perpetuated by scholarly research, including educational evaluations. Villenas, Deyhle, and Parker (1999) advocate for the inclusion of critical race theory analysis that will "provide educational researchers with an interdisciplinary, race-based interpretive framework aimed toward social justice . . . [a] perspective that has generally been absent from mainstream educational research" (p. 32). We agree that this perspective is crucial for addressing racism, for informing development of curriculum that can heal the damage from this history of colonial education (see Deyhle,1992; Deyhle & Swisher, 1997; Siddle-Walker, 1999), and for informing the program evaluation.

Northern Arizona University educates more American Indian students than any other institution in the United States. Institutional rhetoric about commitment to American Indian communities abounds. Serious institutional resource commitment to indigenous education is scarce. Many of the programs touted as successfully serving Indian constituencies reinscribe Western ontologies, epistemologies, and methodologies. Troubled relationships exist with the tribal governments in the area and with the local tribal college. And within this context remains the critical need for educational research that informs educational practice and illuminates how to best serve children.

Understandably, we approached this project with caution considering the kinds of colonial relationships that have typified university involvement with native communities. With David Beaulieu (2000), we believe that "Indian parents, communities, and tribes must define their purposes and goals to guide education with clear directions and . . . they must also assert the criteria for evaluating the success from a tribal and community perspective" (p. 38).

The Hopi Education Summit held in 1995 established a goal of 100% Hopi teachers for all schools on the Hopi reservation. Hopi parents, professionals, and leaders have made their wishes known: they want teachers who have the skills, knowledge, and audacity to proactively change the systems and structures to accommodate schools as communities that meet the needs of their students, and who demand a different structure in a just, caring, and culturally appropriate learning environment.

We created a teacher education program to honor these priorities. Although creating such a program is incredibly complex (see Batchelder, 2000; Beaulieu, 2000; Reyhner, 2001; Senese, 1999; Tippeconnic, 2000; Wallace, 2000; Writer, 2001; Yazzie, 2000), culturally responsive educational practices (see Barta & Schaelling, 1998; Dementi-Leonard & Gilmore, 1999; Elliot, 1998; Jacobs & Jacobs-Spencer, 2001; Lomawaima, 1995; Lyons, 2000; Sparks, 2000; Writer, 2001; Zachold, 2001) are a key component of this program. Educational research confirms that teachers' knowledge of students' language and culture fosters their academic achievement (see Cummins, 1996; Ladson-Billings, 1994; Matthews & Smith, 1994; McLaughlin, 1992/1994; Reyhner, 1988; Willeto, 1999). As explained by Ladson-Billings (1994), this type of teaching strives to "maximize students' learning by using students' cultures as the basis for helping students [to] understand themselves and others, [to] structure social interactions, and [to] conceptualize knowledge" (p. 314). Gay (2000) adds that such teaching liberates students from mainstream cultural pervasiveness, it fosters critical thinking among children, and validates them as knowledgeable. Culturally responsive teachers are involved in the local community and work to foster a nonracist, culturally fit learning environment.

In our model of culturally responsive practice the goal is not merely to increase achievement, but rather to support the transformation of communities. This must begin with providing students with an appropriate civic education that includes equipping them to understand the constitutional status of tribal peoples as distinct nations with sovereign status and treaty rights. While American Indian schools are increasingly being called upon to serve as "sites of American Indian cultural production and reproduction" (Grande, 2000a) by providing culture and language instruction, they must also serve as active players in community development. Some school officials, school boards, and tribal leaders are concerned about making schools better by building on the strengths of their communities. They would teach Indian children to love learning by rooting it in the place they come from and working to improve life on Indian reservations by engaging schools, and specifically the students, in addressing local issues. Far too often schools have focused curricula on individual success, with the consequence that students are inadvertently encouraged to leave home in search of this type of success. As a result, too many of the talented Indian professionals leave the reservation and are employed off-reservation and only a few will ever realize the value of going home to help rebuild their home and communities (Martin, 2000).

There is no question that many Indian students receive a quality education, but the majority of students attend schools that range from good to mediocre, and for large numbers of these young people, schooling is a failure (Hopi Education Summit, 1995). Our goal is not to simply prepare Hopi teachers, but to prepare exemplary certified Hopi teachers who are appropriately trained in culturally responsive pedagogical approaches, methods, and techniques applicable to reservation-based schools. We agree with Hopi parents, professions, and leaders, and with educational researchers who affirm that individuals who know Indian children, speak their language, know the culture, and participate actively in community functions will more effectively provide appropriate instruction to help Indian students succeed academically (see Deyhle, 1989; Deyhle & Swisher, 1997; Gaseoma, 1999; McLaughlin, 1992/1994; Yazzie, 1999).

The program was designed to prepare 20 new exemplary Hopi teachers skilled at providing culturally responsive teaching to be employed as elementary school teachers on the Hopi reservation. Funding from the U.S. Department of Education Indian Education Professional Development Program is crucial to the accomplishment of this goal. The grant funds tuition, books, fees, and a monthly stipend of $1,250 for the student participants. Many of the participants are nontraditional students with children and spouses to support. The stipend is adjusted according to the number of dependents ($200 per month per dependent). This funding is critical, as the cost of living in Flagstaff is much higher than the reservation (in fact, higher than most communities in Arizona). This funding allows the participants to focus more completely on their coursework without having the distraction of a part-time job. Lack of such financial support is often the major obstacle for indigenous students wishing to complete their college degrees.

The program was designed for all of the participants to enroll in the Christensen School-Based Teacher Education Program. Created in 1985, this partnership program includes the following strengths:

- It is informed by the Professional Development School literature (see Abdal-Haqq, 1998; Darling-Hammond, 1994; Goodlad, 1995; Teitel,1996) about how to provide the most effective mechanism for preparing teachers with special attention to the development of an equity-minded, culturally responsive partnership approach (see Murrell, 1998).
- It seeks to produce "teacher-scholars" whose practice is based on critical and reflective inquiry and who recognize, understand, and effectively negotiate the complexities of multiple cultural communities in constant pursuit of educational practices to maximize *all* children's learning and development.
- It is grounded in the real world of the school and classroom through daily internship experiences for students, supervised by trained mentor teachers and university personnel.
- Christensen School has a multicultural student body and the innovative university coursework embraces a critical multicultural focus.

Within the next two sections of this chapter ("Project Goals and Objectives" and "Project Implementation"), we provide a multivocal conversation among the authors. This began with Carolyne briefly outlining the project goals and objectives and her perceptions of the project implementation process. Harvey and Mary read this text and responded with questions and comments. Carolyne added her questions. A representation of this interrogation process is presented in italics.

PROJECT GOALS AND OBJECTIVES

Project Goal

Prepare 20 new exemplary Hopi teachers who are skilled at providing culturally responsive pedagogy to be employed as elementary school teachers on the Hopi reservation. Provide a 1-year teacher induction program.

Specific Goal 1
Initiate a culturally responsive site-based undergraduate program and one-year intensive induction program leading to degree and certification for Hopi elementary educators. *How will we define culturally responsive for this evaluation?*

Objective 1.1.   Activate Project Steering Committee to assist with student recruitment, selection, and project implementation. *What cultural backgrounds do the steering committee members represent? Minutes of the meetings are* *available. Are they important? It seems to Carolyne that few of the committee members were actively involved in the program. They were attentive in the meetings and provided information when asked, but rarely provided critical feedback. Could this be changed? How? Their role seemed to be confined to assisting with program publicity. When invited to interact with the students at special meetings and outings, some attended but because they didn't have deep relationships with the students, meaningful interaction was difficult. This does not appear to be related to culture, except for the possibility that some native students are less eager to interact with strangers before building some foundation of trust.*

Objective 1.2.   Recruit and advise 20 Hopi individuals for acceptance to the Northern Arizona University College of Education Teacher Education Program.

Objective 1.3.   Implement formal program of undergraduate coursework and internships, culminating in student teaching and graduate work; scheduling classes; supervising internships; planning summer coursework.

Objective 1.4.   Implement a 1-year intensive induction program.[2]

Objective 1.5.   Initiate and carry out evaluation procedures for the program.

Specific Goal 2

Provide training for pre-service teachers and mentors in collaborative methods of teaching, mentoring skills, and teamwork practices.

Objective 2.1.   Identify and plan training for Christensen and Hopi mentor teachers.

Objective 2.2.   Implement in-service training for mentors, incorporating multicultural teaching, educational technology, observation skills, mentoring skills, and teamwork skills, to complement the undergraduate and induction program.

Specific Goal 3

Develop an integrated, experiential teacher education curriculum for elementary education teachers for the Hopi reservation.

Objective 3.1.   Prepare integrated coursework and syllabi incorporating indigenous perspectives, issues in multicultural education, rural education, educational technology, and collaborative, reflective practice.

Objective 3.2.   Evaluate the course and curriculum in terms of student learning and achievement of competencies.

Objective 3.3.   Prepare assessment study and implement dissemination activities (e.g., publications, presentations, regional conferences).

Specific Goal 4
   Disseminate project findings.

Objective 4.1.   Develop information about the Project.

Objective 4.2.   Identify effective and efficient dissemination mechanisms.

Objective 4.3.   Develop dissemination materials.

Objective 4.4.   Identify relevant national, state, and local conferences on teacher preparation and Native Education.

Objective 4.5.   Disseminate information about the project at national, regional, and local conferences.

Objective 4.6.   Evaluate dissemination activities.

Objective 4.7.   Revise dissemination activities as indicated.

PROJECT IMPLEMENTATION

As mentioned previously, we had one week to design this program and write the grant proposal that funds it. From her previous work in Cleveland, Carolyne had adopted the metaphor of Jazz Freedom Fighters (see White, Andino-Demyan, Primer, & Storz, 1996), to mark the kind of spontaneous, intuitive, artistic, critical improvisational method necessary for this kind of institutional change work. Improvisation has been crucial to the implementation of this project. Once we were notified of our funding, we faced another challenge with only a couple of weeks to recruit the participants and get them enrolled in classes. This was another time when positive collaboration enabled success. Complicating our recruitment were federal guidelines that required the students be able to receive their degrees within 2 years. As we spoke with students, it became clear that our ideal plan would have to be modified. Some students desired to become secondary teachers, some needed so much prerequisite coursework that the Christensen Program was not viable. We kept our focus on creating the best learning experiences we could while meeting individual student needs. *How important is this question of responding to student needs? Should we have limited project enrollment to only those students who could meet the expectations of the ideal program? Would this have jeopardized our future funding if we were unable to serve the number of students we had said we would serve?*

How will we evaluate the project given that students participated in such different teacher education programs? We have more evaluative data about the students who enrolled in the Christensen Partnership Program than we do about the students enrolled in the other programs. Are we evaluating the whole of their experience in the teacher education program or only those facets for which we had immediate input? If we focus on the students' evaluation of their individual experiences, will that enable us to move beyond this dilemma?

When we realized that we would not be able to fill all of the participants with Hopi Tribal members, it was agreed that we would recruit participants from other tribal communities. The project will graduate 19 students in elementary education and two in secondary education. Fourteen of these students are Hopi, six Navajo, and one Apache. In the *NSF 2002 User-Friendly Handbook for Project Evaluation,* Frierson, Hood, and Hughes (2002) speak to the importance of culturally responsive evaluation, fully taking into account the culture of the program being evaluated and the cultural context within which the program operates (p. 63). For this evaluation, we have Hopi, Navajo, and Apache cultures represented with all of the individual variations of the student participants. We have students who are also part Tewa and part Mexican. We have a staff member who is Kwakiutl/Hixwamis. We have a staff member who is Mormon, one who is a former Mormon, one who holds a combination of native spiritual beliefs, and one who believes in the traditional Hopi way. In addition, we have the dominating white culture overshadowing all of the staff and participants through the mass media, popular culture, and the mandates of university policies, procedures, classroom instruction, state standards, and so on. We have all of the cultural differences among university faculty and staff. We have the differences within each native culture between traditionals, progressives, and others. Then we have the cultural orientation of Mary, the cultural priorities of the Department of Indian Education, the university, the Hopi Department of Education, the multiple cultures of the schools where the students interact in their teacher preparation, and the community members on the Hopi reservation. How might we be responsive to all of these cultural variations without minimizing and/or essentializing any of them?

Project staff members worked closely with university faculty and staff to facilitate recruitment, admission, registration, and retention of the participants. For example, when it was discovered that some of the students were especially challenged in math, Carolyne added a special section of a required math course designed specifically for the participants. The assistant professor hired for this course, Bill Buckreis, taught in a manner that enabled the students to master the material while simultaneously researching how to more effectively instruct math to their future students. Their research resulted in two national conference sessions (at the National Association for Multicultural Education conference and the National Council for Teachers of Mathematics conference) where the students presented their findings with the professor. *Student reactions to these experiences would be useful. What about a written assessment from the professor?*

Given the complex educational needs, the dynamics of language and cultural differences, and the diversity of expectations sought by parents, few people are skilled at engaging in the types of inclusive conversations necessary to facilitate responsible participation between schools and the local Indian communities. However, those dispositions and skills can be learned through critical dialogue and collaboration. One example of this process was when some of the program participants presented at the Hopi Summit on Education in 2004. They had presented previously at professional conferences, but this audience of tribal members included parents and elders. This audience was their most challenging and the one they most wanted to connect with. This audience required that they effectively bridge the university culture and the local Hopi culture. Additional project activities included the following:

- Students received ongoing academic advising and career counseling by the program staff. This included meeting a minimum of once a month. The following are among the multiple issues they may address: family concerns; strategies for speaking with college professors regarding absences related to cultural responsibilities; facilitating access to tutoring and other academic support services; time management; money management; and providing much-needed encouragement and support when coursework and living away from the reservation can find students feeling like they are in "water over their heads." *What other forms of counseling might the students have found useful? Much of this counseling was provided by the project coordinator who is a member of a different native tribe. Would it have been useful to have included counselors from each of the students' cultural groups or is it preferable for the students to ask for such services if they see a need for them?*

- Given the high number of program participants with young children and the difficulties arranging quality child care, the program created opportunities for the children to accompany their parents during workshops and program meetings. *Did this work well? What other forms of student accommodation might the evaluation want to address?*

- Students attended weekly small-group verbal and written reflection conversations during academic coursework and during student teaching. These conversations deepened their understanding of issues related to their professional development and strengthened the learning community as students came to understand that what they may experience as a personal issue is, in fact, a common problem encountered by others in the program and by practicing teachers. By learning to openly discuss these issues, they built the critical reflective dispositions desired for exemplary educators. *Is this just Carolyne's evaluation or did the students agree to this assessment? Transcripts are available of most of these meetings. Would the external evaluator want to examine these?*

- Students participated in special workshops designed to enhance their professional preparation. These included the following: exploring innovative methods for infusing native language and culture into the curriculum, such as a language presentation by the Hopilavayi Project and a workshop on integrating native cultural knowledge into the existing science curriculum; and a workshop on implementing classroom learning expeditions, in-depth investigations of a topic that students engage in the real world through projects, fieldwork, and/or service learning.

- Students presented at national conferences including the National Association for Multicultural Education, the International Reading Association, the National Council for Social Studies, and the National Council of Teachers of Mathematics.

- Students were invited to assume leadership positions. For example, a 2-day cultural immersion trip was planned and implemented by the Hopi student participants for their non-Hopi classmates. This project enabled the Hopi students to reflect upon their communities through the eyes of their native and non-native colleagues.

- Students enrolled in specialized coursework. For example, a course focusing on infusing cultural knowledge into the curriculum was team taught with Hopi Elders and Hopi teachers. This course was offered during the summer following student teaching as a final preparation for their first year of teaching. *Several transcripts from these course presentations are available. Should they be included in the evaluation data?*

- Students participated in an induction-year program. *Transcripts of many of these meetings are available. How should they be used? Transcripts are not available for meetings with all of the students.* Some students were located at a far distance from the program and were difficult to maintain contact with. *What is useful to know about the induction year?* Because we felt that the induction year was not as comprehensive as we wished, we have extended it and added a special summer graduate course focused on tribal sovereignty. *Student papers from this course*

*are available. Students will be presenting papers at the American Education
Studies Association annual conference. They will also be visiting with indigenous groups in Oaxaca, Mexico, to learn about their activities to revitalize
their language and culture, their decision for deschooling. What kinds of data
should we include about this activity.*

STAKEHOLDERS FOR THIS EVALUATION

As we approach this evaluation, we are acutely aware of multiple stakeholders. The Office of Indian Education in the U.S. Department of Education
is the stakeholder calling for the evaluation. Their needs from this evaluation are conventional and fairly straightforward, not nearly as complex as
our task of addressing cultural responsiveness. This task requires that we
address all of the following stakeholders: the Hopi Tribe's Department of
Education; the Hopi Endowment Fund; the Navajo Tribal Office of Education; the NAU College of Education; the student participants; the parents
of the participants; Hopi community members; Hopi Elders; the Hopi
Board of Education; future students of the program graduates; the educational research community; and members of our advisory board. Of these,
we view the Hopi community, Hopi Elders, and Hopi institutions as being
the most crucial and perhaps the most difficult to address. Frierson and
colleagues (2002) advise that "Stakeholders play a critical role in all evaluations, especially culturally responsive ones, providing sound advice from
the beginning (framing questions) to the end (disseminating the evaluation results). It is important to develop a stakeholder group representative
of the populations the project serves, assuring that individuals from all sec-
tors have the chance for input" (p. 65). And, as noted by LaFrance (2002),
"The history of research exploitation in Indian country raises issues for
evaluation . . . evaluation in Indian country should be attentive to community ownership and participation" (p. 66). *How will we gather all of these individuals together to dialogue about the program, program activities, and the kinds of
evaluative information they would like from the program? How about focus groups?
Is there a Hopi cultural activity, like a fair, where we could meet with large groups of
people? Could we run an article in the local Hopi newspaper, an ad on the Hopi
radio station? Perhaps we could present at the Hopi Summit on Education.*

ADDITIONAL TENSIONS FOR THIS EVALUATION

There are numerous factors that have affected the experiences of the student
participants. Most of them are first-generation college students and many are
single parents. There is wide variability in their academic skill preparation.

Although their transcripts would suggest more similarity in their academic skill levels, our experience suggests that many of our students have been mistreated by teachers and professors who gave them good grades without carefully attending to the types of skill development that the students needed. For example, we have students who have earned As and Bs in the English writing courses, and when we work with them on writing a college paper, it is clear that their writing skills are incredibly weak. *What expectations did these former teachers and professors hold for these students?* As we work with them, it is clear that they can develop the needed skills. However, it is extremely time intensive and detracts from the focus the students could otherwise put to their coursework. One way we have addressed this in our courses is that we give the students a grade of "Incomplete" until they are able to achieve the level of writing performance necessary to earn a good grade.

How might we write about other obstacles students encounter, such as spouse abuse or alcoholism, without contributing to negative stereotypes and maintain the students' anonymity in such a small program?

As suggested earlier, how will we address the differences in quality of course instruction given that the students had so many different professors and different program options?

How do we address personality issues, such as difficulties with collaboration among some individuals? Again, the small size of the program makes such information difficult to address in any substantive fashion if we are to maintain confidentiality and anonymity.

Another tension is the continuum of student and staff cultural beliefs and values. Some of the students identify themselves more with Christianity than with any native spiritual belief system. The same is true for members of the Hopi community. These differences complicate discussions of language and culture infusion in the classroom. People who lack a native spiritual grounding find it more difficult to imagine how some of these issues can be infused in the curriculum, and individuals more knowledgeable about the cultural beliefs are also concerned about protecting the sacred knowledge and only sharing the cultural information that is appropriate for broad consumption.

Other tensions relate to changes in program policies dictated by the Office of Indian Education, U.S. Department of Education (OIE/DOE). While increasing the number of culturally responsive Hopi teachers for schools on the Hopi reservation is the priority for the tribe, OIE/DOE decided program graduates could delay their teaching commitment if they choose to pursue full-time graduate study. Our preference would be for the graduates to obtain some teaching experience prior to graduate study, but we are constrained by the OIE/DOE policy. Lack of clear collaboration between OIE/DOE and financial aid regarding their policies has meant that we have faced substantial difficulty facilitating students' receipt of maximum financial support. This difficulty leaves some students questioning our credibility. These are among the many tensions the program negotiates. *How will these tensions be illuminated and how will their relationship to the program operation be understood?*

DECOLONIZING EVALUATION: A BRICOLAGE OF INDIGENIZING METHODS

At this point we envision a culturally responsive evaluation of HTHS necessitating a pragmatic, strategic, and self-reflective methodological bricolage. This bricolage is of a pieced-together, closely knit set of indigenizing research practices that include:

- Focus Group Interviews with Stakeholders (see Madiz, 2000)
- Reflexive Autoethnography (see Denzin, 2003; Ellis & Bochner, 2000)
- Story Telling (see Bishop, 1996; Minh-ha, 1989)
- Testimonies (see Beverly, 2000; Nabokov, 1992)
- Collective Student Reflective Conversations
- Celebrating Survival (see Cajete, 1994)
- Intervening: Collaborative Participatory Action Research (see Kemmis & McTaggart, 2000; Reason, 1994)
- Critical Race Theory/Silences? (see Ladson-Billings, 2000; Parker, Deyhle, & Villenas, 1999; Twine & Warren, 2000)
- Writing as Inquiry (see Richardson, 2000)
- Connecting/Negotiating (see Smith, 1999)
- Envisioning/Reframing (see Smith, 1999)
- Democratizing/Educative (see Gitlin, 1990; White, 1991)

The following are among the multiple data sources that will inform the evaluation:

- Grant Proposal and DOE Reports
- Advisory Board Meeting Minutes
- Autoethnographic Narratives (staff and students)
- Transcripts of Audiotaped Student Reflective Seminars (Weekly)
- Reflection Papers Written by Some of the Student Participants
- Student Demographic Data
- Student Program Applications, Grades, No. of Program Graduates
- Type of Teacher Education Program Students Completed
- Present Employment of Graduates
- Audiotaped Transcripts of Induction-Year Meetings
- Transcripts of Focus Group Interviews

ANTICIPATING THE FINAL REPORT

We seek a new form for presenting the final report of this culturally responsive evaluation, a form that will open different ways of knowing (see Barone, 2001; Scheurich & Young, 1997; White, Mogilka, & Slack, 1998); be more accessible to wider audiences, especially native communities; a form that acknowledges writing as a moral decision that always involves the exercise of power, influence, and authority; a form that acknowledges the real physical, emotional, and moral consequences of scholarship in the lives of real people; a form that can foster solidarity by incorporating multiple truths; a form that will facilitate the making of our students' own histories within the constraints of our postmodern university; an evaluation that will nurture improvement in the program's operation; and an evaluation form that will breathe new life by sharing the experience, strength, and hope of the program participants.

Returning to our metaphor of jazz, we seek a report that will follow Ralph Ellison (1947/1980):

> [Culturally responsive educational evaluation] could be fashioned as a raft of hope, perception and entertainment that might help keep us afloat as we tried to negotiate the snags and whirlpools that mark our nation's vacillating course toward the democratic ideal . . . [we] would have to improvise upon [our] materials in the manner of a jazz musician putting a musical theme through a wild star-burst of metamorphosis. (pp. xx, xxi, xxiii)

NOTES

1. The Hopi Teachers for Hopi Schools Project is a 3-year, innovative, coherent, and sustained teacher preparation program funded by the U.S. Office of Indian Education that includes 2 years of school-based professional teacher education coursework, with a concentration on Hopi history, language, and culture, and a 1-year induction program to prepare 20 exemplary Hopi educators.

2. The carefully organized induction year program we envisioned assumed the program graduates would be graduating at the same time and teaching in Hopi Schools on the Hopi reservation. The reality was that students graduated at different times and were hired in schools located throughout the state of Arizona. This meant that the induction year became more of an individualized experience rather than the collective experience we had anticipated. In addition, because many of the program graduates had worked previously as teacher's aides, the kinds of information and support they needed was different than what is typically addressed in the education literature. Students' strong commitment to cultural activities complicated our efforts to schedule group workshops to support their first year of teaching. No Child Left Behind legislation had a negative impact on the students

efforts to implement the culturally responsive pedagogy they had been taught as many school administrators mandated rigid pedagogical expectations.

REFERENCES

Abdal-Haqq, I. (1998). *Professional development schools: Weighing the evidence.* Thousand Oaks, CA: Corwin Press.

Adams, D. W. (1979). Schooling the Hopi: Federal Indian policy writ small, 1887–1917. *Pacific Historical Review, 48*(3), 335–356.

Adams, D. W. (1988a). From bullets to boarding schools: The educational assault on the American Indian identity. In P. Weeks (Ed.), *The American Indian experience* (pp. 218–239). Arlington Heights, IL: Forum Press.

Adams, D. W. (1988b). Fundamental considerations: The deep meaning of Native American schooling, 1880–1900. *Harvard Educational Review, 58*(1), 1–28.

Adams, D. W. (1995). *Education for extinction: American Indians and the boarding school experience 1875–1928.* Lawrence: University Press of Kansas.

Allen, P. G. (1986). *The Sacred Hoop: Recovering the feminine in American Indian traditions.* Boston: Beacon Press.

Alvord, L. A., & Van Pelt, E. C. (1999). *The scalpel and the silver bear.* New York: Bantam Books.

Axtell, (1981). Dr. Wheelock's little red school. In J. Axtell (Ed.), *The European and the Indian: Essays in the ethnohistory of colonial North America* (pp. 87–109). Oxford, UK: Oxford University Press.

Barone, T. (2001). Science, art, and the predispositions of educational researchers. *Educational Researcher, 30*(7), 24–28.

Barta, J., & Schaelling, D. (1998). Games we play: Connecting mathematics and culture in the classroom. *Teaching Children Mathematics, 4,* 388–393.

Batchelder, A. (2000). Teaching Diné language and culture in Navajo schools. In J. Reyhner, J. Martin, L. Lockard, L. & W. S. Gilbert (Eds.), *Learn in beauty: Indigenous education for a new century* (pp. 1–8). Flagstaff: Northern Arizona University.

Bearden, R. (1997, Spring). *Time* [Special issue: American Visions], p. 67.

Beaulieu, D. L. (2000). Comprehensive reform and American Indian education. *Journal of American Indian Education, 39*(2), 29–38.

Beverley, J. (2000). Testimonio, Subalternity, and Narrative Authority. In N. K. Denzin & Y. S. Lincoln (Eds.), *Handbook of qualitative research* (2nd ed., pp. 555–565). Thousand Oaks, CA: Sage.

Bishop, R. (1996). *Collaborative research stories.* Palmerston North: Dunmore Press.

Bishop, R. (1998). Freeing ourselves from neo-colonial domination in research: A Maori approach to creating knowledge. *International Journal of Qualitative Studies in Education, 11,* 199–219.

Brayboy, B. M. (2000). The Indian and the researcher: Tales from the field. *International Journal of Qualitative Studies in Education, 13,* 412–426.

Cajete, G. (1994). *Look to the mountain: An ecology of indigenous education.* Colorado: Kivali Press.

Chavers, D., & Locke, P. (1989, April). *The effects of testing on Native Americans.* Paper commissioned by the National Commission on Testing and Public Policy.

Cummins, J. (1996). *Negotiating identities: Education for empowerment in a diverse society.* Ontario: California Association for Bilingual Education.

Darling-Hammond, L. (Ed.). (1994). *Professional development schools: Schools for developing a profession.* New York: Teachers College Press.

Dementi-Leonard, B., & Gilmore, P. (1999). Language revitalization and identity in social context: A community-based Athalascan language preservation project in western interior Alaska. *Anthropology and Education Quarterly, 30*(1), 37–55.

Denis, C. (1997). *We are not you: First Nation and Canadian modernity.* Canada: Broadview Press.

Denzin, N. K. (2003). *Performance ethnography: Critical pedagogy and the politics of culture.* Thousand Oaks: Sage.

Denzin, N. K., & Lincoln, Y. S. (2000). *The qualitative inquiry reader.* Thousand Oaks, CA: Sage.

Deyhle, D. (1989). Pushouts and pullouts: Navajo and Ute school leavers. *Journal of Navajo Education, 6*(2), 36–51.

Deyhle, D. (1992). Constructing failure and maintaining cultural identity: Navajo and Ute school leavers. *Journal of American Indian Education. 31*(2), 24–47.

Deyhle, D., & Swisher, K. (1997). Research in American Indian and Alaska Native education: From assimilation to self-determination. In M.W. Apple (Ed.), *Review of research in education* (Vol. 22, pp. 113–194). Washington, DC: American Educational Research Association.

Elliot, I. (1998). Tribal traditions in a basic school. *Teaching K–8, 28*(7), 32–35.

Ellis, C., & Bochner, A.P. (2000). Autoethnography, personal, narrative, reflexivity. In N. K. Denzin & Y. S. Lincoln (Eds.), *Handbook of qualitative research* (2nd ed., pp. 733–768). Thousand Oaks, CA : Sage.

Ellison, R. (1980). *Invisible man.* New York, Random House. (Original work published 1947)

Feagin, J. R., & Feagin, C. B. (1978). *Discrimination American style: Institutional racism and sexism.* Englewood Cliffs, NJ: Prentice-Hall.

Fordham, M. (1998). The politics of language and the survival of indigenous culture: from suppression to reintroduction in the formal classroom. *Equity and Excellence in Education, 31*(1), 40–47.

Frierson, H. T., Hood, S., & Hughes, G. B. (2002). *The 2002 user-friendly handbook for project evaluation.* Arlington, VA: National Science Foundation.

Gaseoma, L. R. (1999). *Hopi oral teachings: A description of what they mean to Hopi Indian students.* Unpublished doctoral dissertation, Northern Arizona University.

Gay, G. (2000). *Culturally responsive teaching: Theory, research and practice.* New York: Teachers College Press.

Gitlin, A. D. (1990). Educative research, voice, and school change. *Harvard Educational Review, 60*(4), 443–466.

Goodlad, J. I. (1995). School–university partnerships and partner schools. In H. Petrie (Ed.), *Professional development schools: Schools for developing a profession.* Albany: State University of New York Press.

Grande, S. (2000a). American Indian geographies of identity and power: At the crossroads of Indigena and Mestizaje. *Harvard Educational Review, 70*(4), 467–498.

Grande, S. (2000b). American Indian identity and intellectualism: the quest for a new red pedagogy. *International Journal of Qualitative Studies in Education, 13*(4), 343–359.

Graveline, F. J. (2000). Circle as methodology: Enacting an Aboriginal paradigm. *International Journal of Qualitative Studies in Education, 13*, 361–370.

Heldke, L. (1998). On being a responsible traitor: A primer. In B. B. On & A. Ferguson (Eds.), *Daring to be good: Essays in feminist ethico-politics.* New York: Routledge.

Hopi Education Summit. (1995). *Summary report of the Hopi education field hearings.* Keams Canyon, AZ.

Horseman, R. (1981). *Race and manifest destiny: Origins of American racial Anglo Saxonism.* Cambridge, MA: Harvard University Press.

Hoxie, (1984). *A final promise: The campaign to assimilate the Indians, 1880–1920.* Lincoln: University of Nebraska Press.

Jacobs, D. T., & Jacobs-Spencer, J. (2001). *Teaching virtues : Building character across the curriculum.* London: Scarecrow Press.

Kemmis, S., & McTaggart, R. (2000). Participatory Action Research. In N. K. Denzin & Y. S. Lincoln (Eds.), *Handbook of qualitative research* (2nd ed., pp. 567–605). Thousand Oaks, CA: Sage.

Kincheloe, J. L., & McLaren, P. (2000). Rethinking critical theory and qualitative research. In N. K. Denzin & Y. S. Lincoln (Eds.), *Handbook of qualitative research* (2nd ed., pp. 279–313). Thousand Oaks, CA: Sage.

Knowles, L. L., & Prewitt, K. (Eds.). (1969). *Institutional racism in America.* Englewood Cliffs, NJ: Prentice-Hall.

Ladson-Billings, G. (1994). *The dreamkeepers: Successful teachers of African American children.* San Francisco: Jossey-Bass.

LaFrance, J. (2002). Networking: How to develop a line of communication. In *The cultural context of educational evaluation: A Native American perspective.* Arlington, VA: National Science Foundation.

Lomawaima, K. T. (1995). Educating Native Americans. In J. A. Banks & C. A. M. Banks (Eds.), *Handbook of research on multicultural education* (pp. 331–342). New York: Macmillan.

Lomawaima, K. T. (2000). Tribal sovereigns: Reframing research in American Indian education. *Harvard Educational Review, 27*, 1–21.

Lopez, G. R. (1998). Reflections on epistemology and standpoint theories: A response to "A Maori Approach to Creating Knowledge." *International Journal of Qualitative Studies in Education, 11*, 225–231.

Lorde, A. (1981). The master's tools will never dismantle the master's house. In C. Moraga & G. Anzaldua (Eds.), *This bridge called my back: Writing by radical women of color.* New York: Kitchen Table: Women of Color Press.

Martin, J. (2000). *Reconnecting schools and communities: Implications for school leadership training and tribal partnership.* Paper presented at the Navajo Nation Economic Development Summit, Flagstaff, AZ.

Matthews, C. E., & Smith, W. S. (1994). Native American related materials in elementary science instruction. *Journal of Research in Science Teaching, 31,* 363–380.

McIntosh, P. (1988). *White privilege and male privilege: A personal account of coming to see correspondences through work in women's studies.* Unpublished manuscript, Wellesley College, Wellesley, MA.

McLaughlin, D. (1994). *When literacy empowers: Navajo language in print.* Albuquerque: University of New Mexico Press. (Original work published 1992)

Mihesuah, D. A., & Wilson, A. C. (2002). Indigenous scholars versus the status quo. *American Indian Quarterly, 26*(1), 145–148.

Minh-ha, T. T. (1989). *Woman Native other.* Bloomington: Indiana University Press.

Murrell, P. C., Jr. (1998). *Like stone soup: The role of the Professional Development School in the renewal of urban schools.* Washington, DC: American Association of Colleges for Teacher Education.

Nabokov, P. (1992). *Native American Testimony.* New York: Penguin Books.

Narayan, U. (1988). Working together across difference: Some considerations of emotions and political practice. *Hypatia, 3*(2), 30–47,

Neumann,A., Pallas, A. M., & Peterson, P. L. (1999). Preparing educational practitioners to practice educational research. In E. C. Lagemann & L. S. Shulman (Eds.), *Issues in education research: Problems and possibilities* (pp. 247–288). San Francisco: Jossey-Bass.

Oldfather, P., & West, J. (1994). Qualitative research as jazz. *Educational Research, 23*(8), 22–26.

Parker, L., Deyhle, D., & Villenas, S. (Eds.). (1999). *Race is . . . race isn't.* Boulder, CO: Westview Press.

Prucha, F. P. (1979). *The churches and the Indian schools.* Lincoln: University of Nebraska Press.

Rains, F. V., Archibald, J. A., & Deyhle, D. (2000). Introduction through our eyes and in our own words—the voices of indigenous scholars. *International Journal of Qualitative Studies in Education, 13,* 337–342.

Rasula, J. (1995). The media of memory : The seductive menace of records in jazz history. In K. Gabbard (Ed.), *Jazz among the discourses.* Durham, NC : Duke University Press.

Reyhner, J. (Ed.). (1988). *Teaching the Indian child.* Billings: Eastern Montana College.

Reyhner, J. (2001). *Family, community, and school impacts on American Indian and Alaskan Native students' success.* Paper presented at the 32nd annual National Indian Education Association conference.

Rich, A. (1978). *The Dream of a common language: Poems, 1974–1977.* New York: Norton.

Rodriguez, C. (2002). Closing remarks. In *The cultural context of educational evaluation: A Native American perspective.* Arlington, VA: National Science Foundation.

Scheurich, J. J., & Young, M. D. (1997). Coloring epistemologies: Are our research epistemologies racially biased? *Educational Researcher, 26*(4), 4–16.

Senese, G. B. (1986). Self-determination and American Indian education: An illusion of control. *Educational Theory, 36,* 153–164.

Senese, G. B. (1999). An unnatural silence: educational access, and achievement in Arizona Native American education. *Planning and Changing, 30*(2), 101–111.

Siddle-Walker, V. (1999). Culture and commitment: Challenges for the future training of education researchers. In E.C. Lagemann & L.S. Shulman, *Issues in education research: Problems and possibilities* (p. 224–244). San Francisco: Jossey-Bass.

Smith, L.T. (1999). *Decolonizing methodologies.* London: Zed Books.

Sparks, S. (2000). Classroom and curriculum accommodations for Native American
students. *Intervention in School and Clinic,* 35(5), 259–263.

Spring, J. (1994). *Deculturalization and the struggle for equality: A brief history of the education of dominated cultures in the United States.* New York: McGraw-Hill.

Stake, R. (1986). *Quieting reform: Social science and social action in an urban youth program.* Urbana: University of Illinois Press.

Swisher, K. C., & Tippeconnic, J. W. III. (Eds.). (1999). *Next steps: Research and practice to advance Indian education.* Charleston, WV: ERIC Clearinghouse on Rural
Education and Small Schools.

Szasz, M.C. (1999). *Education and the American Indian: The road to self-determination*
(3rd ed.). Albuquerque: University of New Mexico Press.

Szasz, M., & Ryan, C.S. (1988). *Indian education in the American colonies. 1607–1783.*
Albuquerque: University of New Mexico Press.

Teitel, L. (1996). *Professional development schools: A literature review* [PDS Standards
Project]. Washington, DC: National Council for Accreditation of Teacher Education.

Tippeconnic, J. W. (2000). Reflecting on the past: Some important aspects of
Indian education t consider as we look toward the future. *Journal of American
Indian Education, 39*(2), 39–48.

Twine, F. W., & Warren J. W. (2000). *Racing research, researching race.* New York: New
York University Press.

Villenas, S., Deyhle, D., & Parker, L. (1999). Critical race theory and praxis: Chi-
cano(a)/Latino(a) and Navajo struggles for dignity, educational equity, and
social justice. In L. Parker, D. Deyhle, & S. Villenas (Eds.), *Race is . . . race isn't:
Critical race theory and qualitative studies in education* (p. 31–52). Boulder, CO:
Westview Press.

Wallace, A. B. (2000). *A reply to "Holding a Mirror to 'Eyes Wide Shut'": The role of Native
cultures and languages in the education of American Indian student.* Available at
http://www.gov/nativeamericanresearch/wallace.html

Warrior, R. A. (1995). *Tribal secrets: Recovering American Indian intellectual traditions.*
Minneapolis: University of Minnesota Press.

White, C. J. (1991). *Experiencing "Upward Bound": An interrogation of cultural landscapes.* Unpublished doctoral dissertation, University of Illinois.

White, C. J. (1995). Native Americans at promise: Travel in borderlands. In S.
Lubeck & B. Blue Swadener (Eds.), *Families and children "at promise."* Albany:
State University of New York Press.

White, C. J., Andino-Demyan, D., Primer, D., & Storz, M. (1996). Constructing a
scholarly community of jazz freedom fighters: (Re)writing the university classroom for the postmodern world. *Planning and Changing, 27*(1/2), 58–73.

White, C. J., Mogilka, J., & Ford-Slack, P. J. (1998). Disturbing the colonial frames
of ethnographic representation: Releasing feminist imagination on the academy. In N. K. Denzin (Ed.), *Cultural studies: A research annual* (Vol. 3, pp. 2–27).
Stanford, CT: JAI Press.

Welch, S. D. (1999). *Sweet dreams in America: Making ethics and spirituality work*. New York: Routledge.

Willeto, A. A. (1999). Navajo culture and family influences on academic success: Traditionalism is not a significant predictor of achievement among young Navajos. *Journal of American Indian Education, 38*(2), 1–21.

Writer, J. H. (2001). Identifying the identified: The need for critical exploration of Native American identity within educational contexts. *Action in Teacher Education, 22*(4), 40–47.

Yazzie, T. (1999). Culturally appropriate curriculum: A research-based rationale. In K. G. Swisher & J. W. Tippeconnic III (Eds.), *Next steps: Research and practice to advance Indian education* (pp. 83–106). Charleston, WV: ERIC.

Yazzie, T. (2000). *Holding a mirror to "Eyes Wide Shut": The role of Native cultures and languages in the education of American Indian students*. Paper commissioned by the Office of Educational Research and Improvement, U.S. Department of Education.

Young, L. J. (2001). Border crossings and other journeys: Re-envisioning the doctoral preparation of education researcher. *Educational Researcher, 30*(5), 3–5.

Zachold, M. G. (2001). Visions and voices: using books on Native American art. *Social Studies and the Young Learner, 13*(3), 21–24.

CHAPTER 8

THE PENAL PROJECT

Program Evaluation
and Native American Liability

Guy Senese
Northern Arizona University

This chapter is an effort to describe two seasons of research in the Dine' Wellness Center evaluation project and an effort to work in harmony with the community and cultural values of the Little Singer school and Birdsprings area of the Dine' (Navajo) Nation. As I work here I cannot avoid finding the contradictions of school life and the expectations of the larger society regarding school goals, ideas of good health, and community solidarity.

In contemplating culturally responsive curriculum and evaluation, the effort must also be responsive to the exploitative conditions of consumerism and capitalism in the so-called New West, which fuel the poverty that leads to family "imbalance" and persistent health problems, including grant-driven health care, as a poor substitute for continual, on-site treatment centers. (As I write this Wellness Center is history, unfunded after 3 years of operation.) This would make the responsive evaluation read as a direct response to problems in the community. As it stands cultural responsiveness read to me like a code language, using "culture" as a placeholder. Culturally responsive evaluations are fixing a problem: the problem is lack

The Role of Culture and Cultural Context in Evaluation, pages 129–147
Copyright © 2005 by Information Age Publishing

of community members conducting evaluation studies. Or creating an educational experience that will sensitize, make the community stranger, more "culturally competent." To many, evaluation problems in Native or minoritiy communities are incorrectly named in the first place. The program environments often reek with unjust, maldistributed resources, an extension of colonial conditions made worse in the collapsing welfare state, amid galloping globalization, that is stripping minority communities of basic living resources. Lacking the will to name this immiserative trend, in comes culture to the rescue. Culture awareness, sensitivity, and responsiveness may be a necessary condition for truthful community pictures to be drawn, but it is not *sufficient*. And worse, it threatens to be a distraction, a feigned move to reclaim lost intellectual territory, but without what DuBois would call the language of freedom, of justice, culture is a more colorful band-aid laid over a 50-stitch wound.

I began to think whether cultural responsiveness was any less a form of administrative surveillance conducted by the university-based liberal establishment. Was it just another penal project, a disciplinary regime pressed on oppressed minority students, where the injustices of the larger society go untouched, unaddressed, while the walls of the prison get painted colorfully with cultural symbols?

I did this work as both a professional but also as an unapologetic friend of the community. I am first aware when I do this work that my 23 years of study and friendship with tribal communities—first in Alaska, then on the Navajo Nation—helped prepare me somewhat to isolate the issues important to people in this community. But my viewpoint is constricted by ideas that were not developed in the heart of this community, but in the world of Euro-centric "study" of Native peoples. Admitting to this weakness did not give me the perspective to write a useful, culturally responsive evaluation. As this chapter explains, it has given me the perspective to write, which is a walk through the ironies of post-colonial schooling.

In 2000 and 2001 I was hired to conduct evaluations of the Dine' Wellness Center at Little Singer Community School, Birdsprings, Navajo Nation, Arizona.

My work here is influenced by 25 years of experience working with Native American school communities, and the education I received from this has informed my understanding of cultural responsiveness. The evaluation consisted of my identifying the stakeholders in the project activities and arranging interviews, identifying pertinent documents relating to project completion goals, and spending significant amounts of interview time with leaders in the community effort to foreground Navajo culture in the school. I interviewed project staff, director, administrators, health workers, teachers, counselors, community treatment recipients and aides in a process of attempting to understand the way in which the wellness concept framed connections with traditional Navajo community spirituality. This report is an effort to understand the project from a culturally responsive perspective.

Several concepts are included in this focus on Navajo culture from a community perspective. +Hozho (harmony), K'e (clanship, interrelatedness), and traditional Navajo peacemaking (the term used here is K'e ye yini nayolshool, translated as: "by feeling our relationship with one another, we can restore peace and harmony").

Principal Lucinda Godinez spoke of the power of the emphasis on K'e or clan responsibility. "Clanship is not a game, it is a way of life," she said. "It is an ethical life and a religious life." She stated that it is the blend of relationship, love, and responsibility that is the center of the harmonious life in the Navajo way. There is no firm boundary between education and wellness. They are inseparable. I asked her what makes a successful educator in this way. She replied that "only those who love" are capable of growing in the "role" of teacher. It is "respect for the role" those students learn. The "ego is left out of it." "The role has its own life." She used the example of a young Anglo teacher from Nebraska, Mr. Thomas, whose combination of hard work, respect for the people, and personal sacrifice in dedication has won him over to the community and parents.

LEARNING FOR LIFE

The mission at Little Singer Community School is: "in cooperation with the home and the parents, to strengthen Dine' cultural values and language to ensure that each student will discover, develop, and strengthen their capabilities for use in meaningful work and family life." The philosophy of Little Singer School prepares students to develop a positive self-image and have better opportunities in life. The bilingual/bicultural life-long learning program builds students' ability to walk with confidence in the Dine' and non-Indian world. Elders past and present believed, and community members today reaffirm, the ideal that children belong at home and the family is the basis for all education. All members of families in the community have a right to an education that will help them reach their goals. The Little Singer Community School service area is located in the southwestern corner of the Navajo reservation in northern Arizona. The Dine' Wellness Center at Little Singer Community School is located approximately in the center of the area, which is about 62 miles by 28 miles. The Little Colorado River forms the southern boundary of this area and since there is no bridge over the river, access is limited.

The core of the Wellness Center and its connection to the community school is expressed in the Little Singer masthead: "Empowering our community through family-based education." This report works to express the complexities of the effort to blend Navajo philosophy of health with contemporary wellness models.

The intent here is to raise questions about the relationship between cultural relevance and the persistent silence in evaluation, and qualitative studies generally regarding the relationship between the question of race in education and the culture of social class in post-industrial capitalism. (Denzin, 2000). I chose PENAL: Program Evaluation and Native American Liability. PENAL is a good acronym and a tip of the hat to the way in which Native American and minority communities generally bear the brunt of educational studies that are stuck on the missed promises of upward mobility. We may give answers in a language of cultural responsiveness but too often avoid what it would take to include a response to the pervasive culture of capitalism and social class disadvantage that goes beyond culture. This affects minority peoples (in this case Navajos) in a variety of ways, one of which would include the "code" of silence in liberal educational evaluation research regarding minority working-class conditions.

My comments here reflect a concern with evaluation of which I was a part for 3 years and that crosses the borders of Dine' culture and the culture of accelerating consumption and capitalist commodity accumulation.

During the period of this evaluation I also worked selling cars in Flagstaff, and would see the large extended Navajo and Hopi families come in to shop. I saw firsthand the relationship between the credit-driven world of auto sales and the realities of these Navajo families. We were encouraged to "qualify" customers according to race. I heard, "Steer the Indians. They go the pre-owned lot and B credit." "Maybe the occasional jeweler has a few bucks." The joke on the floor was a guy looking under the hood of a car was "an Injun looking at an engine." We were encouraged to invite ourselves to the customer's tax preparer for a down payment if we could. You got a rez (reservation) map to the home for the repo (repossession) guy. Two or three months and a missed payment meant you got a big down, a couple of payments, and resold the car as new. Hundreds of solid payment buyers were roped into 28 and 30% loans, which they met. The need for transportation to work is a reality. And work is scarce for many of the above reasons. The financial space between sufficiency and poverty is thin for many.

In this chapter I'm writing about work as a professional education evaluator, and offer some comments about "culturally responsive evaluation. The contradiction I'm exploring here is that between liberal/progressive race-conscious research and the "culture" of contemporary capitalism, which is not typically part of the "response." Race/ethnic culture is the focus, obscuring race/class culture, which is at the base of so much that prevents full participation in a healthy education for, in this case, Native Americans.

I cite the car sales example as a slim but important slice of reality for at least some families in the Little Singer area. Transportation is a life and death matter in a remote community. Payments, accidents, class-based racism in buying, and employment all affect the adults in this Navajo community. As a research evaluator I will spend as much time as I can to try to exercise "cultural competence" from an outsider's point of view. But focus on mores, language, and spirituality without facing post-colonial capitalism is like watching a foundering ship and deciding that it doesn't need a gash in it's hull patched, it needs paint. The holes are under the water, and they are too hard to get at. Besides, as an evaluator, I'm getting paid for paint. If I pay attention to the rot, I might draw attention to conditions that my patrons might rather I ignore.

I did not mention in my report that it is not just the Navajo family—which needs the leveling strength of "balance," or "hozho"—it is the wildly imbalanced capitalist culture of advertising, exploitation, militarism, and violence, which is in need as well. Without this does any family at any kind of prayer have a chance?

I am coldly reminded that peacemaking within the family is affected by racism and poverty. "Liabilities" might not be present if Native American education provided students in reservation schools the skills and histories that illuminate more clearly the distance between their sovereign rights and what is currently available in their "career education" courses. Liabilities would be altered if the smothering consumer culture and entertainment, and advertising industries weren't allowed to stupefy generations of children into a place of value-free passivity, and celebratory, sensational media violence. I wish I could count the number of times I have talked to Navajo teachers who say their cultural teaching is washed away in the daily monsoon of consumer television. To be responsive to Navajo life is to keep one's mind open and supple regarding the differences in culture, but just as much we must keep addressing the culture of structural conditions within media, consumerist, and commercial cultures that affect these communities.

It might not be necessary if we believed in a culturally responsive economy, to go along with the evaluation. But this goes beyond the capitalist faith at the heart of modern liberal education. And this is an American capitalism whose gods are not placed at the cardinal directions, with metaphors for human harmony. It is the god whose eye appears at the apex of the pyramid on the dollar bill.

In all of our studies of race and cultural relevance, why is the culture of capitalism absent? The study here is an evaluation project, which took three years and worked toward a nuanced and "culturally competent" evaluation of the Little Singer Navajo Wellness Center situated in a rural reservation community school near Flagstaff, Arizona. The piece tries to grapple with the culturally "sensitive" evaluator's silence, including my own, regarding the larger culture of globalized consumer capitalism, including rapidly changing conditions of entry-level labor.

The inflation of school credentials, the credit marked that increasingly entraps working-class people, most people in this Navajo community, in a cycle of debt, the commodification of culture, here the decreasing value of community cultural products in favor of cheap foreign copies. The intensive development of a corporate/federal school government attitude, which is hostile to tribal self-determination and sovereignty, has forced centers such as the Little Singer Wellness Center to play conservative defense in order to maintain funding, yet this too is often unsuccessful. The liberal/democratic line in evaluation studies has too often been silent about the way racism goes beyond repair by new curricular and programmatic sensitivities.

It thrives in the economic depredations of the marginalized, here the Navajo, and when the "evaluator" is silent about this "culture" as it effects these people, the evaluator becomes guilty of feeding at the diminishing scraps of what remains of the welfare state edu-business table. This silence is often enforced by the increasingly conservative funding apparatus, a totalizing archipelago of philanthropy that encourages culture awareness where it does not call attention to the way in which the culture of capitalism aids and abets the culture of racism.

The issues I raise here address the confusions of the culture concept as it is applied to communities whose cultural complexes extend to both traditional ways of knowing and living and effects on those ways after a history of state-directed dispossession and the current global cancer of antisocial accumulation. In my own effort to conduct an evaluation with cultural values at the center, I feel like the center did not hold. I was unable to address crucial political economic issues that underlay the family health issues, which were the focus of the Wellness program.

After completing the evaluations of the Little Singer Wellness Center, I have become increasingly aware of the irony in how the educational and health-related liabilities identified in Native Americans are defined. I have also become aware of how, as a liberal educator, I am complicit in the general silence about class and racism as complexes of schooling. Adding a concern for "diversity" and culture in evaluation are OK. The "feds" will at least listen to that and chalk me up as another university goo-goo. I'll get my check. I'll get my publication. And here it is! Even in these "tough economic times" for higher education, maybe this will earn me a *raise* bigger than the annual income of a parent in the Little Singer community.

Including in the evaluation the underlying issues of market and capitalist exploitation of this and other Native American communities, implied in
all that I saw in the community, is not OK. As academics do we benefit
more than our clients? Is this work helping to move education in general
and evaluation specifically in a direction, which is effective in increasing
cultural competence? Or am I just gaming another set of social pathologies
by renaming the solution in culture?

As the Wellness Center was being formed, focus groups in the community identified two health-related issues as their top priority: drug/alcohol
abuse and related family violence. With this in mind I wanted to explore
the silence, including my own here, around social pathologies, which
derive first from systematic antidemocratic, antisocial public policy as it
relates to Native Americans. For example, the funding for the Arizona public health programs, which include the Center, came directly from a tax on
tobacco sales. Sidestepping the complex issues related to "sin taxes" and
their effects, the relationship between the sacred and profane uses of
tobacco in Native America are ironic here. Here a tax on the state-supported drug culture is used to pay for treatment of effects from another
part of the state-supported drug culture. Funds from the same grant also
paid for my evaluation.

I want to claim here that I worked to be "culturally competent" using
what knowledge I have gained of this community, and working closely with
community stakeholders to give power to their vision and definition of
Center and school values. However, my own sensitivity to these values did
not include an element crucial to this evaluation: a frank discussion of the
way in which systematic economic inequality is built into the framework.
Cultural competence is insufficient without political economic competence. Culturally relevant evaluation will remain liberal window dressing
until evaluators have the courage to discuss the economics of inequality,
class, and racism, which Native Americans and others must negotiate daily.

During the evaluation I interviewed Ms. Godinez, the Principal of the
elementary school. Every one of the focus health issues in the Wellness
Center had a counterpart in the educational process at the elementary
level. I asked her how the directionality of Navajo philosophy manifested
itself in her work. She went on to describe a process of piecing together
her Navajo values from a life that included boarding school and strong
Christian influences. She described an intellectual, spiritual, historical process of faith-building amid a sometimes bewildering set of choices.

One thing she said struck me. She said, "Sometimes I put in long days.
I'm out here and it's darkening, all there is is wind, maybe the quiet sound
of a custodian's vacuum in the next building. I get so tired by the end of
some days. But then I think of my family, and my son. His father is Mexican, he goes to school here. Then I think of the Long Walk and Fort Sum-

ner [the captivity narrative that describes Navajo imprisonment in New Mexico in the last century]. And then I sit up straighter. Thinking how tired my great-grandparents must have been. Then I can renew my energy for my son and for the kids at school here."

She described in our interview meeting how culture is a spirit of honoring the past and the future generations. Not as an ideal, or a sentiment, but a living faith. And culture is complicated, woven in freedom and oppression, life and death, same and different language.

In her words I see a complex web of responses possible in a school. The faith of the Long Walk is fortitude in the face of genocide and survival. This hard faith could also be part of the cultural fabric of a school for whom the Long Walk is not over yet. It implies a schooling, which imbues the warrior spirit of the North cardinal direction in Navajo faith. It also emphasizes the poetry of spirituality, the hard awareness that to be Navajo, to be "human," is to protect the space one occupies, to understand that internal colonialism and cultural imperialism is part of the logic of American life.

I see in her fatigue an effort of purpose that can enable clearer choices when the injustices of the colonial past are faced squarely, and new demands are developed toward tribal and community sovereignty, civil and economic equality, and respect for religious freedom. Economic injustices and value choices in the "dominant culture" can be a living part of a critique, which is embodied in curriculum at Little Singer. Both are a fruitful preparation for a new generation better equipped to face the economic and political realities of the future.

SPIRIT TEACHING

The heart of the Wellness Center was Navajo spirituality. Honoring this is to expand our thinking to include as community value our personal responsibility as earth surface creatures related to our position at the nexus of creation. Our sense of balance between warrior and nurturer, male and female, Mother Earth and Father Sky, negotiator, warrior, the balanced sides of our being, helps to manifest our health. We must know/feel we are at that nexus, knowledge, which grounds our self-esteem and health.

With regard to domestic violence and drug abuse, the focus on Wellness from the perspective of Navajo philosophy is healing, not accusing, blaming, or shaming. The Wellness Center incorporated the traditional Navajo peacemaking process to address issues of discord and violence. Thomas Walker, school board president, is a leader in this effort, and he discussed its meaning with me. The peacemaker takes the role of naat'ani, community leader, who draws strength from the assignation and wisdom of the community. This is restorative justice in which the leader/peacemaker is in a search for practical and ceremonial information, which will help the healing process.

I am concerned that the source of disharmony from personal or spiritual imbalance cannot be addressed apart from inherited disharmony in the social conditions that Navajo families inherit. I am thinking of the times past, during which peacemaking principles were developed, when the social and economic conditions were vastly different.

Today young people graduate from schools carrying diplomas with a fraction of the credential value of those a generation ago. Navajo schools like Little Singer are subject to both the impoverishment that comes from inadequate facilities and teachers, to the realities of a labor market, which poorly rewards the minority high school graduate.

OBSERVING STUDENTS

The place where this work was first presented was a conference dedicated to culturally responsive evaluation, a a conference call to change the grounds upon which the cultural capital of school experience is judged. The effort here is to highlight the many positive academic and programmatic efforts to enrich traditionally Anglo-centric evaluation with a fund of empowered cultural signifiers. I see this resting on a foundation that implies this effort will provide educational access previously denied to marginalized African, Native, Latino, and other American students.

As culturally radical as this effort is, I worry that it perpetuates modern liberals' blind faith in working-class upward mobility through education. A multicultural overhaul of the big business of testing and evaluation serves to perpetuate the reformers' faith. However, as Aronowitz (1997) and others have noted, this modern liberal faith requires its own overhaul first.

This faith remains here that student performance—the key variable in occupational mobility—is crucially and causally linked to urban (read poor) schools' unequal access to resources, both institutional and financial. My effort to remain responsive to culture is an extension of this faith. If my work is successful, Navajo student performance will increase for all the right reasons. However, occupational mobility as a function of school success is slipping in its tracks for all students in marginalized and largely working-class communities in the New West as well as in the inner city. Do I put this in my evaluation?

If I think of the Navajo family living in or around Flagstaff, they are affected by the economic troubles of an economy, which has become much narrower. The farming, ranching, herding, timber, and railroad work that was central to Navajo self-sufficiency has diminished due to capitalist automation, globalization, agricultural industrialization, and neoliberal collapse of the idea of commonwealth, and other forces. The area economy is a catch-as-catch-can place where tourism and native crafts are poor places to earn for the primary producer, with possibilities left for "entrepreneurs" who thrive exploiting this labor, and the ever-present advertisement of Native chic. In addition, racism in civil life and economic life is persistent and corrosive.

The *idea* of culture in the context of opening spaces for social and educational achievement in Native America must be expanded to evaluation of the crucial conditions of economic democracy and a politics of rights in the context of treaty right, sovereignty, and economic and environmental sustainability. Is this idea of "culture" our educational commodity now? Does it gratify the liberal conscience of that community of researchers who continue to work and prosper without naming the real foundations of cultural depredation? Does anyone worry that we are parasitic on social injustice when we offer an evaluation (surveillance) that is more "cultural," yet remains disciplinary, and does not ask policymakers to address social injustice and structural underprivilege?

Educational programs can be the seed for a critical space toward discussions across the community toward a politically and economically viable future. This discussion must include students of education and its evaluation as participants and change agents in these communities. Universities are deeply beholden to the Mammon of big testing and educational research contracts, which come from within the heart of monopoly capitalist human resources management. Until this dependency is broken, Native American education sovereignty and indigenous people's educational rights will remain homogenized. In the liberal vision of endless uplift through academic performance, all liabilities addressed in the Wellness Center grant, from family violence through alcohol dependence, are addressed with a new drink. We might call it Manifest Destiny Lite.

MIXING MEDICINES AND MAKING PEACE
IN CULTURAL COMPLEXITY

Art therapy became a part of the tissue of peacemaking and a healing intervention. The school counselor, Miriam Dror, organized a summer poetry reading and art show. It gave me the most powerful experience I had in the 2-year evaluation cycle. I stumbled in on it, actually, when I showed up to visit on an unscheduled day. The reading was part of a counseling art therapy session, and was held in a sunny Hogan-shaped classroom in August 2000.

This experience was a place for cultural memory, continuation, and reinvestment in the value of a holistic education, organic to Navajo culture expression and lived culture values, balance, and emotional and spiritual harmony through poetry and arts. This is a value for the teaching and learning of American Indian children, and hints at quality teaching and curriculum that is culturally responsive. It is also reflexive, reminding the educator of the values of art and spirituality found in American Indian culture, values that have been lost in the instrumentalization and compartmentalization of European literacy and arts in schooling. I see the school as a living space for the development of cultural awareness and lived culture, against culture as noble artifact, culture as commodity.

In this work I see a chance for the development of that crucial discussion of cultural life and its future. I also see the need for the evaluator, the onlooker, to understand the warp and the weft of woven Navajo life, built in struggle with a pre- and a post-colonial past.

The children and parents sat in a ring, and the poet/facilitator introduced the program with emphasis on the connection between the artistic products and the personal/spiritual process. She said, "We can celebrate all of our work of the past week in this reading. Some of our work comes from a playful place, some from a sad place, and all of it from somewhere important in your hearts. Let's wait until everybody is finished to clap." It becomes evident later that she has reviewed all the work and participated in crafting the poems by working on the process of making metaphor. So while building the students' skill and literacy she is aware of the potential for emotional seriousness and even hurt. Her caring and connection to the students is evident. Their honesty, laughter, and tears evidence of a kind of organic, ceremonial experience as being integral to the reading and doing of poetry and art.

Central to the works are reflections on Navajo culture and the students' relationship to their culture, clanship, and family. There are grandparents in their 50s, younger fathers and mothers, middle schoolers of age 12 and 13 and little children in first and second grade.

The poetry teacher worked around the circle. A fourth grader had written about her mom and shows us the picture of her she drew. "Skin the color of the desert/ her hair the color of the dark between the stars." A boy of about 11 writes of a horse, who, like him, he writes, "kicks in the stall 'till it bleeds." His picture is of the horse in its stall, and dancers in a circle, "dancing to protect their village." An older girl of about 13 speaks of a lost cousin, who before he died told her, "Be yourself is the best advice." Her poem contains the lines, "another culture, pounding fear with violence into people's minds." The room was respectfully silent, and her poem comes haltingly, with tears. I noticed the teacher hold her hand, a gesture the girl welcomed. A Navajo girl and a middle-aged Anglo "lady from Vermont." Four days of connection and the mutual respect and caring is palpable. Why is this art/gift in a teacher able to connect with the best of poetry teaching, community feeling, and children's emotional needs? The reading is ceremonial in the most delicate sense of the word.

The values and the losses implied in this poetry float over a terrain of families whose lives are as deeply affected by joblessness and an exploitative economy. This is a place where grandpa is missed in too many cases because he died prematurely or disappeared in an environment of economic privation and political alienation; where mother is valued as a sole resource of comfort when the extended family has been decimated not by lace of cultural values principally, but by the multiple cancers of desperate poverty. The older daughter writes, "Grandma has left me her loom," implying that she does not use it. In my mind I reflect on the constellation of issues raised here, and think, "Should the poem continue…?"

> But my truck payment is too high
> I earn six bucks an hour cleaning motel rooms
> And pay the sitter
> And a 2 hundred hour rug pays
> A hundred bucks.
> And seven hundred for the Big Turquoise guy
> In Sedona.
> The poem "goodbye shi'ma" could be retitled: "I Can't Afford to Weave."

TOBACCO (TAX?)

In one program some students were to make medicine bags after instruction by an elder community medicine man, and school scion, Bennie Singer son of Hatatli Yazhi, (Little Singer). He then gathered the bags and took them into a ceremony for a blessing before being returned to the students.

Traditional lessons on how to use the Circle of Life/Medicine Wheel was illustrated with the four aspects of the circle: the Physical, Mental, Emotional, and Spiritual. Using each aspect, traditional lessons teach how to keep oneself healthy in each segment to form a wholeness of balance.

The traditional talking circle was also used to teach listening skills and patience. All students were given the chance to speak in the circle, and this was indicated when an object—an eagle feather, a cedar branch, or a pebble—was passed.

The Shields model was used to illustrate a method of substance abuse prevention, using shields to represent protection against negative influences.

Tobacco has long been a part of indigenous cultures. The use of tobacco was for ceremonial and medicinal uses only. The history and origin of tobacco was shared with the students as well as the contemporary

abuse of tobacco and the chemical enhancements that are used to acceler-
ate addiction.

A community outreach wellness educator, Ms. Vandrew Jake, was hired
to conduct community outreach. She presented creative classes utilizing
her traditional knowledge to all students. She is a community member and
a certified nursing assistant. Her responsibility was reaching out into the
community and finding out what their health needs were, and telling them
about the services available at the Wellness Center. She made numerous
home visits going door to door in the Birdsprings community.

A counselor was also hired to work with the traditional counselor to inte-
grate Navajo traditional and European counseling models. The school was
able to hire a traditional Navajo peacemaker, Richard Curley, in the last
semester of school. Mr. Curley is a Navajo community member who was
trained by the Navajo Nation as an official traditional peacemaker. This
man and the counselor, working in conjunction with the school's Counseling Circle (consisting of teachers, staff, nurse practitioner), proved to be
highly successful in preventing problems, catching early difficulties, and
dealing with discipline problems.

The Wellness Center was also able to more fully utilize our community
medicine Man as a traditional counselor. He performed traditional ceremonies at the school's traditional Hogan with the permission of, and pref-
erably the participation of, the family. It was agreed that family
participation would be most helpful since so many students had problems
that could be seen as the result of abuse and/or alcohol use in the home.
With family involvement the medicine man believed the student would do
better. We were also asked by a few families to help them arrange for traditional ceremonies outside of the school for their children who were having
behavior problems. The medicine man also worked with the wellness educator, going into the classroom with her to provide a Navajo perspective.
She discussed the teaching of traditional knowledge through prayer and
ceremony, silence and reflection, which all contribute to using our will and
making clear decisions and defining our goals.

FACING RACISM

The prior discussion of the uniqueness of the peacemaking project raises
the issue of interrelatedness and hozho (beauty/harmony). In my interview with the principal, Ms. Godinez, educators who make a special connection with the students and community are the most successful. Ms. Dror
was included among those who successfully made this connection, despite
having been here just 6 months, and having come from Vermont to this
school. She provided many insights about the purpose of the school and

wellness connection. She reflected on her observation that interrelatedness moved broadly to a universal set of indigenous values, where teaching itself is part and parcel of community harmony. This harmony was possible despite the intercommunity religious diversity with the Birdsprings area. The design of counseling services at the school allowed her to work with students and extended family members. This, for Ms. Dror, enables better counseling, since children's troubles are often embedded in surrounding community conditions.

She corroborated parents' oft-cited need for an alcohol awareness program at the Wellness Center. Many of her students felt the pain of parental absence due to this problem. In some cases one or both parents were alcoholic. As a counselor she was involved in the 12-week parent program for family strengthening based on traditional ways of knowing. This program worked with the subject of domestic violence, which in almost every case was alcohol related. The core group of participants, though small, was highly favorable to this experience.

Most of the referrals came as the result of violent or overly aggressive behavior. Some students were also referred for symptoms of social withdrawal, refusal to participate in classroom activities. Forty-one students were seen individually over the prior 5 months, some for only two meetings, others on a weekly basis from the time of referral until the end of the school year. She was a frequent observer of the peacemaking process. One of the disturbing features of school life that she and other teachers observed was bullying and racial epithets based on skin color "status." The "burnt cookies" were teased about their darkness. We discussed the possibility of this distinction deriving from a culture of scarcity, and reflections on the surpluses of the dominant society.

At the beginning of the New Year, utilizing a grant from the Navajo Nation Injury Prevention Project staff presented a program about prevention of domestic violence and the importance of family in basic Navajo teaching. Two Navajo mental health counselors were hired, one female from Winslow and a male from Chinle. Funding was also received to transport people to the center and to take them home after the group discussion and dinner. Each group discussed factors leading to domestic violence, ways to prevent it, and how to get help. The facilitators presented these topics, discussing not only the role of the person in the immediate situation but discussing the role of the family surrounding the place where domestic violence takes place. The same group was not able to meet consistently week after week. Many factors interfere with one's ability to keep appointments, weather conditions, and the health of the person and/or family members, condition of vehicle. The sensitivity of the issues discussed made open conversation a difficult challenge at times.

MIXING MEDICINES

Dietary counselor Linda Willie mentioned that one of the issues she was concerned about regarded the interpolation of Navajo traditional practice (i.e., sweat lodges) was family violence. Some in the community were concerned that it is dangerous to "mix medicines." There is a danger in the possibility of romanticizing Navajo cultural teaching to a point of watering down the complexities of psychic and spiritual treatment. She also, in agreement with Wellness Center nurse Ms. Bayuk, cited the complex and problematic legacy of the boarding school and Christianizing patriarchy. How much of the abuse is the result of the abused having learned to abuse in turn and justify this behavior? How much healing could be accomplished not only by recovering the Beautyway of Navajo spirituality, but also by working through new family roles that were learned in this era, and undermined the value of women in a community, as well as undermining the economic base of Navajo culture?

Finally, we discussed the impact of traditional Navajo peacemaking. The process of peacemaking requires a person or council to act as mediators in resolving conflicts and solving problems. Peacemaking is a programmatic thrust that encompasses the goals of wellness and the process of building harmony in the educational environment. What follows is a description of this program and the way it fits the school mission.

The following discussion developed after a conversation with Wellness Center Director Mark Sorensen and School Board Chair Thomas Walker. The introduction of traditional Navajo peacemaking connects with the combined influences of Hozho, (harmony) and K'e (interrelatedness). This philosophic/spiritual center forms the difference between the cultural responsiveness of Little Singer/Wellness Center policy and standard American school policies. From the dominant cultural perspective, at least reflected in how society has chosen to deal with the issue of student discipline in the schools, peace is the absence of disturbance. Peace is gained by excluding from our presence those who disturb our peace. From a Navajo cultural perspective, indeed from the perspective of many indigenous cultures, peace is the balancing of two poles, male and female, when all elements are in harmony. Early in my work, during a peacemaking conference at Little Singer I noted a remark by Navajo philosopher and peacemaker trainer Philmer Bluehouse, "Peace is the moment of transformation; the balancing of the male and female" energies. From this perspective, peace can be regained by finding a way to reintegrate into the group those that disturb the peace. This person, who has disturbed our peace is not different from us; he or she is part of us. When that person is integrated into the group, we also feel more whole. The goal of Navajo peacemaking in student discipline is to show the student how he or she is imbedded in relationships—clan relatives, close relatives, and friends. The peacemaker's goal is to show the student that he or she is not known except through your "relations" and to get the student to see that your "relations are your medicine."

One challenge is to recognize the importance of spirituality in this process. This depends on the mutual cooperation of family and student in acknowledging the place of reflection and prayer. Prayer is a difficult subject in a public institution. Its appropriateness is centered on the degree of community self-determination that underscores the meaning of "public" for American Indian community schools. Participants are asked to pray in their own way, but the prayer focus is a reflection of the power of universal relation that is at the heart of Navajo philosophy.

The following are reasons articulated by Mr. Walker and Dr. Sorensen for the use of prayer in peacemaking:

1. Prayer articulates the problem.
2. Prayer focuses not on casting blame but rather on seeking a humble solution.
3. Asking for spiritual intervention recognizes that the solution is bigger than any one person.
4. Prayer reminds us that we all have the gift of life from the Creator.
5. Prayer reminds us that we are all related through our Creator.
6. Prayer creates a serious atmosphere.
7. Prayer creates an expectation that good will be the outcome.
8. Prayer recognizes that each person has a gift to share in the solution.
9. Prayer establishes parameters within which all things to be discussed can be placed.

Dine' people, like most Native people, live spiritual lives in which prayer is one of the key ingredients. Native American prayers generally focus on family, life, health, prosperity, and the community.

After the initial prayer the peacemaker should have a good understanding of the situation and the issues involved. The peacemaker restates the problem and begins to negotiate with parties toward a resolution. The peacemaker guides the negotiation:

1. Bring in relevant rules from the larger society to see the connection to the local transgression.
2. Ask questions regarding the students' understanding of the transgression.
3. Draw out feelings.
4. Suggest a consensus solution and search for consensus.

5. Focus shifts to the transgressor's request for forgiveness.

If consensus cannot be reached, another meeting may be requested. Only when this has been exhausted is there a reversion to the progressive exclusion of the student in line with standard discipline policy.

After consensus is reached:

1. The peacemaker restates the settlement and makes sure that everyone knows what he or she is agreeing to.
2. The peacemaker writes down the main points of the agreement, including apologies, referrals, and/or individual assignments on which there is agreement.
3. The peacemaker opens the session up to requests for forgiveness and conciliatory statements.
4. The peacemaker asks everyone to seal the agreement with a traditional handshake (as honored by Navajo common law) and to be willing to sign the written agreement when it is finalized.
5. The peacemaker offers a prayer that acknowledges thanksgiving and transformation: "kodoo hozhoodoo" (from here there is beauty); "aheehwindzin" (thanksgiving); "nas go" (moving on); "hozho nahasdlii" (beauty and harmony restored).

The peacemaker acknowledges that everything has been transformed. Peacemaking is a central tenet of Navajo health in Dine' Philosophy. It reflects the importance of regaining balance and restoring harmony in the body and in the community. It is integral to community. Violence is inimical to health, to wellness. I reflect here on the social and economic violence that is the source of so many of our evaluation "project" concerns. Cultural responsiveness, again is necessary but not sufficient to address the nexus of socio-political issues that impact communities of color. What would evaluation look like that focused on naming, and addressing social violence, and on the elaborate and spiritual quest for peace, distributive and harmonizing justice? It would not be white evaluation, beholden to "funders" and "agencies" looking to simulate attention to "program goals" or basically to ensure that the funds keep rolling.

It would be an "evaluation" named and subscribed to by the community, and supported the way ceremony and here, peacemaking is. It would imply deep change, and would engage all the parties to the violence. There might be speeches, or songs/poems toward healing. Heads might bow, and there may be tears. This vision would disrupt our lucrative positions and the superstructure of state oversight, implied in the university "expert" evaluation industry. The "evaluator" the "peacemaker" would acknowledge "that everything has been transformed."

SOME SONGS TOWARD A CONCLUSION

I am concerned with culturally responsive understanding, which here is facing a discourse paradox, (1) a Navajo way in which there is no separation between physical health, emotional health, and spiritual wholeness, measured against (2) "physical" health issues, which, from my viewpoint, are the result of the depredations of poverty in post-internal colonialist capitalism. Educational problems that are inseparable from both of these issues thrive on neglect of each.

This experience is a place for cultural memory, continuation, and reinvestment in the value of a holistic education, organic to Navajo culture expression and lived culture values, balance, and spiritual harmony through poetry and arts. This is a value for the teaching and learning of American Indian children and hints at quality teaching and curriculum that is culturally responsive. It is also reflexive, reminding the educator of the values of art and spirituality found in American Indian culture, values that have been lost in the instrumentalization and compartmentalization of European literacy and arts in schooling.

The readings were accompanied by a show of related artworks that the students and their parents made. It took over an hour. It was learning in the best sense, a true "performance" and not a scholastic role play. It was congruent with Navajo values and culture, and was a ceremonial expression of a 4-day process of building both art and trust. One of the mothers read her poem haltingly, emotionally:

> I forgive you grandma for not being here
> when I was born.
> I wish you could be here
> to teach me my language and culture.
> You left your loom
> I see your never-ending black hair.
> Beautiful and strong
> Like the Great Spirit, never wrong.

I could not help imagining what took this lady's grandma. Was it diabetes? Addiction-related illness? Loneliness? How many elders leave sooner than their more affluent peers? What effect does poverty, globalization, conservative immiseration, and its depredations have on any culture any evaluator would wish to serve? Yet the quality of the silence in qualitative evaluation research is deafening.

REFERENCES

Aronowitz, S. (1997). A different perspective on educational inequality. In H. Giroux & P. Shannon (Eds.), *Education and cultural studies: Toward a performative practice* (pp. 179–196). New York: Routledge.

Denzin, N. K., & Lincoln, Y. S. (Eds.). (2000). *Handbook of qualitative research* (2nd ed.). Thousand Oaks, CA: Sage.

Pavel, D. M. (1995, Fall). Comparing BIA and tribal schools with public schools: A look at the year 1990–91. *Journal of American Indian Education,* pp. 10–15.

Pertusati, L. (1988, January). Beyond segregation or integration: A case study from effective Native American education. *Journal of American Indian Education,* pp. 11–19.

Robinson-Zanartu, C., & Majel-Dixon, J. (1996, Fall). Parent voices: American Indian relationships with schools. *Journal of American Indian Education,* pp. 33–54.

CHAPTER 9

IT STARTS WITH A MACHETE

The Politics and Poetics of Space in Urban School Reform

Nona M. Burney
Roosevelt University

Carolyne J. White
Rutgers University

Mary E. Weems
John Carroll University

---

*"poetic language" . . . is an unsettling process—
when not an outright destruction—
of the identity of meaning and speaking subject,
and consequently of transcendence or,
by derivation, of "religious sensitivity."*

—Julia Kristeva (quoted in Minh-ha, 1989, p. 5)

*No one can any longer separate knowledge from power, reason from performativity,
metaphysics from technical mastery . . . certain members of the university can play
a part there (in pockets within the university campus) irritating the insides
of the teaching body like parasites.*

—Jacques Derrida (Soussloff & Franko, 2002, p. 29)

The Role of Culture and Cultural Context in Evaluation, pages 149–178
Copyright © 2005 by Information Age Publishing

An evaluation is culturally responsive if it fully takes into account the culture of the program that is being evaluated. In other words, the evaluation is based on an examination of impacts through lenses in which the culture of the participants is considered an important fact . . . [and] attempts to fully describe and explain the context of the program . . . being evaluated. (Frierson, Hood, & Hughes, 2002, p. 63)

This chapter embraces poetic language to irritate and stimulate a questioning of a modernist evaluation project invested in a positivist paradigm, a project that embraces the possibility of neutral and objective knowledge devoid of power. Concerned with how to conduct a culturally responsive evaluation of our collective work in radical urban school reform, here we follow Frierson, Hood, and Hughes (2002) and explore new ways to illuminate the culture of the program context and the culture of the participants. As with Susan Krieger (1991), the science we speak from is "not hard, objective, standard, dispassionate, nor is it about measurement, data, clear-cut models of behavior, or procedures for testing. It is soft, subjective, idiosyncratic, ambivalent, conflicted, about the inner life, and about experiences that cannot be measured, tested, or fully shared" (p. 2). This is evaluation research that seeks "other" ways of knowing. Following Miron (2003), we move toward the aesthetic in educational research, toward ways of knowing that may better illuminate the cultural facets of radical education reform.

The African American artist Romare Bearden faced a similar challenge in his work. He adopted artistic collage as a method that was identical to his meaning. We present a written collage here to represent the rich complexities of culturally responsive educational practice and evaluation; to reflect our belief in the power of imaginative space; and to mirror the multifaceted form and content of our shared urban journey.

Bearden's meaning is identical to his method. His combination of technique is in itself, eloquent of the sharp breaks, leaps in consciousness, distortions, paradoxes, reversals, telescoping of times and surreal blending of styles, values, hopes, and dreams which characterized much of Negro American history. Through an act of creative will, he has blended strange visual harmonies out of the shrill, indigenous dichotomies of American life and in doing so reflected the irrepressible thrust of a people to endure and keep its intimate sense of its own identity. (Goings & Boulware, 1993, p. 5)

CONTEXTUAL BACKGROUND:
CREATIVE, IMAGINATIVE, UTOPIAN SPACE

Sherman Alexie (1993) writes that "Imagination is the politics of dreams" (p. 152) and each day Nelson Mandela asks everyone in South Africa to repeat this sacred intention:

> *Let us take care of the elders,*
> *for they have come a long way,*
> *Let us take care of the children,*
> *for they have a long way to go,*
> *And let us take care of those in between,*
> *for they are doing the work.*

Children all over the country can be heard singing it on the way to school. Imagine the kinds of spaces created in the minds and hearts of people as they share this prayer.

> *It doesn't interest me to know*
> *where you live or how much money*
> *you have. I want to know if you can get up*
> *after the night of grief and despair,*
> *weary and bruised to the bone,*
> *and see what needs to be done*
> *for the children.*
> —Oriah Moccatain
> Dreamer, Native American Elder

This Elder's words open space in our minds and hearts. The creation of utopian space is our focus. We write to illuminate the strategies we employed to do so, and to invite you into spaces we encountered on our journey. These are innovative, supportive, creative, symbolic, disjointed spaces of possibility, frustration, silence, defeat, and partial victories.

Our text title borrows from Gaston Bachelard's book, *Poetics of Space*. We argue that embracing the poetic is needed in both urban school reform

The images I want to examine are the quite simple images of felicitous space. In this orientation, these investigations would deserve to be called topophilia. They seek to determine the human value of the sorts of space that may be grasped, that may be defended against poetic shadings, this is eulogized space. Attached to its protective value which can be a positive one, are also imagined values, which soon become dominant. Space that has been seized upon by the imagination cannot remain indifferent space subject to the measures and estimates of the surveyor. It has been lived in, not in its positivity, but with all the partiality of the imagination. (Bachelard, 1969, pp. xxxi–xxxii) and for the creation of culturally responsive evaluation practices. Otherwise, the universe of science and reason might constuct us as naive to even venture into the terrain of urban school reform (see Anyon, 1995, 1997; Ben-Peretz, 2001; Britzman, 2000; Gay, 2000; Henig et. al, 1999; Hess, 1998; Ladson-Billings, 2000; Lipman, 1998; Murrell, 1998; Nieto, 2000; Popkewitz, 1991; Rothman, 1993; Sarason, 1993; Senese, 1995; Sleeter, 2001; Weiner, 2002; White & Burney, 1994). For us it is not a choice. It is what needs to be done for the children. We write from a particular set of experiences, in particular cultural spaces in Cleveland, Ohio.

Space

For fresh intellectual air

where "what-I-want-to-be-the truth"
is changed to an honesty that starts
as a sharp wake up! Call, but
ends with new openings. Re-create spaces
for teaching new warriors to use the lance
of questions, diversity, and open discussions,
as space for vandalizing only-white walls.

It starts with a machete.
Straight rows are slashed down to the root
of the problem and voices are pulled into circles
where it's safe to let your heart down, and answer "no"
in the space marked "yes".
Space for taking a chance is the only place
for changing the

Anything that exists in abundance in the classrooms
and halls where many of our children are kept
like spoiled lunches, and obsolete furniture—
only getting attention when it's time to
throw them out.

The results are as complex as revolution.
some hold their privilege around them like
a warm, white shawl, return their chairs
to the row, fan the circle with an all-too-familiar
flame, but others listen, exchange, risk one space
at a time,
fill their pockets with change
turn out the white.

—Mary E. Weems

We found that the spaces we sought to create (and the spaces that we needed to sustain ourselves) in the terrain of radical urban school reform were increasingly informed by imagination, poetry, and aesthetics. With Audre Lorde (1984), we find poetry "a revelatory distillation of experience... the way to help give name to the nameless so it can be thought.... It lays the foundations for a future of change, a bridge across our fears of what has never been before (pp. 36–39).

The poetic spaces we created encouraged us to stay present and engaged, to know differently, and to invite others into these ways of knowing. Our work then and our work now as we write this text resonates with Bachelard. He writes that people crave spaces that inspire them to dream. These were the utopian spaces Nona encountered in the creation of Martin Luther King Law and Public Service Magnet High School (MLK/ LPS) and the spaces we sought to create through communal dialogue in the CCPE Network.

But how do people engage this creative, imaginative, utopian process? Within what follows we revisit and illuminate our journey through a decolonizing feminist methodological bricolage (see Denzin & Lincoln, 1994, 2000) deeply informed by critical race theory (see Ladson-Billings, 2000). We

> ... thinking that refuses mere compliance, that looks down roads not yet taken to the shapes of a more fulfilling social order, to more vibrant ways of being in the world. This kind of reshaping imagination may be released through many sorts of dialogue: dialogue among the young who have come from different cultures and different modes of life, dialogue among people who have come together to solve problems that seem worth solving to all of them, dialogue among people undertaking shared tasks, protesting injustices, avoiding or overcoming dependencies or illnesses. (Greene, 1995, p. 5)

include auto-ethnographic (see Ellis & Bochner, 2000) and poetic reflections (see Richardson, 2000), elements of vulnerable, performative, interpretive ethnography (see Lincoln & Denzin, 2000; Weems, 2003; White, Mogilka, & Slack, 1998), what Laurel Richardson (1997) terms "narrative knowing and sociological telling." We write from within multiple culturally responsive lenses and seek to enact on the written page our continued insistence on maintaining unresolved, indeterminate, imaginative space for more culturally responsive practices.

NONA CREATES SACRED SPACE

I come to this work as an American woman of African descent, spiritual activist in the traditions of Jesus and Gandhi, groomed by Deweyian teacher educators, nurtured by unconditionally loving parents and siblings, and mentored by practitioner-scholars. My "sacred space" is carved out each morning as I pray for guidance, meditate, and reflect on the preceding day's events.

I lived the teachers' dream as the head planner of the Martin Luther King Law and Public Service Magnet High School (MLK/LPS). Established in 1982 through a partnership between Cleveland State University's Colleges of Law and Urban Affairs and the Cleveland Public Schools, this Grade 9–12 social studies–oriented public school "choice" prepared students for careers in law, law enforcement, public administration, and related areas. Curriculum was integrated and executed through an array of experiential components encapsulated in our vision "the school is a community and the community is a school." The school's motto was "preparing leaders for the next millennium." Students, faculty, and staff created a strong sense of community, a sacred space within the school building.

> Laurel Richardson (1993) describes sacred space as being space that is not "innocent" but space where minimally four things happen: "people feel safe within it, safe to be and experiment with who they are and who they are becoming; people feel 'connected'--to each other, and/or a community; people feel passionate about what they are doing, believing that their activity makes a difference; and people recognize, honor, and are grateful for the safe-communion" (pp. 15, 17).

Data collection was a way of life for the school. Students kept journals, teachers administered pre- and posttests and collected field experience evaluation data, and graduating seniors completed exit surveys. The magnet school's success was documented in various ways over the first 10 years of its existence, from formative evaluations by consultants who examined the process of its implementation to the various reporting systems of the school district, comparing schools by attendance, dropout rates, and standardized test scores (Rak, 1994; Stroempl, 1993). This magnet program was unique in that there were no entrance criteria, except an anticipated interest in social studies. Mainstreamed from

> An MLK/LPS student observed, "If you want to get some part of ninth grade life or some procedure in the building changed, first...you should do something with the students, start a petition... and then when you think you have enough signatures, go to the principal or assistant principal. That's what I always do. Even for a ninth grader. Everybody can have power if they want it" (Burney, 1997, p. 82).

special education and/or honors classes at another school, all MLK/LPS students took the same rigorous coursework: extra social studies and English classes, no study halls, and mandated internship experiences, beginning in ninth grade. Cornwell's (1993) case study of the school cited the student internship, the conflict mediation program, and the student government as activities that empower the students. Essentially, this school was the epitome of a "restructuring" high school before that term was coined (Burney, 1997).

CAROLYNE ENCOUNTERS SACRED SPACE

Sacred space is what I encountered in the Four Cities Urban Professional Development School Network. In September 1993 I was invited to represent Cleveland at the network's inaugural meeting. A white traitor and first-generation college graduate, a new assistant professor embracing decolonizing forms of research (White, 1991) and pedagogy (White, 1988), fearful about the upcoming tenure process, I was skeptical. A former director of an Upward Bound Program in the Southwest (see White, Sakiestewa, & Shelley, 1998), I knew well the ways radical educational reform work can reform the worker. At that first meeting, I walked into a room of strangers representing Chicago and Milwaukee. One exception was George Lowery, the then dean of the College of Education at Mercy College in Detroit. Seeing George, also a former Upward Bound warrior, convinced me to give the network a try. A core group engaged in utopian thinking, we read and critically analyzed the current literature relative to professional development schools. Our critical analysis was richly enhanced by our multiple cultural differences—differences across gender, ethnicity, disciplinary background, academic rank, geographical locations, and differences in developmental phases in our creation of school/university partnerships. Some of us had been intimately involved with partnerships over a number of years and others—like me—were just beginning to contemplate such work. Thus, we were able to learn from the successes and failures of colleagues. We collectively rejected any ideal "model" approach and talked honestly and openly about our doubts and our concerns for being able to do more good than harm as we engaged work in educational reform.

> As I learn more about the way that white racism has constructed the world and my understandings of it, and as that learning comes increasingly to inform the way I live in the world, I become an "unreliable" white person who cannot be trusted by other whites to act appropriately. (Heldke, 1998, p. 94)

North American Time

I am thinking this in a country
where words are stolen out of mouths
as bread is stolen out of mouths
where poets don't go to jail
for being poets, but for being
dark-skinned, female, poor.
I am writing this in a time
when anything we write
can be used against those we love
where the context is never given
though we try to explain, over and over
For the sake of poetry at least
I need to know these things.
                    —Adrienne Rich (2004)

Through our honest and open dialogue, we built a deep level of trust, such as I had rarely encountered in any professional endeavor. We were a critical and vital learning community. We put issues of social justice at the center of all of our work. George consistently asked us, "How will this work benefit children in classrooms?" and our gifted facilitator, Amy Otis-Wilborn, guided our process.[1]

MARY EXPOSES SACRED SPACE

An African American poet/scholar/activist who loves exploring the power of language through reading, creative writing, and dramatic performance, I shared Carolyne's commitment to teaching future teachers to honor the culture and language of their students, beginning with establishing a safe, caring, noncompetitive learning community environment.

From my cultural perspective, space for learning is sacred because my ancestors fought and died for the right to learn, because the racist foundation of public schooling is designed to inhibit imagination-intellectual thinking while enabling rote memory, regurgitation, and testing. In the urban school setting it is crucial to reach out to students, to let them know that their words have the power to shape their cultural response to schooling, that one of the main barometers of an educated people is its ability to create.

CAROLYNE INVITES COLLECTIVE UTOPIAN VISION

Challenged, stimulated, informed, and supported by the Four Cities community of learners, I pursued the possibilities of radical educational reform work in Cleveland. Beginning with conversations with Florence M. Hall and Carole A. Allore, Cleveland Public School teachers with whom I had worked on a Foxfire Project (see White, 1992, 1993), we called a meeting of Cleveland Public School (CPS) teachers, counselors, and

CCPE Vision Statement

(1) Promote a climate of critical, collaborative scholarly inquiry about school reform in Cleveland, with special emphasis on issues of race, class, and gender equity;

(2) Promote collaborative partnerships between all educational stakeholders in Cleveland: students and teachers (CPS and CSU), parents and teachers, social service agencies and schools, the business community and schools, various funded projects, etc.;

(3) Promote the novel professional development of CSU and CPS administrators, staff and teachers, with special emphasis on pre-service and in-service teacher education;

(4) Promote participatory action research (through the Collaborations Journal) as a mechanism to critically evaluate and document how well students are learning, how well teachers are teaching, how successfully pilot projects are performing;

(5) Promote pilot projects (such as the Urban School-Based Teacher Education Program) to explore novel and innovative approaches to school restructuring, the development of conflict-based, problem-posing, culturally sensitive curriculum and pedagogical approaches, and equitable uses of technology in schools.

administrators, and Cleveland State (CSU) faculty members and graduate students to explore the idea of pursuing projects of radical urban school reform in Cleveland. From this meeting, a planning grant was written[2] and we received $2,000 from the Joyce Foundation. The group that evolved to address how Cleveland educators and community members could work for antiracist, positive school reform was known as the Cleveland Collaborators for Positive Education (CCPE) Network. Over the next 5 years, we received more than $342,000. This funding enabled an extensive group of Cleveland professors and graduate students, public school teachers, administrators, parents and students, community artists, and business people to intersect in novel, dynamic ways, addressing issues of racism and school reform.

Given our social justice focus, CCPE goals centered on scholarly inquiry and communication, collaborative partnerships, professional development, participatory action research, and the promotion of pilot projects with innovative approaches to educational reform. A centerpiece of our work was the creation of USTEP, a praxis-oriented Professional Development School collaboration between Martin Luther King Law and Public Service Magnet School and Cleveland State University. We created a scholarly journal, *Collaborations: A Journal of Education in Cleveland,* to provide a forum for conversations stimulated through CCPE activities.[3]

CCPE became an example of radical urban educational reform where, on the basis of mutual respect and trust, people created critical and innovative ways to think about and to do more authentically democractic schooling.

ENTERING THE SPACE OF WARRANTED DESPERATION

Borrowing words from Donna Haraway (1989), this vision statement was to "produce a patterned vision of how to move and what to fear in the topography of an impossible but all-too-real present, in order to find an absent, but perhaps possible, other present" (p. 295).

> There are many kinds of hope . . . one bad kind of hope is manic hope in the unjustifiable. While it is more immediately energizing than desperation, warranted desperation can lead to a form of hope realistically matched to the level of sacrifice needed to actually realize it. Warranted desperation is, in fact, righteously dangerous if it springs from an education about the abrogation of justice, fairness, and opportunities for legitimate life chances. (Senese, 1995, p. 85)

We were only too aware of the colonial landscape we were entering as we sought "a possible other present" of a decolonized and socially just learning community.

We sought to embrace *warranted desperation* and avoid what Guy Senese (1995) terms "manic hope in the unjustifiable." But how do we invite people to join us in the land of warranted desperation? Even if we agree that manic hope is dangerous, it remains more familiar, more comfortable, less threatening. Manic hope invites a feel-good sentimentality that effectively suffocates the possibility of real change—and in fact can further limit the life chances of children. Warranted desperation is much harder as it requires recovery from collective denial about the realities that severely limit the life chances of our children, and collective recovery from denial about the realities that severely limit our chances of making a significant difference in those lives. Warranted desperation requires a different definition of our work, a different kind of orientation and commitment. It requires discomfort. Witnessing the plethora of educational reform efforts that function within the realm of manic hope (see Murrell, 1998), the CCPE Network sought the creation of something different, the creation of spaces for edifying communal conversation about the harsh realities encountered by all of the stakeholders.

> **Mary:** I felt the desperation of the school space the first and every time I walked into Martin Luther King Law and Public Service Middle Schools and Magnet High School.

NONA REFLECTS ON CCPE AND MLK/LPS

The introduction of the CCPE to MLK/LPS through Carole Close and Carolyne was a new benchmark in the magnet's relationship with Cleveland State University's College of Education (COE). When we first planned the magnet, that college's dean was not interested in participating. Conflicts among the original planners regarding decision making led to the wise choice of a COE faculty member to serve as arbiter and evaluator (Rak, 1994). But CCPE offered much more, for it provided a vehicle for collaborative professional development for MLK/LPS's seasoned faculty.

> To handicap a student by teaching him that his black face is a curse and that his struggle to change his condition is hopeless is the worst sort of lynching. It kills ones aspirations and dooms him to vagabondage and crime. It is strange, then, that the friends of truth and the promoters of freedom have not risen against the present propaganda in the schools and crushed it. (Woodson, 1933/1990, p. 2)

First, there was the introduction to the Four Cities Network. Our long-standing partnership with CSU's Colleges of Law and Urban Affairs enabled us to occupy a unique seat at this table where we could test our practices against the experiences of other urban PDSs and broaden our exposure to practitioners and scholars with a critical perspective of reform in urban schools. It was exhilarating to travel to Chicago, room with colleagues in nice "digs" (treated like the professionals we were), and to have substantive conversations with well-known, inspiring educational scholars from across the country.

THE POLITICS OF RACIALIZED SPACE

A social justice lens was central to all of the work of CCPE. Given our Cleveland urban school context where a majority of the students were being miseducated through multiple practices of institutionalized racism, interrupting racism was an integral focus of the work.

Mary: I entered work with CCPE having been one of those miseducated students within the Cleveland Public schools, and having 5 years of field experience teaching oral-literate performance-based, creative writing workshops to students in the Cleveland Public Schools. As an African woman, mother, activist, artist educator, and performance poet, I am not interested in scholarship that is disconnected from the active struggle for social change. True change requires word-power, backbone, blood, risk, and movement in a direction that is ongoing, resistant, and result-oriented.

Carolyne: I encountered the following questions as I engaged this work: How do I as a white woman, beneficiary of white privilege, agent of the academy, educated to valorize epistemologies of whiteness, enter this work? How do I rework what Audre Lorde named "the master's tools" for use in this crucial anti-colonial work for social justice? How do I equip myself for the land of warranted desperation?

"Revolution"

When the man is busy
Making niggers
It doesn't matter
What shade
You are
If he runs out of one particular color
He can always switch to size
And when he's finished
Off the big ones
He'll change to sex
Which is after all
Where it all began.
        —Audre Lorde (1992)

CLEVELAND'S JAZZ FREEDOM FIGHTERS

In his book *Race Matters,* Cornel West (1993) invites his readers to become jazz freedom fighters who "cultivate an improvisational mode of protean, fluid, and flexible dispositions toward reality suspicious of 'either/or' viewpoints, dogmatic pronouncements, or supremacist ideologies" (p. 105). Early in the formation of CCPE, Carolyne started using the phrase *jazz freedom fighters* to symbolize the nature of the work we were imagining. Colleagues responded with quizzical looks, as if asking, *What is she talking about?* But this changed with many CCPE participants after hearing Cornel West speak at a NACCP function.

A group of us (that included a security guard and four middle school and high school teachers from MLK/LPS) team-taught three graduate courses one summer at Cleveland State University. The security guard, Tim Roberts, was so excited by West's *Race Matters* (1993) and Joel Spring's *Deculturalization and the Struggle for Equality: A Brief History of the Education of Dominated Cultures in the United States* (1994), that he vowed to give the books as Christmas presents to all of his family and friends. Vivian Robinson-Lee, a biology teacher, reflected upon this experience as "promoting a notable time to read and discuss revolutionary philosophies and views of various distinguished authors, which allows existing teachers to revisit theory and stimulate new classroom practices" (Lee, 1998, p. 1). Collaborative university teaching facilitated our development of shared conceptual language and understanding, and the space of trust required for collective, critical dialogue about our teaching practices.

Members of the CCPE network (including university and middle/high school students) gave several national conference presentations (American Association of Colleges of Teacher Education, American Educational Studies Association, National Coalition of Education Activists, American Educational Research Association, and the University of Pennsylvania Ethnography Forum) where we referred to ourselves as *jazz freedom fighters*. Before long the term had taken root. We were Cleveland's Jazz Freedom Fighters, seeking to nurture others to join us through the development of the Urban School-Based Teacher Education Program (USTEP).

THE URBAN SCHOOL-BASED TEACHER EDUCATION PROGRAM

As we considered entering into a professional development school partnership, MLK/LPS was the obvious choice because of the extraordinary faculty and the multiple ways they exemplified the positive educational practices we hoped future teachers would emulate. During the summer of 1995, as we (with MLK/LPS teachers and CSU faculty) were planning for the implementation of the USTEP, the Cleveland Public School District office was also making plans.

Nona: Our progressive school operation was interrupted by a school district office decision to move the magnet school out of its original and appropriate site to a condemned middle school building in order to accommodate an overpopulation of middle school students in the community. Having habitually chronicled my MLK/LPS experience daily since 1982, I find that "journal memory" is the best vehicle for retelling the rest of this story. I sent the faculty a memo that looked like the minutes of that "ambush," naming names and seeking the best in our faculty's ability to do alternative searches in a situation that was "a clear and present danger" to the magnet's continued suc-

May 17, 1995 Spent AM with parents; spent the PM with "bandits" planning to move MLK/LPS. Ambushed, unaware, spoke as best I could. Back to rally staff and friends of the school.

May 18, 1995 Eventful—from rallying support, holding our tiger (Councilwoman Fanny Lewis) by the tail, taking the heat for the right thing and seeing the staff and students exemplifying our mission.

May 19, 1995 A lot happening—students were at City Hall with parents ready to picket. Most touching—they sang the school song together to anyone who would listen. Opportunity to speak to the audience—"If I perish . . ." Too stressed in the afternoon as staff examined alternative proposal. Listen to help. . .

cess. I suspect copies were forwarded to those same central office persons because I got a call from the assistant superintendent accusing me of "not being a team player," even though the true team of this school was composed of parents, teachers, students, and community partners and supporters. We started the "Save our Schools" campaign—the city councilwoman, "a tiger" on behalf of quality education in her ward, made an inspiring speech to the assembly of students and faculty. In response, students made signs and marched. The faculty and I developed alternative proposals for the central office.

Facing the reality that central office personnel were intent on accommodating the overflow of middle school children at our expense, the faculty of the magnet school developed options with the help of the Center for School Improvement, the school district's professional development unit. We proposed phasing in a middle school population beginning with approximately 300 seventh and eighth graders. The central office accepted our proposal to incorporate a middle school component in our program with a few modifications—doubling the number of students and including sixth graders!

In July 1995, out of warranted desperation, I began tapping my network to prepare faculty and staff for the new configurations. I met with a retired principal with expertise in middle school development, giving her the same recommendations I had submitted to others. Ironically, she headed the "intervention of a team of educators," whose 2-day visit in October 1995 resulted in their making the same requests I had made months earlier—"parallel universe" or "déjà vu"?

> May 22, 1995   Superintendent Boyd expressed interest in our proposal—thinks I'm insubordinate?

I had submitted a comprehensive proposal to the chief operating officer, with copies to others who might provide collateral support. This plan included seven recommendations on curriculum and instruction, teacher training and professional development, parent and community involvement, and administrative structure, substantiated by research, practice, and my own experience. The socioeconomic data for the community from which the middle school children would come warranted extraordinary intervention, if this new configuration was to be beneficial. The percentage of high school graduates in the Hough statistical planning area was 37.65% (1990 Census). The poverty rate for the community was 78.2%. The ethnic makeup of the area was 97.92% African American (1990 Census) (Council for Economic Opportunities in Greater Cleveland, 1991).

No response to the proposal had been received when the school started in August, but I was determined to implement parts of the proposal with whatever resources were at my disposal. I "bootlegged" a list of the middle school children newly assigned to MLK/LPS after requests to the central office person processing this information were met with a "not available at this time" response. A committee of high school students, an activist parent, and I planned a mini-orientation for the children. Next, the parent and I went door to door in the community, delivering invitations and talking to parents about our expectations of success for the children. This gave me a firsthand scan of the ways children would come to our school. Cultural responsiveness in a nonresponsive school district? The first week's challenges were harbingers of the year's obstacles.

The middle school staff of approximately 40 individuals was not identified until mid-August. I only had time to plan one comprehensive team-building in-service, the week before opening day. Drawn from lay-off lists of persons with K–8 certification but experience in K–4, or closed programs, or adjustment transfers, these teachers were joining a magnet school faculty that was feeling betrayed by the central office, and by me, too (because my focus shifted to making the middle school program viable).

Facilities requests made in May 1995 were not completed at the opening of school in August. My request for a staggered opening to allow middle schoolers some time alone in the building to become acclimated was denied. All 1,000+ children reported at 7:45 AM with TV cameras rolling because the superintendent chose to make us his "first day of school" feature. The fire marshal said it was the best opening he had ever seen.

Carolyne: USTEP moved into this overcrowded building. Far from the model experience we had anticipated for our apprentice teachers, the feel of the building as we entered to begin our innovative program can only be described as akin to the kind of setting that stimulates posttraumatic stress disorder reactions. As I would walk into the building, I was often aware of a dissipating sense of presence, overcome with confusion, distraction, disassociation, sensory overload. I had to continu-

Mary: When Carolyne invited me to USTEP, I walked into the building hearing ambulance alarms, the hard clink of prison doors, hope falling to the floor like shards of milk-bottle glass—the building vibe so bad it literally stank.

ally call upon myself to attend, to come back, to be present. High school students resented the presence of the middle school "children." Fire alarms were set off intermittently throughout each day. What was to be our ideal classroom turned into a makeshift instructional space created with a pretense of a room divider that left just enough room between its top and the ceiling that middle school students could take turns throwing items into our space. Our goal to prepare exemplary urban educators required incredible and unimagined adjustments. In place of the stimulating scholarly conversations we had envisioned, much of our time with teachers was devoted to providing emotional support. Sustained by our shared vision and unbelievably strong relationships, we persisted.

Nona: The 1995–96 school year saw MLK/LPS changing from a model magnet high school of 450+ high school students to an embattled program challenged to coexist with 600 middle school students and 40 new faculty whose experience with this age group ranged from "none" to "not recently." It was like a sci-fi parallel universe. As the principal of this new configuration, I was so embroiled in the challenges of making this impossible situation work for the children's sake I was only peripherally aware of CCPE's or USTEP's inroads. My most arduous task was helping the adults weather the transformation of MLK/LPS (Burney, 1997).

High school and middle school teachers, except for a dedicated core from both constituencies, were overly hostile about sharing spaces. The "prima donna" demeanor of high school faculty only exacerbated the middle school teachers' frustration and diminished esteem. The dedicated core, which Vivian Robinson Lee, Tim Roberts, Diane Jenkins, and Matt Chinchar personified, remained strong. More than 100 parent and community volunteers collectively contributed more than 600 hours to help us generate a facsimile of an educative environment. At that time, a culturally responsive evaluation and a culturally responsive sensitivity would have helped my immediate supervisor understand the impact of this new configuration at MLK/LPS (Burney, 1997; Tichy & Devanna, 1986).

In April 1996, I spoke with Carolyne about ways to get the staff and students to define what we, MLK/LPS/MS want to be. She contracted with Willie Bonner and a group of CSU graduate students to assist. During an in-service meeting, teachers were asked to convey their feelings about the changes that had occurred, using symbols drawn on transparencies of the school mascot, the unicorn. Students in Grades 6–12 were given a writing prompt that asked them to write a letter to a friend describing their feelings from the beginning of the school year. Willie designed a six-panel storyboard of teachers' symbols and excerpts of students' essays that had been coded by the graduate students (Simon & White, 1996). The level of maturity and the astute nature of the students' writings were particularly striking. The whole installation remained in the main hall of the school for more than 2 weeks, generating necessary and important conversations, especially among the adult stakeholders—teachers, parents, and administrators. Subsequent analysis of this evaluation revealed critical stages of transformation that teachers had not fully processed or accepted (Burney, 1997).

Carolyne: Within this space of incredulous chaos also existed individuals of incredible vision, stamina, resilience, spirit, and commitment. Two of these individuals were Vivian Robinson Lee, a biology teacher, and Tim Roberts, the school security guard. They decided to carry out an intervention on behalf of the young women and men in the school. Their models of peer mentoring were met with enthusiasm and appreciation by the students and suspicion and critique by many of the MLK faculty. Together they designed the "Stick" Program with the following mission: "to empower faculty, staff, community liaisons, parents, and guardians to design student-centered projects that will promote and create a safe, nurturing, and loving school environment that will improve and foster academic performance; promote and sustain self-esteem; enhance one's character; develop and maintain positive personal relationships; promote the importance of teamwork and being a team player; advance school pride and instill a sense of ownership and community." This program included the following projects: Project BRICK, a mentoring program for middle and high school males; Project HALL MONITORS for Grades 9, 10, and 11; Project GIRL TALK for middle school females; Project PRECIOUS STONES for high school females; and Project WRAP AROUND for a middle school and high school in-house suspension program. Original funding for all of these projects came primarily from Tim and Vivian's pockets. Given the flexibility of the Joyce Foundation, CCPE was able to provide some financial support, and Tim and Vivian actively sought funding from other sources in the community. (See White, 1998, for more information about Project BRICK.) Tim Roberts named his Project BRICK for "Brotherhood, Respect, Intelligence in Conduct, and Knowledge." As a second father for all of the young men enrolled in BRICK, Tim modeled all of the of the above characteristics. He also modeled writing poetry as a way to know yourself in the world. One of the young men, Basheer Jones, realized his talent as a result of working with Tim. Winner of the Editors Choice Award from the National Poetry Forum, Basheer's poem, "Tell Me Why?" was accepted for publication in

B.R.I.C.K.

"Lean on me, when you're not strong
I'll be your friend,
I'll help you carry on . . ."
Instead of kids raising themselves,
raising Hell A man tall as a tenement house steps in
Drawing his own road to success
For them to follow believing
Be-loving them these young brown limbs
Lingering under his shade
Hugging his legs
Stepping a little taller
Stepping out.
One young man, a poet
Putting his feelings to rhyme
Out lines meet across time
Folding like hands—his eyes
On this one man
They stand together
Like bricks.

—Mary E. Weems

TEACHER

I wanna give thanks to the teachers that's teaching my people
And my peers you should get it because your knowledge is lethal
And the teachers who try their best may god bless you
And if you don't know who I'm talking to believe me they know who
Some of these teachers aren't nothing but a fake
They think they can treat my peers like they're a piece of cake
Teachers know students can't have your way
My peers, try to learn because if you sit around
They're still going to get their pay
No disrespect some times you teachers act crazy
And you don't teach us nothing so you can call us plain lazy
Only reason I come to school is to get an education
My mother told me to stay patient my detention
And suspensions is my only vacations
And these teachers want to show everybody that they're
The best you only have to prove to god because he's the
Only one that gives you his test
And my peers don't let these teachers hold you down
Just get good grades so they can have
A frown and feel like a clown I wanna give thanks to a
Lady when I did bad she never leave me alone
Didn't have any money so she gave me a loan
This lady I give thanks to by the name of Mrs. Jones
And despite the children that's bad and Pulling pranks to
All the teachers who try their best I wanna give thanks

—Basheer Jones (1997)

their poetry anthology, *Passionate Whispers*. Another of his poems, "My Mother," was accepted for inclusion in the Poets' League of Greater Cleveland's Writers & Their Friends *First Stage Production*. His work is the dream that BRICK brings to life.

SPACE FOR PREPARING URBAN JAZZ FREEDOM FIGHTERS

Carolyne: I redesigned my qualitative research course in the CSU Urban Education Doctoral Program to focus on an examination of the social construction of whiteness (see White, Andino-Demyan, Primer, & Storz, 1996). Three doctoral students from this course—Didi Andino-Demyan, Dena Primer, and Mark Storz—became instructors in USTEP and Mark wrote an auto-ethnographic dissertation (Storz, 1998) that explored the processes

Like an African mother, the blues has birthed many children, and has un-selfishly breast fed many others not her own. And in the final analysis, the blues is nothing more than dreams delayed, hopes deferred, emotions and feelings suppressed and sometimes forever unfulfilled. We all have them, every human being of us. And ours are no different than yours, and certain-ly no more important. The Blues? It is any song that has at its core the ques-tion, 'When will it end?' The personal pain, man's unhumanity to man, and above all, the suffering of children.

—*It Ain't Nothin But The Blues* (1995)

by which preservice teachers came to construct and interrogate their under-standings of racism. USTEP faculty became skilled at incorporating issues of racism and oppression into all of the classes. They were not hesitant to enter into difficult discussions with their students. Developing a consistent thread that addressed racism and other foundational issues became a difficult, criti-cal project for faculty teaching in USTEP. Traditionally, faculty members who teach methods courses have not been well prepared for this type of teaching. We often engaged team-teaching to address this issue. USTEP students were vocal about ways in which discussion about racism became a part of their program. For the European American students in the USTEP group, this was the first time that most had been in an urban school and the first time that they were in the minority in a CSU class. For the African American and His-panic students, the USTEP class generally was the first CSU class they had that did not shy away from issues of race and discrimination.

While some educators appear to support a notion of professional develop-ment schools as needing to be "ideal" models of master teaching, our work at MLK focused more upon equipping students to understand and negotiate the multiple realities of one urban school in Cleveland. MLK teachers were invited to assist with the instruc-tion of the teacher educa-tion courses and they were invited into critical conver-sations with the university students about their prac-tice. This ability for all of us to critically interrogate our own practice became a key focus of our work.

The one thing I could tell you about the USTEP program is it's not afraid to look at the big picture. Meaning it's not afraid to call it the way it is. It's not going to sugar-coat it. It's going to present it and we're going to deal with it. It's not of the "Oh, let's all get along. Oh, we're just in this big old melting pot." No, we're going to deal with the issue. With regards to race, we're going to deal with issues in regard to discrimination. With regards to gender discrimination. Right on down the line.
(African American USTEP student Storz, 1998)

ENCOUNTERING SPACES OF RACIALIZED RESISTANCE

Critical reflection characterized the actions of CCPE members, whether teaching a USTEP class or dealing with a question from the audience during a conference presentation. Mary, Carolyne, and Willie Bonner presented a session at the *Reclaiming Voice: Ethnographic Inquiry and Qualitative Research in a Postmodern Age Conference* in 1997 at the University of Southern California. Our session, *Reclaiming Voice: At Play in the Fields of the Lord,* included showing a video we had been creating to contextualize and document our work in CCPE. Drawing upon the "mystory" form of Gregory Ulmer (1989), we sought to create a video that moved across discourses of our personal experience, scholarship, and popular culture. Our video included clips from the films *Shaka Zulu, Green Pastures,* and *At Play in the Field of the Lord;* paintings by Willie, poetry by Mary; and scholarly quotes selected by Carolyne. We gave a powerful multivocal performance. At the end of the presentation, an African American woman in the audience asked, in effect, what Mary and Willie, as African Americans, were doing with Carolyne, a white academic. We explored our reflections on this work together and the woman's question in an article published in *Collaborations.* Included in the article was a poem that Mary was moved to write. Obstacles to CCPE's infusion of an obvious, antiracist stance in everything we undertook came in a variety of forms—sometimes through the resistance of white USTEP students to confront their white privilege; sometimes, as the poem suggests, through the resistance of an African American to trust in someone white. In general, however, it seemed that once people got over their surprise of openly discussing racism and other forms of oppression and felt safe to express themselves, they hungered for this level of discourse as they grew through relationship to others in the class, to coauthors, or to CCPE coworkers.

CREATING SPACE FOR CULTURALLY RESPONSIVE
COLLABORATIVE EVALUATION

Nona: What culturally responsive evaluation could be employed to address our situation? My challenges as a "talking back" administrator had exponentially increased (White & Burney, 1994). Despite what was allegedly a collaborative performance evaluation process of my work as principal, my immediate supervisor summarized my work that year from her perspective alone. She refused my offer of an alternative, more balanced statement. Therefore, I submitted a 160+ page document to this supervisor, her supervisor, the superintendent, and the director of personnel. This evaluation documented how I had met or exceeded our agreed-upon standards of

What are you doing with her?

The sista said (meaning that white woman)
taking me back in a single question, stripping me of my
extravagant African headwrap,
my dress made of hand dyed strips of mud cloth
sent back from the Africa of my blood and dreams,
making me think Uncle Tom and Thomasina that just
us really is blind, that we must be out our minds
to think that change is gonna come. I remember
blood rushing to my brown face, cutting my eye
to my white woman colleague, touching base with my African American
brother colleague
giving the invisible high five that said "What is this? and
where is it coming from?"
I mumbled somethin that sounded intelligent,
that covered my shock like a raggedy dress.
My response was fulla holes that needed darning
even now because I only know one answer
and knew the moment I thought it that nothing
I said would do because due to over 500
years of racism as varied as a spoiled vegetable
soup covering everything from our hair to our language,
our art, our history, our freedom, our way of making
a living, a thousand hard knocks on invisible glass
ceilings, millions of dollars stolen for our labor,
and one hundred million reasons we shouldn't, in the mind
of this sistah and millions like her, be with Carolyne
of-all-last-names White, she didn't want to hear
it, but wanted us to disappear like a bad scene
taking our kick ass presentation on knocking down
the walls of institutionalized racism.
with us.

(Weems, in White, Weems, & Bonner, 1997, pp. 23–24)

performance. Subsequently, the central office "evaluated" all administrators based on criteria other than those performance standards they had promulgated. I received a 1-year contract, the optimum being a 3-year one. Only "talking back" through CCPE initiatives and embracing the space of warranted desperation did I find hope.

Carolyne: Approximately 5 years after the CCPE journey had begun, we faced the end of our funding from the Joyce Foundation and the prospect of an external evaluation. The evaluator was scheduled to visit Cleveland for 2 days to evaluate our accomplishments. How could one person visit with all of the key participants and stakeholders in this network in only 2 days? What about the viability of having one white woman conduct an evaluation about a collaborative multicultural urban education effort? Seeking a remedy, I asked Mary and Willie Bonner to conduct a 6-week summer workshop for MLK middle and high school students. Mary would teach creative writing and interviewing skills, Willie would teach videotaping skills. The students would conduct and videotape interviews with key CCPE collaborators. The students would create the evaluation questions from their cultural lenses. This project resulted in approximately 20 hours of videotaped interviews that were sent to the evaluator before her visit. While these interviews informed her understanding of the program, the problem remained of how to organize so much diverse data into the one brief report desired by the Joyce Foundation. The evaluator wrote a concise report that was extremely positive about the merit and worth of our work. She told an evaluation story that communicated to the foundation audience that we had used their money well and we had succeeded in accomplishing the objectives we had set forth in the proposal. However, as Greene (2000) writes, "The need is not to find the one correct way to do program evaluation, but rather to conduct our craft so that it responds to multiple audiences, includes multiple perspectives, constructs multiple and diverse understandings and equally diverse representations of those understandings, and encourages dialogue and conversations" (p. 995). That has been our goal in this chapter, to explore another way to conduct this craft, a way that might open new stories for broader public audiences (see Ryan & Hood, 2004).

> July 26, 1996   Spent the AM getting my "Response" together. Went to NCEA [National Coalition of Education Activists] Conference. Encouraging to hear the results of USTEP in the lives of the pre-service "teachers." There is *victory*.

As we consider the evaluation activity engaged by the middle school students in their summer workshop, we see that they formed a tight and supportive community among themselves as they learned new skills and also gained extensive exposure to university life. Their evaluation activity had a positive educative outcome for them.

Nona: Evaluating the process and product of the CCPE venture that we Jazz Freedom Fighters shared, our quest to re-form—no, transform—an educational environment for the benefit of children who have been made disadvantaged takes a machete. Not unlike the two-edged sword, this metaphorical truth-seeking, truth-telling blade would have to cut through the overgrowth of bureaucratic complacency that had ignored the initial proposals to effectively implement the Grade 6–12 configuration of MLK/LPS. Just to clear a path to the minds and hearts of teachers, administrators, children, parents, and community leaders who were trying to find a way out of this choking underbrush and canopy of reproducing miseducation, the team of evaluators could not employ the typical "agent orange" of psychometric strategies. These demand much from participants/objects and leave nothing behind to sustain the survivors who must still "do school," regardless of the report. It would take an artist's vision, a poet's voice, to discern and communicate the warranted desperation that impelled us all to act. My immediate supervisor could not see the bridge between team-building and effective instruction of children; the "smoke screen" of standardized test scores obscured the power of B.R.I.C.K. where black boys of the middle school literally danced around Tim Roberts to show off their 2.5 and better GPAs. That school district evaluator had no way to measure the growth of white, female K–3 teachers who overcame their fear of these sixth-grade "hough tough" charges to promote decorum in the midst of the chaos Mary so aptly perceived.

No, the CCPE team would have to cut their way in to the eye of this storm, stand with us in the center, where children and their teachers are the focus, and *with* us, expand the sacred space *around* us so that transformative education could prevail. They would have to be culturally responsive in the broadest sense—not just cognizant of the GRECSO (gender, race, ethnicity, class, sexual orientation) paradigm, but of school culture, the macro-district mentality as well as the micro-MLK/LPS psyche (Stroempl, 1993).

Even their reports would have to reflect culture in its most inclusive terms—poetry, visual arts, music. That is how Carolyne, the scholar/activist; Mary, the poet; Willie Bonner, the artist; and USTEP teacher candidates helped MLK/LPS's community begin to process the pain of this transformative set of events—primeval, therapeutic self-expression. One of the first workshops I presented upon my return to MLK/LPS was a performance of a segment of the *Post-Modern Tragedy*, featuring middle and high school teachers using the students' voices. Humorously cathartic, this method of delivering the findings of that study facilitated the adults' revisioning process.

We end this piece where we began, modeling an expanded cultural response to the issue of culturally responsive evaluation...

EMERGENCY ROOM: A SCHOOL IN CRISIS

Blood, School, Books

The vibe was bad the first day
like garbage day in the summer,
or the air of a dirty nursing home
My feet moved forward tracing Carolyne's
feet, tracing Willie's feet, stepping in the shoes
of all the students' who'd walked in these doors
wiping their dreams on the floor mats, leaving
their raps, and flows, and cartoons, and sketches,
and new words, and life behind them as if
school has nothing to do with life NOT because
they know that, but because they don't and few
behind these stripped walls help them see

there are no separations life as seamless as a steel
sheet, as the face of their principal serene in his
militant ignorance, calmly moving the couches and
tables and books out of the emergency room we built
for the students, a little carved corner where we tried
to say welcome! sit, chill, discuss, read, school is cool
come in, come in

behind these stripped walls help them see
we kept coming back, I kept coming back, kept coming
back like an old song trying new lyrics, whistling,
performing, poems falling from my fingertips like leaves
writing with students rushing to catch up with their
imaginations, fussing, fed up, excited, disappointed, amazed

each time the front doors looked the same dirty, barred,
my metaphor shifting position to hospital, prison to hospital,
prison to hospital

one day I needed our emergency room. I was in the library
filled with books, each book a Dreamkeeper, no one was reading

sharing my work, the students, seniors with eyes older than me
their arms crossed in "we gon' see," their legs stretched out,
me in the middle doing "B.B. Blues" not knowing about the blood

my head stopping me, a red light in my eyes, the students' voices,
the teacher's voice, my head hurting like lye, I moved out of the room
hearing an alarm, smelling the halls, moving to a different space
not thinking, just moving trying to leave my headache behind

I reached the couch, rested my head, closed my eyes
and waited for the ambulance to come and stop the blood
from boiling.

—Mary E. Weems

OPENING NEW SPACES

Much of our work in the CCPE Network appears to have turned to dry cloth. The grant funding ended. The Urban School-Based Teacher Education Program ended. Many of the CCPE collaborators moved to new positions. Nona Burney moved to Roosevelt University where she is now an Associate Professor. Mary moved to the University of Illinois to pursue her doctorate in Educational Policy Studies. Today, she is a Visiting Assistant Professor at Ohio University. Carolyne moved to Northern Arizona University to become Chair of Instructional Leadership in the Center for Excellence in Education.

One of our collaborative projects with students, a Youth Power Project called "School as Second Home," had resulted in the purchase of leather couches as part of our creation of a "living room" space near the entrance to the school building. This living room included a plaque acknowledging that the purchase of the couches was funded by a student-initiated grant project. However, since the installation of a new administration at the school, the leather couches had been moved to a new location, behind glass sliding doors where students can view them, but not sit on them.

However, the living space of politics and poetics continues to grow within us and between us. The vision embodied in the CCPE Network continues to breathe through us and, we hope, in those with whom we worked and struggled. In place of manic hope in the unjustifiable, we have discovered the powerful space of a more modest hope: hope for the company of like-minded "Jazz Freedom Fighters" to work alongside us, and hope for resilience in the face of the new challenges we encounter in new spaces of warranted desperation. Our "patterned vision of how to move and what to fear" grows as we continue to work for "an absent, but perhaps possible other present."

POSTSCRIPT

As we were completing this manuscript, Carolyne received an email message from a USTEP student she had taught. The message was addressed to both Carolyne and Nona. The former student, Robert K. Early, wrote: "Happy New Year. I hope this email finds you both in the best of health and joy. After a little searching, I located email addresses for you on the University website. Oh the power of technology. I thought you both would like an update on our special USTEP class." Robert then listed each student and the urban schools where they are currently employed. He ended the message with, "I thought you both would like to know that the Jazz Freedom Fighters are out in the fields spreading the word."

TALKING BACK TO OUR TEXT

Crafting a culturally responsive program evaluation is incredibly complex scholarly work. This chapter offers an exploratory look at a few of the multiple elements of the CCPE project. It is in no way comprehensive. Intentionally disjointed, our goal has been to argue for and enact the power of new scholarly forms of knowing, in particular poetic space (see Barone & Eisner, 1997; Cahnmann, 2003; Eisner, 1991, 1997; Glesne, 1997; Richardson, 2000), for better illuminating crucial cultural components of transformative educational reform work in this urban setting.

NOTES

1. This group grew to include more university faculty and public school teachers and administrators from Chicago, Detroit, Milwaukee, and Cleveland. We met quarterly and hosted a yearly conference with guest speakers who included Tom Russell, Christine Sleeter, Carl Grant, and Peter C. Murrell, Jr. Teachers from urban schools in the four cities attended and presented at these conferences.
2. Primary contributors included CSU faculty members Kathy Bickmore and C. Lynne Hannah and CPS faculty member Carole Close.
3. Published for 3 years, the *Collaborations Journal* solicited collaboratively written articles from teachers, parents, students, university faculty, civic leaders, and community members. It was distributed free of charge to every Cleveland Public School and through many community organizations.

REFERENCES

Alexie, S. (1993). *The lone ranger and tonto fistfight in heaven.* New York: Atlantic Monthly Press.

Anyon, J. (1995). Race, social class, and educational reform in an inner city school. *Teachers College Record, 97*(1).

Anyon, J. (1997). *Ghetto schooling: A political economy of urban educational reform.* New York: Teachers College Press.

Bachelard, G. (1969). *Poetics of space.* Boston: Beacon Press.

Barone, T. (2001). Science, art, and the predispositions of educational researchers. *Educational Researcher, 30*(7).

Barone, T., & Eisner, E. W. (1997). Arts-based educational research. In R.M. Jaeger (Ed.), *Contemporary methods for research in education* (2nd ed.). Washington, DC: American Educational Research Association.

Ben-Peretz, M. (2001). The impossible role of teacher educators in a changing world. *Journal of Teacher Education, 52*(1).

Britzman, D. P. (2000). Teacher education in the confusion of our times. *Journal of Teacher Education, 51*(3).

Burney, N. M. (1997). *A postmodern tragedy: Reform of education for children who have been made disadvantaged.* Unpublished doctoral dissertation, Cleveland State University.

Cahnmann, M. (2003). The craft, practice, and possibility of poetry in educational research. *Educational Researcher, 32*(3), 29–36.

Cornwell, T. L. (1993). Revitalizing the public service: The secondary school curriculum. In T. L. Cornwell & S. O. Ludd (Eds.), *Excellence in Ohio: Revitalizing the public service, an occasional paper series. Vol. 11: Civic education* (pp. 49–65). Bowling Green, OH: Bowling Green State University, Center for Governmental Research and Public Service.

Council for Economic Opportunities in Greater Cleveland. (1991). *Poverty indicators, 1991.* Cleveland, OH: Author.

Denzin, N. K., & Lincoln, Y. S. (1994). *Handbook of qualitative research.* Thousand Oaks, CA: Sage.

Denzin, N. K., & Lincoln, Y. S. (2000). The discipline and practice of qualitative research. In N. K. Denzin & Y. S. Lincoln (Eds.), *Handbook of qualitative research* (2nd ed., pp. 1–29). Thousand Oaks, CA: Sage.

Eisner, E. W. (1991). *The enlightened eye: Qualitative inquiry and the enhancement of educational practice.* New York: Macmillan.

Eisner, E. W. (1997). The promise and perils of alternative forms of data representation. *Educational Researcher, 26*(6), 4–10.

Ellis, C., & Bochner, A.P. (2000).Autoethnograhy, personal narrative, reflexivity. In N. K. Denzin & Y. S. Lincoln (Eds.), *Handbook of qualitative research* (2nd ed., pp. 733–757). Thousand Oaks, CA: Sage.

Frierson, H. T., Hood, S., & Hughes, G. B. (2002). *The 2002 user friendly handbook for project evaluation.* Arlington, VA: National Science Foundation.

Gay, G. (2000). *Culturally responsive teaching: Theory, research and practice.* New York: Teachers College Press.

Glesne, C. (1997). That rare feeling: Representing research through poetic transcription. *Qualitiative Inquiry, 3*(2), 202–221.

Goings, R. L., Jr., & Boulware, E. N. (Executive Producers) & Hotton, J. (Director). (1993). Griots of imagery: A comment on the art of Romare Bearden and Charles White [Videotape]. New York: Praise Song on a Shoe String, Inc.

Greene, J. C. (2000). Understanding social programs through evaluation. In N. K. Denzin & Y. S. Lincoln (Eds.), *Handbook of qualitative research* (2nd ed., pp. 981–999). Thousand Oaks, CA: Sage.

Greene, M. (1995). *Releasing the imagination.* San Francisco: Jossey-Bass.

Haraway, D. (1989). *Primate visions: Gender, race and nature in the world.* New York: Routledge.

Heldke, L. (1998). On being a responsible traitor: A primer. In B. B. On & A. Ferguson (Eds.), *Daring to be good: Essays in feminist ethico-politics.* New York: Routledge.

Hollins, E. R., & Oliver, E. I. (1999). *Pathways to success in school: culturally responsive teaching.* London: Erlbaum.

Jones, B. (1997). *Teacher.* Unpublished poem.

Kolodny, K. A. (2001). Inequalities in the overlooked associations in urban educational collaborations. *Urban Review, 33*(2), 151–178.

Krieger, S. (1991). *Social science and the self: Personal essays on an art form*. New Brunswick, NJ: Rutgers University Press.

Ladson-Billings, G. (2000). Racialized discourses and ethnic epistemologies. In N. K. Denzin & Y. S. Lincoln (Eds.), *Handbook of qualitative research* (2nd ed., pp. 257–277). Thousand Oaks, CA: Sage.

Lincoln, Y. S., & Denzin, N. K. (2000). The seventh moment: Out of the past. In N. K. Denzin & Y. S. Lincoln (Eds.), *Handbook of qualitative research* (2nd ed., pp. 1047–1065). Thousand Oaks: Sage.

Lorde, A. (1981). The master's tools will never dismantle the master's house. In C. Moraga & G. Anzaldua (Eds.), *This bridge called my back: Writings by radical women of color*. New York: Kitchen Table: Women of Color Press.

Lorde, A. (1992). *Undersong: Chosen poems old and new revised*. New York: Norton.

Lorde, A. (1984). Poetry is not a luxury. In *Sister outsider: Essays and speeches*. Freedom, CA: Crossing Press.

Minh-ha, T. T. (1989). *Woman, native, other*. Bloomington: Indiana University Press.

Miron, L. F. (2003). The cultural images of public schooling and the emergence of plurality in research. *Cultural Studies Critical Methodologies, 3*(2), 203–228.

Murrell, C. P. (1998). *Like stone soup: The role of the professional development school in the renewal of urban schools*. Washington, DC:AACTE.

Nieto, S. (2000). Placing equity front and center: Some thoughts on transforming teacher education for a new century. *Journal of Teacher Education, 51*(3).

Popkewitz, T. (1991). *A political sociology of educational reform: Power/ Knowledge in teaching, teacher education and research*. New York: Teachers College Press.

Rak, C. F. (1994). *The Cleveland Public Schools Law and Public Service Magnet High School: A research report*. Cleveland, OH: Cleveland State University, College of Education.

Rich, A. (1973). *Diving into the wreck: Poems, 1971–1972*. New York: Norton.

Rich, A. (1978). *The dream of a common language: Poems, 1974–1977*. New York: Norton.

Rich, A. (2004). *North American time*. Retrieved March 25, 2004, from http://www.emilydickinson.org/titantic/rich6.html

Richardson, L. (1993, April). *Poetics, dramatics and sacred spaces*. Paper presented at the Redesigning Ethnography: Responses to Postmodernist, Feminist and other Critiques Conference, University of Colorado at Boulder.

Richardson, L. (1997). *Fields of play: Constructing an academic life*. New Brunswick, NJ: Rutgers University Press.

Richardson, L. (2000). Writing: A method of inquiry. In N. K. Denzin & Y. S. Lincoln (Eds.), *Handbook of qualitative research* (2nd ed., pp. 923–948). Thousand Oaks, CA: Sage.

Rosenberg, P. M. (1997). Underground discourse: Exploring whiteness in teacher education. In M. Fine, L. Weis, L. C. Powell, & L. M. Wongs (Eds.), *Off white: Readings on race, power, and society* (pp 78–79). New York: Routledge.

Rothman, R. (1993). Obstacle course: Barriers to change twart reformers at every twist and turn. *Education Week*, 9–12.

Ryan, K. E., & Hood, L. K. (2004). Guarding the castle and opening the gate. *Qualitative Inquiry, 10*(1), 79–95.

Sarason, S. (1993). *The case for change: Rethinking the preparation of teacher educators.* San Francisco: Jossey-Bass.

Senese, G. (1995). *Stimulation, Spectacle, and the ironies of education reform.* Westport, CT: Bergin & Garvey

Simon, M. E., & White, C. J. (1996). *CCPE Partners with MLK* (Urban Child Research Center Report). Cleveland, OH: Maxine Goodman Levin College of Urban Affairs, Cleveland State University.

Sleeter, C. E. (2001). Preparing teachers for culturally diverse schools: Research and the overwhelming presence of whiteness. *Journal of Teacher Education, 52*(2).

Soussloff, C., & Franko, M. (2002). Visual and performance studies: A new history of interdisciplinarity. *Social Text, 73*, 29–46.

Spring, J. (1994). *Deculturalization and the struggle for equality: A brief history of the education of dominated cultures in the United States.* New York: McGraw-Hill.

Storz, G. M. (1998). *Constructing understandings of race: Tales from an urban professional development schools foundations course.* Unpublished doctoral dissertation.

Stroempl, R. H. (1993). Ethnographic interpretation of faculty perspectives on school culture: Site-based implications for school reform (Doctoral dissertation, Cleveland State University, 1993). *Dissertation Abstracts International, 54,* A1629.

Taylor, R. (1995). *It ain't nothin' but the blues.* Taken from a play in Cleveland, Ohio.

Tichy, W. G., & Devanna, M. A. (1986). *The transformational leader.* New York: Wiley.

Ulmer, G. (1989). *Teletheory: Grammatology in the age of video.* New York: Routledge.

Weems, M. (2003). *Public education and the Imagination-Intellect: I speak from the wound in my mouth.* New York: Peter Lang.

West, C. (1993). *Race matters.* Boston: Beacon Press.

White, C. J. (1988). Conversation as text. *Educational Foundations, 22*(3), 87–105.

White, C. J. (1991). Institutional racism and campus climate. In D. W. LaCounte, W. Stein, & P. W. Head (Eds.), *Opening the Montana Pipeline: American Indian higher education in the nineties* (pp. 33–45). Sacramento, CA: Tribal College Press.

White, C. J. (1992). *Awakening moral wisdom: Re-visioning urban landscapes with Foxfire.* Evaluation Report for Cleveland Education Fund. Cleveland, OH: Author.

White, C. J. (1993). *Communicating across differences: A collaborative learning adventure.* Evaluation Report for Cleveland Education Fund. Cleveland, OH: Author.

White, C. J. (1998). Project BRICK: Moral wisdom in action. *Association for Childhood Education International, 11*(2), 1–3, 6.

White, C. J., & Burney, N. M. (1994). Urban educators "talk back" across discourse of empowerment. *Collaborations, 1*(1), 86–100.

White, C. J., Burney, N. M., & Lee, V. R. (1998). *At play in Cleveland's schooling fields: Exploring social justice PDS work through the Urban School-Based Teacher Education Program.* Symposium presented at The Holmes Partnership annual meetings.

White, C., Andino-Demyan, D., Primer, D., & Storz, M. (1996). Constructing a scholarly community of Jazz Freedom Fighters: (Re)writing the university classroom for the postmodern world. *Planning and Changing: An Educational Leadership and Policy Journal, 73*(1-2), 27–58.

White, C. J., Mogilka, J., & Slack, P. J. (1998). Disturbing the colonial frames of ethnographic representation: Releasing feminist imagination on the academy. In N. K. Denzin (Ed.), *Cultural studies: A research volume* (Vol. 3, pp. 3–27).

White, C. J., Sakiestewa, N., & Shelley, C. (1998). TRIO: The unwritten legacy. *The Journal of Negro Education, 67*(4), 444–454.

White, C. J., Weems, M. E, & Bonner, W. J. (1997). Reclaiming voice: At play in the fields of the lord. *Collaberations, 3*(1), 20–26.

Woodson, C. G. (1990). *The miseducation of the Negro.* Nashville, TN: Winston-Derek. (Original work published 1933)

CHAPTER 10

USING THEORY-DRIVEN EVALUATION WITH UNDERSERVED COMMUNITIES

Promoting Program Development and Program Sustainability

Katrina L. Bledsoe
The College of New Jersey

When I presented my thinking concerning the use of theory-driven evaluation with underserved and often diverse communities at the Relevance of Assessment and Culture in Evaluation (RACE) 2003 conference in January 2003, I had been reflecting upon my experiences with the approach for nearly 2 years and had written two opinion articles in *Mechanisms* (Bledsoe, 2003; Donaldson, 2001), the newsletter of the Program Theory and Theory-Driven Evaluation Topical Interest Group, a division of the American Evaluation Association (AEA). My goal then had been to defend the theory-driven evaluation approach from the critiques that it lacks realism (Scriven, 1997; Stufflebeam, 2001) and is unable to provide useful information for communities that often cannot afford the time and expense that

The Role of Culture and Cultural Context in Evaluation, pages 179–199
Copyright © 2005 by Information Age Publishing

evaluation, especially theory-driven evaluation, supposedly can require (Scriven, 1997). I also had taken the discussion a step further by suggesting (perhaps rather boldly) that the theory-driven approach was also a mechanism to promote program sustainability (Bledsoe, 2003). I had significant success using theory-driven evaluation with several community-based programs designed for communities of color and thus wanted to reflect upon and share with others those experiences (e.g., Bledsoe, Gilbert, Fischbein, Cervantes, & Dragan, 2001; Bledsoe & Graham, 2005). The current chapter is a result of those reflections and experiences, and is designed to expand the knowledge and usefulness of the theory-driven approach beyond the "ivory tower" of academia.

Theory-driven evaluation (TDE) has long been considered a valuable evaluation approach in the field (Chen & Rossi, 1987; Lipsey & Pollard, 1989; Weiss, 1997). Considered part of the overarching "discipline" of theory-based evaluation (Gargani, 2003), TDE has been hailed as either a significant answer to many evaluation challenges and problems (Chen, 1990; Chen & Rossi, 1987; Donaldson, 2003), or a waste of precious time and resources (Scriven, 1997; Stufflebeam, 2001). At times, theory-driven evaluation has been dismissed as insensitive or unrealistic in understanding the needs, unique perspectives, and circumstances of organizations and communities, especially underserved ethnic communities (Scriven, 1997; Stufflebeam, 2001). Of course, the truth lies somewhere in between (e.g., Weiss, 1997). Those who are dismissive of the approach purport that the use of TDE is unrealistic, especially for groups who would not be able to pay for such an evaluation and/or don't have time for an iterative approach to evaluation. Stakeholders who fall into either of the aforementioned categories (or both) are identified as communities with programs in need of immediate implementation (see Figure 10.1). These programs are often social service–focused, designed to address an immediate and impending need such as health education or drug prevention (e.g., Orlandi, 1994).

The current discussion is centered on how a theory-driven approach to evaluation and assessment is effective in identifying and exploring the subtleties and nuances unique to underserved communities, thus leading to more relevant and community-specific programming. Specifically, I suggest that theory-driven evaluation is useful in assisting program designers, gov-

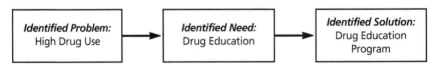

Figure 10.1.   How needs are turned into programs.

ernments, funders, and consumers in understanding the nuances and the subtleties of the program, the consumers it serves, and the community in which it operates. This increase in precision helps to improve program design, which subsequently promotes program sustainability. Specifically, it is proposed that theory-driven evaluation has the ability to (1) elicit stakeholder "program theory," thereby providing an opportunity to voice unique perspectives by those who otherwise might be ignored (e.g., communities of color, high-risk populations); (2) delineate the links that are vital for program functioning (e.g., cultural influences); and finally, (3) take information from other areas—including other programs, documented literature, evaluation approaches, and the like—and use it to develop a comprehensive model of how the program works (and/or should work) and whom it may affect (Chen, 1990; Donaldson, 2001).

In many cases, theory-driven evaluation can clearly identify specific program components that are most useful to underserved communities, especially for communities of color. This is especially important in the 21st century where the quest for cultural sensitivity and competence is at the forefront of program development, program evaluation (Mertens, 1995; 2003; Orlandi, 1994), and program sustainability in social concerns such as health and drug intervention and prevention (e.g., Vega & Gil, 1998). These are issues that often have high consequences for communities of color (e.g., high mortality; New Jersey Health and Human Services, 1998) but only a few seem to have documented what contributes to those consequences (e.g., racism, cultural beliefs; Guzman, 2003).

This chapter serves as a starting point for discussion among program designers, researchers, and practitioners concerning the ability of a theory-driven approach to listen and use the perspectives of those who are most affected by the program, and to clearly articulate when and why programs work. I include case studies from both my and others' experiences to provide examples of how theory-driven evaluation is conducted. Finally, I also discuss the usefulness of the approach in combination with others that are more participatory, empowering, and transformative.

Before I begin, it is important to have general understanding of TDE, including its origins and procedures.

THE THEORETICAL UNDERPINNINGS: A BRIEF TUTORIAL OF THE THEORY-DRIVEN EVALUATION APPROACH

Theory-driven evaluation can be described as a cousin of what has been often termed theory-based evaluation, and has been used, at least on some level, since the early 20th century. Educational theorist Ralph Tyler (1909, cited in Gargani, 2003) in describing how to enhance educational programs noted that effectiveness would be greatly improved by understanding the mechanisms of a program and the manner in which it works. Theory-based evaluation acknowledges that there are theoretical underpinnings to the design and, by extension, the evaluation of the program. Although theory-driven evaluation is used synonymously with theory-based evaluation, it is best defined by Weiss (1997) as examining the mechanisms that mediate the process and outcomes of a program or an evaluand. Specifically, she defines the TDE approach as evaluation that combines the use of scientific and stakeholder theory to delineate the inner workings of a program and how they are related to the outcome (Weiss, 1997). This definition has been the most frequently cited to define approaches ranging from logic modeling (Stinchcomb, 2001) to conceptual modeling (Scriven, 1997).

Although others discussed TDE throughout the 1980s and 1990s (e.g., Bickman, 1989; Lipsey & Pollard, 1989; Patton, 1989), it was Chen (1990) who identified six types of theory-driven evaluation. Chen focused specifically on intervening mechanism theory (others are treatment theory, implementation environment theory, outcome theory, impact theory, and generalization theory; see Chen for a detailed discussion of these approaches), which has been the most commonly used (Donaldson, 2001). When one refers to TDE it is this latter approach that comes to mind. The intervening mechanism approach focuses on defining *how* and *why* a program works to produce some kind of outcome or change.

One of the reasons the intervening mechanism approach is used so often is because of its reliance on both social science theories and methodologies and stakeholder "theories" (ideas and perceptions of how the program works) and "methods" (strategies that are used to implement the program). Like social science, one of the purposes of using a TDE intervening mechanism approach is to identify the components that make the program work and in what way those components are most effective. This also includes those components that are either unintentional positive or negative outcomes of the program, or factors that influence the strength and magnitude of the program components, such as program dosage (under what conditions the program works best or worst; Lipsey, 1990).

Thus the draw to the TDE intervening mechanism approach is precisely its ability to clearly delineate the components of a program and when and why they work rather than to simply say, "The program works." That is, rather than evaluating a program within a "black box" context and not being able to define the specific working (and non-working) program components, the mechanisms of a program are defined and illuminated. Figure 10.2 provides an illustration of black box evaluation. Program A, a drug prevention program for adolescents, is presumed to lead to some change in B, say reduced drug use among adolescents. We know that the program affects drug use in some way but are unsure exactly in what manner (see Figure 10.2).

In theory-driven evaluation, however, the drug prevention program is presumed to affect drug use through some mechanism. Between the two is a mediating factor, some aspect that is considered to be the actual reason or link (e.g., increased knowledge of the physical health consequences of drugs) to the final desired outcome. The program is linked directly to the mediator(s), which in turn is linked directly to a reduction in drug use (the outcome; Donaldson, 2001). Donaldson's (2001) article on mediator and moderator analysis illustrates the usefulness of an intervening mechanism theory approach in determining the contribution of each aspect that is hypothesized to cause the program outcome (see Figure 10.3).

Additionally, moderators such as environment, culture, gender, socioeconomic status, and the like can also be taken into account. A moderator is a factor that can affect the strength of the program intervention and strategy. For instance, what if the program is more effective for those of a higher socioeconomic status than those of a lower status? Specifically, what if adolescents from a higher socioeconomic status are more likely to benefit from the program because of having school resources than adolescents from a lower socioeconomic status without access to such resources? Using a theory-driven evaluative approach, these moderators can be accounted for early in the evaluation and possibly in the program design/development stage and provide strategies to address the realities and needs of both adolescent groups (see Figure 10.4).

Donaldson (2001) and others (e.g., Chen, 1990) have noted that there are typically three steps to conducting theory-driven evaluation: (1) devel-

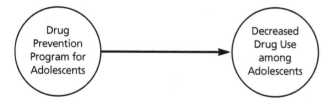

Figure 10.2. Conceptual model of black box evaluation.

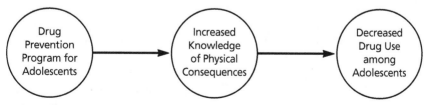

Figure 10.3. Theory-driven intervening mechanism evaluation.
Models adapted by permission from Donaldson, 2001.

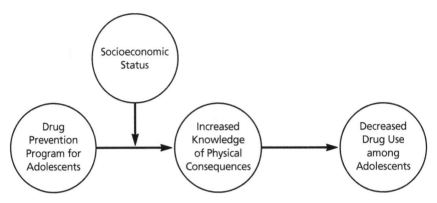

Figure 10.4.   Theory-driven intervening mechanism evaluation with a moderator.

oping program theory, (2) formulating and prioritizing evaluation questions, and (3) answering evaluation questions. In the development of program theory, evaluators work closely with stakeholders to try to delineate the actual program components and the manner in which they work. Evaluators and stakeholders then attempt to prioritize the types of questions that would yield useful information for program development and/ or finetuning of an existing program. Such questions might focus on who is being serviced and in what manner it would be best to serve them. Finally, collaborators explore possible methods by which to answer the evaluation question in an appropriate and feasible manner (e.g., is the community more amenable to the use of interviews or surveys?). This strategy not only allows for the identification of components that define the program, but also allows for a more representative evaluation, one that clearly represents the community the program serves. Thus evaluators have a clear understanding of the mechanism they should measure and what method is best for measuring it (Donaldson, 2001).

Mercier, Piat, Peladeau, and Dagenais (2001) demonstrated how a theory-driven approach contributed to the identification of the program theory and formulation of evaluation questions at the formative stages in the development of a "drop-in" youth center. Specifically, they found that the use of concept mapping, a graphing technique used to map out knowledge links of how the program works, was helpful in articulating the specific components, such as time of program operation (when the drop-in center was opened and closed), that might contribute to the success of the program (Mercier et al., 2001).

In our work for a local nonprofit agency in New Jersey (Bledsoe & Graham, 2004), we have found that a theory-driven approach (logic model development, evaluation question formulation, use of stakeholder program theory, and testing of appropriate evaluation questions) has been especially useful in providing necessary feedback not only for the program evaluation of a literacy program, but also for long-term program development, sustainability, and future funding. Using the approach we have been able to clearly identify what program components are and in what manner they are working, which ultimately informs operators and funders about the viability of the program in the long term.

But why is such clarity in programming necessary? Organizations are constantly asked for measurable outcomes to prove that the program works and this accountability is still quite basic, the program either works or it doesn't. Despite this basic focus on measurable outcomes, program administrators find themselves in the unique position of having to answer other questions before answering the overarching question of program effectiveness. "Other" questions include (but are not limited to), what short-term change (mediator) leads to the long-term change (outcome)? Those additional questions are a direct result of the changing nature of programs and program evaluation.

THE CHANGING NATURE OF PROGRAMS AND EVALUATION

Evaluators for some time now have commented on the effectiveness of social programming. For instance, theorists and practitioners (e.g., Wholey, 1979), have expressed skepticism about the effectiveness of social programs, and have provided suggestions for making them more effective. Such skepticism is not unwarranted. In our evolving global society, programs are often ill equipped to address and serve the needs of highly diverse communities (Guzman, 2003).

The changing nature of the global society has been of top priority of evaluators (American Evaluation Association, 2003). Because of the increase in diversity of culture and thought, as well as in community, program development, evaluation, and sustainability have been key concerns for not only the organizations that work on a daily basis in these highly dynamic atmospheres but for professional evaluators and organizations such as the American Evaluation Association (AEA). These groups are finding that a "one size fits all" approach to programming is less viable in attaining program fidelity than approaches that consider the cultural context in which the program is developed and executed (Bledsoe, 2001).

With programs coming to terms with increased diversity, so too must the field of evaluation. Evaluators are finding that they must become flexible and adept at using a variety of approaches that are sensitive to extracting and fostering understanding of the context in which the program is operating (Mertens, 1995, 2003). Thus when programs and evaluations are being developed they must now consider how they will be perceived and implemented in diverse settings by diverse stakeholders with varying needs. This is especially true for community-based organizations that are often operating with limited budgets, time, and resources, but face the challenge of serving large, diverse, and underserved populations with "a cornucopia of needs" (Bledsoe, 2001). Consequently, issues of culture, language, socio-economic status, education, and the like all must be considered in program development and evaluation.

For example in our work with a nonprofit agency (Bledsoe & Graham, 2005) we have grappled with the issue of not only the interrelationship between dominant and minority groups, but also the relations between historically underserved groups such as Latino and black communities. Rather than the dominant and minority cultures competing for resources, the focus now is on minority groups competing against each other. All are competing for access to valued community treasures such as education, health services, and political power, but their unique circumstances, needs, and approaches differ. For example, in our work with a local phil-anthropic organization in New Jersey, we have found that both African American and Latino communities both have limited access to health programs. However, issues for African Americans may revolve around perception of discrimination due to stereotypes generated through historical racism (Lipsitz, 2002), while for immigrant Latino populations the discriminatory barrier may be attributed to language (Foley, 2002).

Across the country, demographics are changing significantly. Areas that were once dominated by one historically disadvantaged group are also witnessing this change. This change requires the addition of resources that communities who are already underserved may not be in a position to generate (Guzman, 2003). Such concerns as the former illustrate the increasing demand for programs and *program evaluation* that address the specific issues of underserved communities, and their unique perspectives. Communities cannot be neatly packed under the umbrella term of "multiculturalism." Each community of color has its own needs that must be included in developing programs that will be able to effectively service a diverse group. Thus terminology such as "inclusiveness" and "pluralism" has now become standard when designing social programs and social program evaluation in particular (e.g., Guzman, 2003; Mertens, 2002).

For instance, Mertens's (2002) use of the transformative approach in the program design and evaluation process calls for evaluators of social programs in underserved communities to serve as community advocates and social change agents. Green (1997) corroborates this approach through her use of qualitative methods that she has used in her work in advocacy evaluation in educational settings. Such acknowledgment of the need for multiple perspectives acquiesces that program design is indeed value-laden. If program design should undoubtedly reflect the values of communities being served, it seems reasonable to extend that expectation to program evaluation theory and practice.

THE NEED FOR EFFECTIVE EVALUATION APPROACHES IN UNDERSERVED COMMUNITIES

Crano (2002) notes that program evaluations often fall short in their methodological approaches. In his view, evaluation approaches are not useful in promoting issues such as construct validity. Construct validity is defined as having variables and measures that are representative of the phenomena of interest (Vogt, 2001). This type of validity is especially useful in designing effective approaches for underserved communities.

For example, we are currently designing a program on obesity for local high school students in Trenton (Trenton, Teacher's Network, in preparation). While the concept of obesity seems straightforward (defined by the group as being significantly overweight as defined by body mass weight and height index charts), ethnic populations such as the black community do not have the same outlook toward weight and height proportion. In fact, researchers (e.g., Frisby, 2004; Rubin, Fitts, & Becker, 2003) have found that ethnic communities often have higher self-esteem than whites at larger body sizes. Therefore, measuring the concept of obesity using a dominant cultural paradigm may not be an appropriate construct measurement. We have had success not in framing obesity in terms of pounds overweight, but as a construct of future health consequences for both the teen and their family.

Such a focus on construct validity is especially important because it aids in the development of methodology that can accurately measure the phenomena of interest (e.g., culture and eating habits). If the measures and therefore measurements are accurate, the likelihood of pinpointing the usefulness of the program is high (Vogt, 2001). Crano's (2003) view is important given that program designers and program evaluators (especially external evaluators) are often accused of not providing accurate representation of the program, the environment in which the program occurs, and the population that is most effected by the program.

The trend of the federal government for the last 10–15 years has been to fund programs that encourage clients to be self-sufficient, especially since program consumers and administrators are more equipped and knowledgeable to deal with community needs than the larger, more distant federal government. It is presumed that program administrators and consumers can make use of resources rather than rely on charity and philanthropy from organizations who often don't have the level of understanding of the context that is needed to develop and evaluate community-based programs (Guzman, 2003; Lincoln, 2003; Mertens, 2003). Given this realization, the need for sensitive evaluation approaches that can provide accurate and representative results of the program is salient.

Additionally, programs are being required by local government and private funders to be more accountable by providing evidence that programs are achieving their goals and objectives. Evaluation approaches that are flexible, collaborative, representative, and rigorous are necessary to accurately describe and evaluate provide true representation and accurate evaluation of community-based programs. Such approaches should provide an opportunity for those who are most affected to be heard, illuminate and illustrate the program workings and nuances, and make use of existing and factual knowledge of the community and the people who reside in it. So the question is not only how effective is the program, but also how and in what way?

THE TDE APPROACH: GIVING VOICE TO THOSE WHO OTHERWISE MIGHT BE UNHEARD

The theory-driven evaluative approach can be an effective tool in giving "voice" and credibility to the needs of underserved communities. It accomplishes this by providing the opportunity for underserved populations to express their "theory" of the needs of the community and in what manner those needs might be addressed. Therefore, the focus of the evaluation is not only the social scientific theoretical perspectives but one that also includes the practical perspectives of both those who design and administer such programs (high-level stakeholders) and program consumers (downstream stakeholders), TDE can incorporate the perspectives of those who would otherwise be silent and passive recipients or program services.

For instance, our work in Los Angeles with a crime prevention program for Latino adolescents (Bledsoe et al., 2001) was successful in using a TDE approach. Because the team put forth a significant effort in working with stakeholders ranging from city officials to program recipients, we were able to hear the stories of an ethnic community that would otherwise go unheard. Stakeholders with a theory of how a program should or is operating provide insight and information into the context in which a program is operating (Chen, 1990; Donaldson, 2001).

Our work in Trenton, New Jersey, exploring racism, stress, health, and infant mortality among African American women continues to benefit from using a theory-driven approach (Bledsoe & Gilbert, 2003). Health program providers, designers, administrators, and funders have been grappling with the question of what can be done to increase services to women of color, and especially African American women.

Health providers had speculated on reasons for the high rate of infant mortality in this African American community (lack of health care, lack of caring toward prenatal care, etc.). However, a focus group discussion with program recipients noted other startling aspects such as the degree of perceived racism toward African American women from health providers, degree of access to health care facilities, and belief in home- or community-based remedies. Each was found to be a contributing factor as to why these women were limited in their use of what is considered to be proper prenatal care techniques. Such information could be critical in the design and the formative evaluation of programs of this type. With a formative evaluation, we consider the needs and extenuating circumstances and build them into the program prior to implementation so that we can measure the effect of those circumstances.

In the case of the Trenton prenatal program, program design might incorporate a diversity training course for health education providers about the existing stereotypes that pervade and limit the delivery of good prenatal care. Program evaluation can measure the effectiveness of the training and subsequent behavior but also can measure changes in stereotypes. TDE is useful in being able to account for such factors and measure the degree to which they moderate or mediate the relationship between the program and the distal goal of diminishing infant mortality.

DISCERNING THE INNER WORKINGS OF THE PROGRAM THAT ASSISTS IN PROGRAM FUNCTIONING

One of the fundamental flaws of a black box evaluation approach is that there is little need (or room for that matter) for valuing why a particular outcome has (or has not) been obtained. For example, if a drug prevention program for adolescents of color has a cultural component (e.g., cultural pride training) that is considered key to the outcome of the program (abstention from drug use), black box evaluation can express that the program was successful or unsuccessful, but not in which manner (e.g., is the program's success due to the cultural component or not?). With the use of theory-driven evaluation the black box is demystified. We can clearly understand how the cultural component serves to create the abstention of drug use (e.g., by instilling the belief that there are alternatives other than drugs). Thus, TDE serves to discern the actual components, the manner in which they are supposed to elicit change or the desired outcome.

Again, Mercier and colleagues' (2001) example is key here. The use of a theory-driven approach was helpful, specifically through the use of concept maps, focus groups, and literature searchers of previous programs' evaluations focusing on youth centers. Using these strategies led to the development of a theory or logic as to how the program would presume to work.

Working with the crime prevention program in Los Angeles, we found that the use of TDE allowed for the articulation of cultural subtleties such as the concept of "machismo" (Latino concept of manliness). Machismo has been found to be a factor in the precipitation of violence in Latino culture (e.g., Lee, 1995; Welland-Akong, 1999). Hence, the program designer was able to understand it as a sense of honor, rather than the primary reason for violent behavior of Latino and Hispanic adolescent males.

We have also found that developing a program logic model, inclusive of some of the cultural and gender characteristics that affect the program, was helpful in providing a more effective model to evaluate an urban literacy program designed to serve communities of color (Bledsoe & Graham, 2004). The short-term outcomes and the long-term goal is in-home reading, thereby increasing the likelihood of pre-literacy in children ages 0 to 6. Using a theory-driven approach we were able to discern the rationale of how such goals might be accomplished. The program consists of 3 hours of services per week of group and individual reading, a meal, music, and crafts. Such interaction leads to more in-home reading, which leads to preliteracy skills before arrival to K–12 education (e.g., Britto & Brooks-Gunn, 2001; Diamond, Reagan, & Bandyk, 2000).

The program administrators have described the program as providing pre-literacy skills, but in what ways does this occur? A theory-driven approach helps to identify the inner workings of the program as well as accounting for sometimes-overlooked aspects such as culture, gender, socioeconomic status, and the like. Based on numerous meetings with stakeholders, the literacy program is thought to lead to cognitive stimulation, reduced parental stress, and increased nurturing interaction which leads to in-home reading, which in turn leads to the distal goal of school readiness (see Figure 10.5).

Additional moderators such as language or socioeconomic status may affect the execution and fidelity of the literacy program. For instance, in addition to serving African Americans, the program also serves Latino(a)s and Polish immigrants who speak English as a second language. Consequently both Polish and Spanish were utilized to provide services as well. Other related moderators thought to enhance success might be culture (e.g., is physical closeness a cultural more?) or the availability of transportation for parents to attend weekly activities.

Specific links (indirect and direct), can be mapped and assessed in terms of the relationship to the short- and long-term goals (Donaldson,

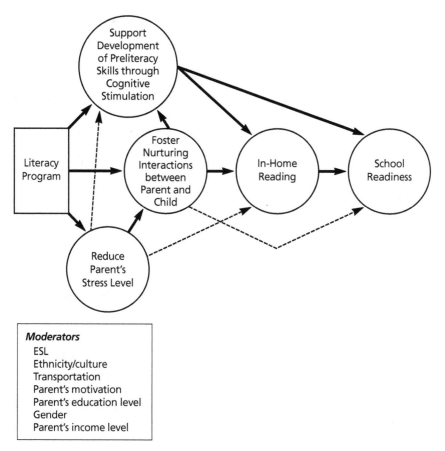

Figure 10.5.   Model of urban family literacy program. The bold lines indicate a strong link to the outcomes; dotted lines represent possible links to the outcomes.

2001). Figure 10.5 attempts to discern the mechanisms of how the program works, while acknowledging the influence that a community's cultural and economic environment might have on the implementation of the program and the long-term outcomes. For example, if the program is found to be effective for African American communities but not for Latino communities, steps can be taken to refine the program so that it accounts for cultural differences. At the same time, stakeholders (with the technical assistance of evaluation consultants) can design instruments and methodology that enables the evaluator to discern true change in the community (see Figure 10.5 for illustration). Taking into consideration these cultural differences in model and method, for example, can be facilitated by the use of social science theory in areas such as community and cultural psychology.

THE TDE APPROACH: MAKING USE OF SOCIAL SCIENCE INFORMATION ON UNDERSERVED COMMUNITIES

One of the most useful assets of the TDE approach is its ability to incorporate information from other venues, including other programs, scholarly research literature, and evaluation approaches, and use this information to develop a comprehensive model of how the program works and whom it may affect (Chen, 1990; Donaldson, 2001). In their work with African American women, Lauby, Smith, Stark, Person, and Adams (2003) found that designing programs that catered to some of the cultural nuances of the African American community, research on the cultural mores of African American women, and their views on sex was helpful in providing program administrators with strategies on how best to implement an AIDS prevention program and evaluate its effectiveness.

The approach has also worked well in areas such as drug prevention. For example, Edwards, Seaman, Drews, and Edwards (1995) tried to establish a theoretical framework for planning a culturally sensitive drug and alcohol prevention model (inclusive of relevant community and social factors) for Native American adolescents. They suggested that program effectiveness could be improved by focusing on and including positive social factors (e.g., educational opportunities), economic indicators (e.g., SES), and cultural factors (e.g., how the culture views drug and alcohol use). That is, by recognizing and addressing the influence of factors such as lack of educational opportunities, low SES, or cultural acceptance of drug use (e.g., cultural acceptance of drinking in some Latin cultures) on drug use and abuse, prevention programs might be more effective.

STRATEGIES USED IN CONDUCTING THEORY-DRIVEN EVALUATION

Chen (1990) has described TDE as part science and part art. The science of conducting evaluation involves a best practice, scientific, and iterative process, working to identify and clearly articulate components that can be accurately represented and measured. However, the art of conducting TDE is its inclusion of relevant program stakeholders and consumers in the evaluative planning and process, while also making use of their personal theories of how the program works and the methods in which to measure its effectiveness.

In our work with a community arts program (Konzal, Graham, & Bledsoe, 2003) we have found that including relevant stakeholders such as program consumers, staff, and administrators has proven useful in conceptualizing the type of constructs to measure (e.g., the influence of an after-school academic and arts program on the health practices of adolescents of color) and in exploring methodological approaches (e.g., qualitative methods).

In our experience program participants are more responsive to evaluators when providing insight on concerns such as literacy and delinquency as a *community* rather than *individually* (e.g., Bledsoe et al., 2001). In this case, the use of survey methodology can prove to be a challenge. In some culturally diverse communities, conducting a survey might not be appropriate due to the varying degrees of literacy among potential participants. Consequently, a focus group or community narrative might be more useful in identifying the needs (e.g., specialized tutorials for students) and the cultural context in which those needs exist (e.g., servicing a 50% Latino immigrant population).

One strategy that has proven useful has been the logic modeling process. Programs often have a "logic" or step-by-step process that must be completed for an outcome to occur. Logic modeling often helps organizations articulate this process to determine what the program is truly attempting to accomplish (Fetterman, 2003). In some instances, as Donaldson (2001) has noted, we have found that this might be the only step that is completed in the evaluative process. The step is useful determining the evaluability of the program (the program's readiness to demonstrate concrete outcomes). Because the process is iterative, it allows vested team members to continue to identify the true program components, monitor program improvement, and provide accurate *measurement* of components.

Another approach that is useful is "benchmarking." Benchmarking allows the exploration of other programs that may be accomplishing the same goals using similar strategies. We found this strategy to be helpful in our work with the family literacy program in Trenton, New Jersey (Bledsoe & Graham, 2004). For instance, many nonprofit agencies and schools throughout the United States are developing and administering pre-literacy programs. Benchmarking can serve to identifying critical competitors who may compete for similar clientele (Scriven, 1997).

Finally, we have found that using a variety of evaluation approaches throughout a project can serve to increase the capacity and fidelity of program results. This latter strategy has been especially important, for it underscores the need for evaluation approaches to be flexible. The use of multiple evaluation strategies is addressed in the following section.

THE USEFULNESS OF THEORY-DRIVEN EVALUATION
WITH OTHER APPROACHES

Evaluators are often polarized as to the type of approaches they use. They can become a little like woodworkers who see every project as one that needs a hammer. While this alliance with a specific approach is often supported in theory, in practice, evaluators know that one may use a variety of techniques when working with organizations, especially community organizations, at varying times. Thus, approaches should be flexible enough to work effectively with others.

The utility of the theory-driven evaluation approach lies within its versatility in working with others. For instance when combined with approaches such as empowerment evaluation (Fetterman, 1996) and utilization-focused evaluation (Patton, 1997), both of which are commonly used in community-based settings and underserved communities, the marriage between the two works well to foster interactive discourse between program developer, administrators, and evaluators.

In a recently funded statewide initiative in California focusing on work and health, both empowerment and theory-driven evaluation strategies were used to help stakeholders and evaluators articulate the program expectations (in this case, development of computer centers in low-income, ethnically diverse communities) and also allowed stakeholders to understand and take ownership in program development and program evaluation (Donaldson & Gooler, 2002).

In our own work with the family literacy program (Bledsoe & Graham, 2004), we made use of four approaches: theory-driven evaluation (Chen, 1990), empowerment evaluation (Fetterman, 1996), inclusive evaluation, and consumer-based evaluation (Mertens, 1995, 2003). Each was used at varying points in the project to produce an evaluation that provided information not only about the inner workings of the program, but also highlighted the unique cultural and socioeconomic needs of the community (a predominantly black and Latino population).

The use of theory-driven evaluation allowed the identification of specific mediating and moderating aspects, which presumed either to affect or lead to a particular phenomenon. Our use of an empowerment approach recognized that the organization needed to learn and understand evaluation procedures and be empowered to monitor the program after external evaluation. The use of an inclusive approach helped us to make use of the knowledge and expertise of the communities by including program staff and administrators in the development of the evaluation plan. The use of an inclusive approach was especially helpful because we worked to solicit feedback from sources that are rarely considered when evaluators discuss using a TDE approach: those who would actually be program implementers and clientele of the program (Bledsoe & Graham, 2005). Finally, a consumer-based approach was used to solicit direct feedback from consumers about the evaluation measures and procedures.

This combination of approaches has helped to increase utilization of the evaluation results and encourage ownership of the program and the evaluation procedures, as well as increasing the likelihood of gaining future funding.

THEORY-DRIVEN EVALUATION AS A MECHANISM TO PROMOTE PROGRAM DEVELOPMENT AND PROGRAM SUSTAINABILITY

One of the issues in community-based programming, especially those programs that are designed to service the underserved, is sustainability and long-term program functioning. Although program sustainability is perhaps one of the most pressing concerns, it is often elusive to both evaluators and stakeholders because of the lack of real knowledge of what the program is and how it works.

In the evaluation project in New Jersey concerning the rate of Sudden Infant Death syndrome (SIDS) among African American women (Bledsoe & Gilbert, 2003), the use of a theory-driven approach has been key to providing the link as to why this community suffers diminished health outcomes such as infant mortality (the rate of SIDS is twice that of whites). The incidence of infant mortality cuts across all economic and educational backgrounds of the African American population (New Jersey Department of Health and Senior Services, 1998).

Although program administrators have found the phenomena puzzling, they have been at a loss for strategies to combat it. However, in working with community program developers and staff, we are finding that organizations are now beginning to entertain possible reasons as to why this occurs (such as perceived access), and to consider the effects of racism and the subsequent stress of that racism as a possible link to SIDS. By making such links clearer, it becomes possible to talk about addressing the needs of the community in real and concrete ways that promote long-term sustainability. This is particularly important for community-based organizations that are often operating on limited budgets and limited funds, lacking in time and resources, and servicing large, diverse, and underserved populations (Bledsoe, 2003).

Thus we are finding that the articulation of program theory based on the realistic and representative information from stakeholders and from social science theory (be it past evaluations and/or theoretical models) can help increase the chances for long-term funding and sustainability.

CONCLUDING THOUGHTS

One of the more memorable comments I received at the Relevance of Assessment and Culture in Evaluation (RACE) 2003 conference in Arizona concerning the use of TDE in underserved communities was one in which a conference attendee was wondering what I would say concerning TDE that had not been said before. I am hopeful that this prescriptive piece has answered that question. My thoughts here are designed to provide a new direction for the approach and encourage theorists and practitioners of TDE to explore the road less traveled (conceptualizing the approach beyond the ivory tower), but one that is surely becoming its own distinctive path, especially in its use with underserved communities.

I believe TDE has tremendous appeal in communities and is useful in determining relevant and best practice in method design and measurement. As well it works with other approaches such as empowerment evaluation to enable program stakeholders to assist in the development of logic models as well as realistic and feasible evaluation plans.

Those who have been detractors of TDE cite TDE's use of academic and stakeholder program theory as limiting and time consuming (Scriven, 1997; Stufflebeam, 2001). Yet the use of program theory is probably its greatest appeal. TDE can help evaluators to understand the communities and cultures that are most affected by social programming, while stressing the importance of inclusion and self-determination as crucial to providing the impetus of having relevant stakeholders be a part of the evaluation conceptualization process.

Rather than limiting this useful approach to the theorists and ivory tower practitioners, let us begin to broaden the scope of TDE to real-world settings and not dismiss it as being too limiting for underserved communities. Let theory-driven evaluation be the bridge in bringing evaluators and communities together for a common goal—providing representative program design and evaluation to those who will benefit most.

AUTHOR'S NOTE

The author would like to thank Barbara J. Lehman of the Department of Psychology, University of California, Los Angeles, for her insightful comments and editing. All comments concerning this chapter can be sent directly to the author, Katrina L. Bledsoe, The College of New Jersey, Department of Psychology, Box 7718, Ewing, New Jersey 08628, email: Bledsoe@tcnj.edu.

REFERENCES

American Evaluation Association. (2003). *AEA policies and procedures manual: Diversity Committee.* Available at http://www.eval.org/Publications/publications.html #Policies

Bickman, L. (1989). Barriers to the use of program theory. *Evaluation and Program Planning, 12,* 387–390.

Bledsoe, K. L. (2001). Why I believe theory-driven evaluation is useful in program development for underserved and diverse populations. *Mechanisms: The Newsletter of the Program Theory and Theory-driven Evaluation Topical Interest Group, 5,* 3–6.

Bledsoe, K. L. (2003). Using theory-driven evaluation to promote program sustainability in community-based settings. *Mechanisms: The Newsletter of the Program Theory and Theory-driven Evaluation Topical Interest Group, 6,* 4–6.

Bledsoe, K. L., & Graham, J. A. (2005). Using multiple evaluation approaches in program evaluation. *American Journal of Evaluation.*

Bledsoe, K. L., Gilbert, C. K., Fischbein, K. M., Cervantes, A. I., & Dragan, A. B. (2001). *Final Report on Evaluation Activities: The Hathaway Resource Center COPS Program.* Claremont Graduate University.

Bledsoe, K. L., & Gilbert, C. K. (October, 2002). *Race, stress, and health among African American communities.* Presentation at Children's Futures, Trenton, NJ.

Britto, P. R, & Brooks-Gunn, J. (2001). Beyond shared book reading: Dimensions of home literacy and low-income African American preschooler's skills. In P. R. Britto & J. Brooks-Gunn (Eds.), *The role of family literacy environments in promoting young children's emerging literacy skills: New directions for child and adolescent development.* (pp. 73–89). San Francisco: Jossey-Bass/Pfeiffer.

Chen, H. T. (1990). *Theory-driven evaluation.* Newbury Park: Sage.

Chen, H. T., & Rossi, P. H. (1987). The theory-driven approach to validity. *Evaluation and Program Planning, 10,* 95–103.

Crano, W. D. (2003). Theory-driven evaluation and construct validity. In S. I. Donaldson & M. S. Scriven (Eds.), *Evaluating social programs and problems: Visions for the new millennium* (pp.145–157). Mahwah, NJ: Erlbaum.

Diamond, K. E., Reagan, A. J., & Bandyk, J. E. (2000). Parents; conceptions of kindergarten readiness: Relationships with race, ethnicity, and development. *Journal of Educational Research, 94,* 93–100.

Donaldson, S. I. (2001). Mediator and moderator analysis in program development. In S. Sussman (Ed.), *Handbook of program development for health behavior research.* (470–496). Newbury Park, CA: Sage.

Donaldson, S. I., & Gooler, L. E. (2002). Theory-driven evaluation of the Work and Health Initiative: A focus on Winning New Jobs. *American Journal of Evaluation, 23,* 341–346.

Edwards, E. D., Seaman, J. R., Drews, J., & Edwards, M. E. (1995). A community approach for Native American drug and alcohol prevention programs: A logic model framework. *Alcoholism Treatment Quarterly, 13,* 43–62.

Fetterman, D. M. (1996). Empowerment evaluation: An introduction to theory and practice. In D. M. Fetterman, S. J. Kaftarian, & A. Wandersman *Empowerment evaluation: Knowledge and tools for self-assessment and accountability* (pp. 3–49). Thousand Oaks, CA: Sage.

Fetterman, D. F. (2003). Empowerment evaluation strikes a responsive cord. In S. I. Donaldson & M. S. Scriven (Eds.). *Evaluating social programs and problems: Visions for the new millennium* (pp.63–76). Mahwah, NJ: Erlbaum.

Foley, N. (2002). Becoming Hispanic: Mexican Americans and Whiteness. In P. S. Rothenberg, *White privilege: Essential readings on the other side of racism* (pp. 349–360). New York: Worth .

Frisby, C. M. (2004). Does race matter? Effects of idealized images on African American women's perceptions of body esteem. *Journal of Black Studies, 34,* 323–347.

Gargani, J. (2003). *A historical review of theory-based evaluation.* Unpublished Manuscript, University of California, Berkeley.

Green, J. C. (1997). Evaluation as advocacy. *Evaluation Practice, 18,* 25–35.

Konzal, J., Graham, J. A., & Bledsoe, K. L. (2003). Ready, Set, Go: The GET SET Tutorial Program. Trenton, NJ.

Lauby, J. L., Smith, P. J., Stark, M., Person, B., & Adams, J., (2003). A community-level HIV prevention intervention for inner-city women: Results of the women and infants demonstration projects. *American Journal of Public Health, 90,* 216–229.

Lee, R. S. (1995). Machismo values and violence in America: An empirical study. In L. L. Adler & F. L Denmark, (Eds). *Violence and the prevention of violence.* (pp. 11–31). Westport, CT: Praeger.

Lincoln, Y. S. (2003). Fourth generation evaluation in the new millennium. In S. I. Donaldson & M. S. Scriven (Eds.). *Evaluating social programs and problems: Visions for the new millennium* (pp. 77–90). Mahwah, NJ: Erlbaum.

Lipsey, M. W., & Pollard, J. A. (1989). Driving toward theory in program evaluation: More models to choose from. *Evaluation and Program Planning, 12,* 317–328.

Lipsitz, G. (2002). The possessive investment inwhiteness. In P. S. Rothenberg, *White privilege: Essential readings on the other side of racism* (pp. 349–360). New York: Worth.

Mercier, C., Piat, M., Peladeau, N., & Dagenais, C. (2001). An application of theory-drive evaluation to a drop-in in youth center. *Evaluation Review, 24,* 73–91.

Mertens, D. (1995). Identifying and respecting differences among participants in evaluation studies. *New Directions for Program Evaluation, 66,* 91–97.

Mertens, D. L. (2003). The inclusive view of evaluation: Visions for the new millennium. In S. I. Donaldson & M. S. Scriven (Eds.). *Evaluating social programs and problems: Visions for the new millennium* (pp. 91–108). Mahwah, NJ: Erlbaum.

New Jersey Department of Health and Senior Services. (1998). *Blue Ribbon Panel report on infant mortality reduction.* Trenton, NJ: Author

Patton, M. Q. (1997). *Utilization-focused evaluation: The new century text.* Thousand Oaks, CA: Sage.

Rubin, L. R., Fitts, M. L., & Becker, A. E. (2003). "Whatever feels good in my soul": Body ethics and aesthetics among African American and Latina Women. *Culture, Medicine, and Psychiatry, 27,* 49–75.

Scriven, M. (1997). Minimalist theory: The least theory that practice requires. *American Journal of Evaluation, 19,* 575–604.

Stinchcomb, J. B. (2001). Using logic modeling to focus evaluation efforts: Translating operational theories into practical measures. *Journal of Offender Rehabilitation, 33,* 47–65.

Stufflebeam, D. (2001). Evaluation models. *New Directions for Evaluation, 89.*

Trenton Teacher's Network (in preparation). *Program design of an intervention to prevent obesity among Trenton Central High School.* Trenton, NJ: Author.

Vega, M. A., & Gil (1998). *Drug use and ethnicity in early adolescents.* New York: Plenum Press.

Vogt, P. (2001). *Dictionary of statistics and methodology.* Thousand Oaks, CA: Sage.

Weiss, C. H. (1997). How can theory-based evaluation make greater headway? *Evaluation Review, 21,* 501–524.

Welland,-Akong, C. G. (1999). A qualitative analysis of cultural treatment components for Mexican male perpetrators of partner abuse. *Dissertation Abstracts International, 60*(6-B), 2967.

Wholey, J. S. (1979). *Evaluation: Promise and performance.* Washington, DC: Urban Institution.

CHAPTER 11

CULTURAL REFLECTIONS STEMMING FROM THE EVALUATION OF AN UNDERGRADUATE RESEARCH PROGRAM

Michelle Jay
Dedra Eatmon
Henry T. Frierson
University of North Carolina at Chapel Hill

Established in the summer of 1988, the Summer Pre-Graduate Research Experience Program (SPGRE) at the University of North Carolina at Chapel Hill offers undergraduate students throughout the country the opportunity to work full time on self-selected research projects under the direction of university faculty members. The program is designed for students who are interested in pursuing graduate studies, particularly the PhD degree. The program's main objective is to address the obvious shortage of PhD recipients from underrepresented groups, particularly those from African American, Native American, Mexican American, and Puerto Rican populations.

To reinforce and promote interests in the pursuit of graduate study, the SPGRE program immerses participants in an environment intended to

The Role of Culture and Cultural Context in Evaluation, pages 201–216

help prepare them for those critical research aspects associated with graduate study while engaging them in innovative and original research projects. For 10 weeks, beginning in late May and ending in late July, participants are involved in research ranging from fields in the basic biomedical sciences to the humanities and the physical sciences to the social sciences. The range of research options is extremely broad and is tailored to students' interest. In addition to their research task, participants attend weekly seminars that explore various aspects of life in the academy as well as GRE preparation courses. Financial support is provided for participants in the form of a stipend, food allowances, and travel reimbursements. In addition, the program covers the cost of housing as well as all university fees, giving participants full access to the university's resources.

THE STATUS OF UNDERREPRESENTED MINORITIES IN PHD PROGRAMS

Currently, African Americans, Hispanic/Latino Americans, and Native Americans comprise more than 25.3 % of the U.S. population (U.S. Census Bureau, 1996), yet members of those groups received only 7.6% of all science and engineering doctorates awarded to U.S. citizens in 2002 and a mere 4% of all doctorate degrees in those fields awarded by U.S. universities (Hoffer et al., 2003). Specifically, in the life sciences, of the 8,350 doctoral recipients in 2002, African Americans, American Indians, Mexican Americans, and Puerto Ricans together constituted only 4.3% (359) of the recipients, and a mere 2.9% (170 of 5,715) of all doctorates received in the physical sciences (Hoffer et al., 2003). Indeed, these groups are truly underrepresented as doctoral recipients and consequently as researchers and academicians in science and engineering fields. Thus concern over the small presence of U.S. minorities in the sciences is clearly warranted.

The need to increase the number of underrepresented graduate students of color enrolled in and earning doctoral degrees continues to be a major concern in post-secondary education, despite previous calls to address this matter by individuals such as Wyche and Frierson (1990). In assessing possible explanations for the paucity of minorities in graduate programs, Wyche and Frierson argue:

> A significant reason why there is such a disproportionately small number of African American, American Indian, Mexican American and Puerto Rican students going to graduate school and getting Ph.D. degrees may simply be because they are rarely told they should do so, nor provided experiences leading to such paths. Ironically, the latter is particularly true at our nation's major research universities. (p. 989)

While recruitment of minority students into graduate programs, particularly in STEM fields (science, technology, engineering, and mathematics), has seen some improvement over time, given the relatively small number of enrolled students from those groups, retention is critical. Inadequate mentoring relationships, campus climate, and financial burdens are but a few of the factors that can negatively affect a student's ability to successfully complete doctoral study, and those factors are particularly pressing for students of color (Golde & Dore, 2002; Martinez, Durham, Philbrick, & Melenez, 1992).

Research enrichment and intervention programs, such as SPGRE, hold significant potential for successfully engaging minority students in academic and research activities to overcome those barriers. Consequently, constant evaluation of these programs is essential in determining their effectiveness and for providing possible directions for improvement in their efforts to address the shortage of underrepresented minorities in STEM and other fields. Accordingly, the evaluation study presented in this chapter sought to add to the body of literature that examines intervention programs for underrepresented minority students and their effectiveness.

THE SPGRE PROGRAM

The SPGRE program is a component of the larger Research Education Support (RES) Program at the University of North Carolina at Chapel Hill. Consisting of multiple components involving both undergraduates and graduate students, the RES Program enhances, strengthens, and supports the university's long-term commitment to addressing the underrepresentation of minority students in graduate programs at the university. The cornerstone of the RES program is the mentor/mentee relationship that develops between faculty preceptors and their students. Based on two major funding sources, the National Institute of General Medical Sciences and the National Science Foundation, RES builds on the strengths of the University's strong research activities and its efforts to enhance and promote diversity among its student body. The short- and long-term goals of the RES program are to increase the number of underrepresented minorities acquiring the skills, knowledge, and background preparing them for research careers and enhancing the completion of the PhD.

SPGRE, the summer undergraduate component of the RES program, invites undergraduate students from a diverse range of colleges and universities across the county to participate in summer research. A concerted effort is made to match students, according to their research interests, with relevant research projects and faculty research mentors. To ensure such a match, students and faculty members are required to communicate prior to the students' acceptance into the program and their subsequent arrival on campus.

In addition to providing students with research opportunities, the SPGRE program provides an experience similar to that of graduate students who attend large research universities. Students are required to participate in writing workshops and attend weekly seminars that focus on life in the academy. UNC faculty and staff, as well as other professionals working in the Research Triangle, lecture on topics ranging from "Women in the Academy" to "Creating a Successful Presentation." Program participants are also provided with free GRE preparation courses. When students are not engaged in research or attending seminars, they are free to take advantage of university life. In addition to university-sponsored events, SPGRE's program staff hosts several social events, from barbecues to field trips, to enhance participants' experience.

By the end of the program, students are expected to have produced a paper as their finished product and present their work visually at the end-of-the-program poster session. In addition, a number of students make oral presentations of their work during the course of their program. It is expected that all participants will leave the program as attractive prospects for major graduate research programs.

EVALUATING THE SPGRE PROGRAM

Since its inception in 1988, the SPGRE program at UNC Chapel Hill has conducted evaluations that have employed the reflections of its program participants (through questionnaires, surveys, and personal interviews) to assess the worth and effectiveness of the program and to identify the extent to which certain program variables affect the perceptions of participants (Frierson, Hargrove, & Lewis, 1992, 1993, 1994; Frierson & Riggins, 1998; Frierson & Zulli, 2002; Hargrove & Frierson, 1994). These studies indicate that race, gender, and the racial composition of their home institutes are among some of the central factors that can affect the perceptions and attitudes of students in the program. As SPGRE and its umbrella program, RES, are targeted toward underrepresented minority students, most evaluation or research studies conducted on the program would provide a "minority perspective" on their findings. However, a literature review indicates that no prior research questions or evaluations have been designed that focus directly on the impact of the program's cultural context on program participants. However, as summer research experiences for undergraduate students appear to have a significant influence on program participants' decisions to pursue doctoral studies, not only should program outcomes be examined, but assessing the quality of participants' personal experiences during the course of the program can yield important and useful information as well. For example, a previous evaluation study of the SPGRE program investigated the impact of a preceptor's race and gender on their students' experience. Interview results indicated that students with African American or female preceptors reported more positive perceptions of research and their individual research environments than those with Caucasian male preceptors (Frierson et al., 1994). As the program's ultimate goal is to increase minority students' desire to pursue research-based graduate degrees, any insight into heightening participants' experiences can be valuable in increasing participation in, and success of, the program. Extending the work of previous studies, the objective of this evaluative study was to explore how student perceptions, attitudes, and experiences were affected by the cultural context of the program, a program variable previously unexplored. For the purposes of the study, culture was defined as "a cumulative body of learned and shared behavior, values, customs and beliefs common to a particular group or society. In essence, culture is that which makes us who we are" (Frierson, Hood, & Hughes, 2002).

Within the context of an enrichment or intervention program like SPGRE, the presence of program staff, peers, and in some cases, faculty preceptors who understand and reflect the specific type of cultural background that program participants bring with them can have a substantial impact on their experience. As Stent (1973) noted, minority professionals are especially attuned to the educational, social, and emotional needs of minority students within academic environs and are thus uniquely positioned to design and lead these types of programs. In particular, the cultural and social capital imparted by program directors, staff, program assistants (graduate students), and faculty mentors of color to program participants with whom they share a similar cultural background can provide them with significant insight into the types of intellectual and personal support systems that minority students are generally inclined to need.

This study investigate the perceived benefits that students garnered from participating in the SPGRE program, and in particular, to identify those benefits that were related to the ways in which shared backgrounds and cultural similarities enhanced their academic and personal experiences within the program. Essentially, the study, one of an evaluation nature, sought to begin the process of uncovering the significance of the cultural context and subsequent cultural influences on the experiences of program participants.

RELATING TO PROGRAMS SUCH AS SPGRE
TO CULTURALLY RESPONSIVE EVALUATION

According to Frierson and colleagues (2002), it is critically important to fully take into account the culture context in which a program operates; or in other words, to conduct a cultural responsive evaluation. They assert that an evaluation is culturally responsive if "it is based on an examination of impacts through lenses in which the culture of the participants is considered an important factor, thus rejecting the notions that assessment must be objective and culture free, if they are to be unbiased" (p. 63). Conducting a culturally responsive evaluation protects the evaluation of a program from being significantly flawed or skewed.

When designing and conducting an evaluation, cultural responsiveness can potentially play a role at each of the phases of the evaluation process. For example, Frierson and colleagues (2002) argue that in the preparation stage of a culturally responsive evaluation, the assembling of the evaluation team is critical to the evaluation process, particularly when the programs involve ethnically diverse participants. Employing culturally responsive evaluators "who honor the cultural context in which an evaluation takes place by bringing the needed, shared life experience [between evaluators and participants] and understandings to the evaluation at hand" can enhance the likelihood that those shared lived experiences ensure that the evaluators truly hear and understand what is being said.

Thus, given the importance of the creation of a cultural responsive evaluation team, the individuals who composed the team for this evaluation study included two female research and evaluation assistants employed by the Research Education Support Program who worked in collaboration with the program director. One of the evaluators, an alumnus of the SPGRE program, is intimately familiar with the program and its staff. The other holds both undergraduate and graduate degrees in engineering, a field where minority students remain underrepresented. All of the individuals involved in the evaluation were of African American heritage. Moreover, each has a strong commitment to culturally responsive evaluation and understands the necessity of being responsive to the cultural context of the program.

Another phase of evaluation that can employ cultural responsiveness is in outlining of the intents and purpose(s) of the evaluation. Summative evaluations, such as the one conducted in this study, attempt to provide information about the program's effectiveness and its impact on its participants. Culturally responsive summative evaluations "examine the direct effects of the programs implementation on the participants and attempt to explain the results within the context of the program" (Frierson et al., 2002, p. 67). In this study not only was the cultural context of the program taken into consideration, but it served as the main variable (as it related to the program experience of 17 African American students) under investigation.

EVALUATION DESIGN AND DATA COLLECTION METHODS

At the request of the RES program director, this evaluation study was undertaken during the fall of 2002 involving former SPGRE participants enrolled in doctoral programs at UNC-CH. The specific purpose of the study was two-fold: (1) to explore the relevance and importance of the program staff's racial and cultural backgrounds (as key components of the program's cultural context) for program participants; and (2) to explore the participants' perceptions of their experiences as they related to their ability to see their own culture reflected in various facets of the program, including fellow participants, faculty mentors, and program activities. These explorations went beyond simple program assessment to identify less obvious factors that may contribute to program success and impact students during and after participation in the program.

To obtain a thorough description of participants' experiences, personal interviews were conducted. As Frierson and colleagues (2002) note, culturally responsive evaluation makes substantial use of qualitative evaluation techniques. Because qualitative methods rely heavily upon the data collector(s), "when collecting qualitative data directly from individuals, e.g. via interview or observations, if those who are collecting and recording the data are not attuned to the cultural context in which the program is situated, the collected data could be invalid" (p. 68).

In addition, cultural responsiveness is reflected in the nature of the questions pursued in this study. Recognizing that the culture of this particular program is uniquely shaped by the backgrounds of the participants and the program staff stimulated the evaluators' desire to see what affect the shared backgrounds between staff and students and between students and their peers had on the program environment and culture and thus the experiences of the students.

Most evaluation questions, including those previously posed of the SPGRE program, focus on issues related to the program's success in reaching its goal, or in other words, about the program's worth. However, because the evaluators understand that the process of reaching those goals entails an examination of the students' actual experiences in the program in order to ascertain why they did or did not experience success, the evaluation questions were tailored to focus on the substance of their experiences. In addition, as evaluators of color (and graduate students) we acknowledge and understand the importance of seeing people of color reflected in academic communities as being critical to minority students' decisions to pursue, and persist in, graduate school. Thus, the evaluators desired to examine that salience of that importance and its influence by focusing on the students' perceptions of the importance of their shared background with program staff and fellow participants.

Because the important role played by culture in the SPGRE program was a major facet of this study, the evaluators were sensitive to the lived experiences of its participants. Thus, the types of questions posed to the study participants may not have been included in an evaluation that did not acknowledge its cultural context. Moreover, while a nonculturally responsive evaluation team may have asked questions about the cultural significance of the program, they may not have done so in a manner that would have revealed the subtle nuances in participants' experiences and the tangible and intangible ways in which they were impacted in the process.

The study participants included 17 African American SPGRE alumni who had attended the program between 1998 and 2001 and were now pursuing their doctoral degrees at the University. Of the 17 students, 10 (58.8%) were women and seven (41.2%) were men. At the time of their participation in the SPGRE program, 12 (70.6%) were attending a historically black college or university (HBCU), and five (29.4%) were attending a predominantly white institution (PWI). Also at the time of their participation in the program, all students had completed their junior year and were entering their senior year at their undergraduate institutions.

The interviews for this evaluation were based on seven broad questions that explored the relationship between the cultural context of the program and (1) the students' decision to spend the summer in the program, (2) the academic and social experiences provided by the program, (3) the students' overall satisfaction with their program experience, (4) the students' subsequent decision to attend UNC-CH for doctoral study, and (5) their transition to graduate school. Students were asked to answer the questions as completely and as honestly as possible and were informed that the purpose of the study was to gain information about their experiences in an effort to improve the SPGRE program specifically, and to provide information that may promote further studies of similar support programs for underrepresented minorities students in general. Interview questions are provided in the Appendix to this chapter.

The interviews ranged from 20 to 30 minutes. Qualitative analysis of the interviews involved exploring participants' responses to uncover any emergent themes in the narrative content and coding the responses accordingly. The first section of the interview focused on the impact of racial and cultural similarities between program staff and participants on the participants' decisions to attend the program and on their academic and personal experiences in the program while the second part explored participants' perceptions of the graduate student experience, their transition to graduate school, and subsequent acclimation to their surroundings. The various ways in which the participants' experiences in the program were positively affected by the shared similarities became general themes in and of themselves. The resultant themes reveal a number of intangible benefits derived from what was perceived as the shared cultural capital of the participants and staff.

EVALUATION FINDINGS

Importance and Impact of Racial Reflection

The results indicated that some of the program participants (41%) were knowledgeable of and influenced to attend the program based on the fact that it is specifically directed at underrepresented minority students. One program participant commented:

> I think that it played a major role [in their decision to attend the program]. I was interested in being in a program with other minority students who were interested in going to graduate school. Also, being exposed to minority professors and getting their input and advice on graduate school was important.

Another participant noted that the program's focus on minority students ranked "very high" for him, "because I had attended other internships before and I was the only person of color and I felt very alone. I didn't feel that I had the support that I felt I needed to actually enjoy my summer experience." Also influential in their decision to attend the program was prior knowledge of the program from former participants, the opportunity to engage in meaningful research experiences, and having been recruited to the SPGRE program by its director. Interestingly, the most popular motive mentioned by the participants (47%) was the opportunity for them to gain research experiences in their area of interest *specifically at the University of North Carolina at Chapel Hill*. Expressing a sentiment that rang true with several participants, a student explained, "I just knew that I was coming to the University of North Carolina and that was something that I was very interested in."

Notably, very few of the students were initially aware that the SPGRE program directors and administrative staff were people of color. However, more than half (59%) indicated that they were pleasantly surprised by the fact and were favorably impressed upon making the discovery. One participant recalled, "I thought it was definitely a good thing. It was a support issue for me. It felt good to be working with people who are like you and know what's best for you and who have traveled the road you are on. It definitely increases your comfort level." Another stated that they felt that obtaining a PhD was now achievable as a result of having seen program staff and faculty of color who were in the process of completing, or had already earned, their own degrees. Adding to these positive perceptions was a professional culture among the program faculty and staff that participants felt a part of that was "positive to experience." One student intimated that they were particularly pleased to see "black professionals who are good at what they do."

An additional benefit of the program frequently cited by participants was the presence of graduate and post-doctoral students of color who served as additional mentors in their research settings. Moreover, as the participants had ample opportunity to interact with the SPGRE graduate assistants (who represented a variety of different departments and who performed duties such as acting as liaisons between the participants and the program director), their ability to witness the daily grind of graduate school via the graduate assistants gave the participants a fairly accurate portrayal of what is typically expected of graduate students at what is commonly referred to as a Research I institution.

Importantly, all of the participants noted that the administration and execution of the SPGRE program by faculty and staff of color had a significant impact on their experience in the program. In addition to feeling a general sense of encouragement and inspiration throughout the program, students cited a relationship between their increased levels of comfort and having program staff with whom they were able to relate and vice versa. As one participated intimated:

> It [having the program staffed by people of color] had a positive impact. They had a perspective that I think people who are not of color would have lacked. And I think that as a result, they really wanted to see us succeed, so there was more of a personal investment on their part that I felt. And I still keep in contact with the program directors so I feel that they are personally invested in me and having them be in charge of the program made it more personal for me. They definitely wanted to see us succeed.

Moreover, participants felt that they could be "honest" and "straightforward" about their experiences in the program, secure in their ability to approach, confide in, and garner advice from the program director and support staff.

Though less than half of the students (41%) felt that it was not important that their fellow participants reflect their own racial or ethnic background, most (88%) did agree that it created an enjoyable environment. The participants indicated that it was easy to relate to one another because of their shared backgrounds and similar educational and personal experiences. Indeed, participants often took comfort in knowing that after a hard day in their respective labs or research settings, they could look forward to spending their evening relaxing in an enjoyable social atmosphere. Several of the students interviewed mentioned a sense of real camaraderie among their fellow participants and made mention of the fact that they were still in communication with some of the friends that they had made during their time in the SPGRE program.

Significantly, some participants mentioned the considerable value of not being the "odd man out" or being "othered" and having to prove oneself academically and intellectually as the sole minority student in an academic program. In sharing her thoughts on the importance of having fellow participants from similar racial or ethnic backgrounds, one former participant noted:

> It think it was important for me to feel comfortable in the program ... that I got to interact with other people of color because it tended to happen at other places that I've been to that you end up being the one black person and in SPGRE you got the feeling that you weren't the only smart African American going for something and that was really nice. That was a nice thing to see.

There was a general sense of contentment among participants in seeing that it was "okay to be black and smart."

When questioned about the role they perceived culture had played in their SPGRE experience, the interviewees' answers were mixed.[1] In many ways, the SPGRE program offered the same activities that any typical summer enrichment program might have such as social outings, GRE preparatory courses, and a variety of seminars. However, students stated that their personal experiences outside of the work setting were made more enjoyable because of the presence of their fellow participants and the SPGRE graduate assistants, whose cultural backgrounds were similar to their own. For those students who had come to the program from HBCUs, the social atmosphere that existed among African American students was not unfamiliar to them. However, those who attended PWIs encountered a unique setting and dynamic rarely experienced at their home institutions. As one participant explained, she "used the experience to bond" and was "envious of sisters at HBCUs" who were able to experience the unique social setting created when surrounded by a majority of students of color on a daily basis.

Another manifestation of the cultural context of the program, as perceived by the participants, was the way in which the topic of race was openly addressed. Specifically, students felt that they could be honest about the role of race and ethnicity in academia. As one participant explained, "People would talk more freely about how your race plays into what you are going to be doing in the future ... it made things a whole lot more colorful and a whole lot less restrained." Elaborating on the influence of the program in preparing students for the unique experience of being a minority in academia, one student commented:

> [I think culture played a role in the program in] the way we were made to feel like family, in a community sense. So people were looking out for you and they told you the truth and laid out the expectations for you so you knew what to expect. Yeah, in a community sense, we were told how things went down so we wouldn't embarrass ourselves or the group, you know?

Graduate Environment and Transition

From their responses, through their participation in SPGRE, program participants gained exposure to and became familiar with the UNC-Chapel Hill campus, worked in academic departments, and gained a fuller understanding of the expectations for students in graduate school. While only one of the participants interviewed had decided to apply to and attend UNC-Chapel Hill for graduate school prior to participating in SPGRE, many (88%) agreed that the experience was a significant factor in their ultimate decision to apply to UNC. As one participant recalled:

> I think that my decision to apply was directly affected by SPGRE because I applied almost immediately after the program was over. While I was working in the lab that summer, I went and visited professors from other departments and I basically interviewed with them. I was also familiar with the area and felt comfortable in the environment.

Indeed, several participants pointed out that they were recruited by faculty members of the departments in which they (the participants) worked. The majority of the participants made important connections to professors and graduate students in their prospective departments and were able to work closely with faculty members, many of whom currently serve as their advisors. Additionally, many participants noted that their exposure to influential individuals in their department made getting recommendations easier and shortened the application response time.

All but one participant agreed that participation in the SPGRE program aided in their transition to graduate school.[2] Elaborating on the program benefits regarding transition, one participant noted:

> Having participated in the program, we had several experiences that helped aid in the transition like presenting our work in an oral format...that was definitely a good experience. Writing a manuscript was something we had to do at the end of the summer that was also helpful. Doing a poster was a good experience because I presented that poster at two different conferences....

And just having a better idea of what graduate school was like and being in a situation with other members of the academy really helped.

As was reflected in the above statement, many students felt they had a good idea of what was expected in an academic research setting and how research was conducted as well as what was expected of graduate students, specifically at UNC-Chapel Hill. Ultimately, the interviewees indicated that, as a result of their positive experiences in the SPGRE program, they felt more "mentally and emotionally prepared" for graduate school life.

Finally, as a result of their SPGRE participation, some of the study participants were also invited to participate in RES's Initial Summer Research component prior to their first semester in graduate school at UNC-Chapel Hill. The 10-week component provides students with the opportunity to come to campus early and begin conducting research projects in their respective departments. For these SPGRE alumni, the Initial Summer Research component reinforced the independent research environment to which the students were introduced during the SPGRE program. Of particular interest are the comments made by study participants, particularly those who had made the transition from an HBCU to UNC-Chapel Hill, regarding the absence of any "culture shock" as a result of having been exposed to the UNC-Chapel Hill environment during their SPGRE experience. Participants noted that familiarity with the program and department into which they were accepted, familiarity with the campus and its resources, and a ready friendship base of SPGRE peers placed them at ease as they began their graduate study.

CONCLUSIONS

To overcome the barriers that prevent minorities from being so gravely underrepresented in STEM and other fields as researchers and academicians, programs that are designed to introduce students from those groups to the responsibilities and activities involved in such positions should become a major feature of universities and colleges across the country, a notion posed by Wyche and Frierson (1990) almost 15 years ago. However, not only is it important to create and maintain enrichment and research education programs for minority students, but considerable attention should be given to what this study argues is the significant importance of the racial, ethnic, and cultural backgrounds of program faculty and staff.

The evaluators of this study concur with Stent (1973) that the minority professional must be used as a "key to institutional change" by becoming involved in the development and implementation of programs and activities that will challenge and engage minority students. Minority professionals, particularly university faculty members, and graduate students are uniquely positioned to provide the kind of leadership, guidance, and mentorship needed to help enrichment and intervention programs like SPGRE achieve their goals. As this study illustrates, the presence of minority professionals—from graduate students to faculty members to key program administrators—makes a significant impact, not only on program participants' general experiences in the program, but on their personal beliefs about their capabilities to attend graduate school and successfully complete doctoral study.

Indeed, the importance of racial and cultural reflection as a facet of these programs is a topic worthy of further investigation, particularly as it relates to program implementation and effectiveness. Conducting a culturally responsive evaluation, such as the one presented here, offers additional measures for assessing program worth beyond successful implementation and achievement program goals. As verified by this evaluation study, participants experienced increased levels of comfort and were encouraged by a sense of genuine concern for their success as the result of the presence of minorities in key positions in the SPGRE program. The participants felt that the staff had a personal investment in them, were genuinely concerned about their present experiences and their futures, and had their best interests at heart. Having staff with similar backgrounds gave the students a "richer experience" in which they felt more comfortable, and more inspired, than they might have in a different setting.

Moreover, the students felt a sense of pride in seeing professionals of color cultivating an independent and self-directed work ethic through a unique program with a motivated group of students, many of whom (not interviewed for this study) have since gone on to pursue and complete doctoral degrees in not only STEM fields, but also humanities and the social and behavioral sciences. The enhanced personal experiences of the participants in SPGRE resulting from the cultural context of the program can only add to the academic and research skills acquired through participation in the SPGRE program and others like it. Capturing and qualifying the personal experiences of program participants enhances a program's evaluation and gives evaluators insight into future program assessment strategies.

NOTES

1. For this question, the word "culture" was intentionally left undefined so as to allow interviewees a variety of ways to respond as they saw fit. However, based on interview responses, participants' conceptualization of culture embodied common reference points regarding learned and shared behav-

iors, values, and beliefs common to the minority groups that the program participants represented.

2. The one participant who did not share this sentiment stated that the social interactions that she experienced during SPGRE differed from the social interactions she was presently experiencing in her graduate program.

APPENDIX:
Interview Questions

1. In what ways was your decision to attend SPGRE affected by the fact that it is specifically directed at underrepresented minority students like yourself?

    (a) What were some of the other critical decisions that most influenced your decision to attend SPGRE?

2. What were your impressions when you discovered that the SPGRE program staff were people of color?

    (a) Did you know this prior to your decision to attend the program?

3. In light of the fact that the program was directed by people of color, what impact do you believe that had on your experience?

4. How important was it to you that your fellow participants reflected your own racial or ethnic background?

    (a) What difference do you think that it made in terms of your experience?

5. What role do you think that culture played in general in your SPGRE experience? (i.e., your own, that of the participants, that of the staff, etc.)

    (a) If you think that culture played a role, which aspects do you think were most influential and why?

6. Had you already decided to apply to or attend UNC for graduate school when you applied to SPGRE

    (a) If you had not, what factors contributed to your decision to apply to and attend UNC?

7. Do you think that your participations in the SPGRE program aided in your transition to graduate school? In what ways?

REFERENCES

Frierson, H. T., Hargrove, B. K., & Lewis, N. R. (1992). *Preceptor race and gender: Effects on black undergraduates' attitudes and perceptions in a summer research program.* Paper presented at the annual meeting of the American Educational Research Association, San Francisco.

Frierson, H. T., Hargrove, B. K., & Lewis, N. R. (1993). *Gender and type of school attended: Effects on African American students' perceptions related to a summer research program.* Paper presented at the annual meeting of the American Educational Research Association, Atlanta, GA.

Frierson, H. T., Hargrove, B. K., & Lewis, N. R. (1994). Black summer research students' perceptions related to research mentors' race and gender. *Journal of College Student Development, 35,* 475–480.

Frierson, H. T., Hood, S., & Hughes, G. B. (2002). *The 2002 User-Friendly Handbook for Project Evaluation.* Arlington, VA: National Science Foundation.

Frierson, H. T., & Riggins, T. A. (1998). Male and female minority students' perceptions and satisfaction concerning a short-term research and mentoring program. In H. T. Frierson (Ed.), *Diversity in higher education, Vol. 2: Examining protégé–mentor experiences* (pp. 183–193). Stamford, CT: JAI Press.

Frierson, H. T., & Zulli, R. A. (2002). Examining the perceptions of minority undergraduate students participating in a university-based research program. *African American Education, 2,* 119–132.

Golde, C. M., & Dore, T. M. (2001). *At cross purposes: What the experiences of today's graduate students reveal about doctoral education.* Philadelphia: The Pew Charitable Trust.

Hargrove, B. K., & Frierson, H. T. (1994). Assessing African American students' attitudes toward research and perceptions of preceptors as outcomes of a summer research experience. In S. Hood & H. T. Frierson (Eds.), *Beyond the dream: Meaningful program evaluation and assessment to achieve equal opportunities for minorities at predominantly white universities.* Greenwich, CT: JAI Press.

Hoffer, T., Sederstrom, S., Selfa, L., Welch, V., Hess, M., Brown, S., Reyes, S., Webber, K., & Guzman-Barron, I. (2003). *Doctorate recipients from United States universities: Summary Report 2002.* Chicago: National Opinion Research Center.

Martinez, R., Durham, R. L., Philbrick, P., & Melenez, D. (1992). Minority graduate education: An encouragement program. *Equity and Excellence, 25,* 31–34.

Stent, M. D. (1973, February). *Researchers, consultants and urban schools: a black perspective.* Paper presented at the annual meeting of the American Educational Research Association, New Orleans, LA.

U.S. Bureau of the Census. (1996). *Population projections of the United States by age, sex, race, and Hispanic origin: 1995 to 2050* (Current Population Reports, P21-1130). Washington, DC: U.S. Government Printing Office.

Wyche, J., & Frierson, H. T. (1990). Minorities at majority institutions. *Science, 249,* 989–991.

CHAPTER 12

THE USE OF CONTEXTUALLY RELEVANT EVALUATION PRACTICES WITH PROGRAMS DESIGNED TO INCREASE PARTICIPATION OF MINORITIES IN SCIENCE, TECHNOLOGY, ENGINEERING, AND MATHEMATICS (STEM) EDUCATION

Elmima Johnson
National Science Foundation

Increasing demands for a society fluent in science and technology have both focused attention on science, technology, engineering, and mathematics (STEM) education and generated a myriad of programs in these fields. Programs have been developed, implemented, revised, adapted, and institutionalized to address the growing demand for a competent, diverse STEM workforce. These programs are based on best practice as well as new ideas, and many have resulted in some measure of success. Nevertheless,

The Role of Culture and Cultural Context in Evaluation, pages 217–235
The opinions, findings, and conclusions or recommendations expressed in this material are those of the author and do not necessarily reflect the views of the National Science Foundation.

much remains to be done. There is also an ongoing demand in STEM education and program evaluation to explore avenues to meet new expectations for increased participation and productivity and attainment of parity by a broader group of learners. While these programs have provided some success, the education community has much to learn about diversity and how to meet the long-standing needs of diverse groups, including minorities, women, and persons with disabilities.

This chapter addresses how the evaluation community can respond to these challenges through the use of evaluation strategies that are culturally relevant to these diverse groups. It reviews evaluation practices in STEM education, with specific attention paid to programs designed to broaden participation in science technology, engineering, and mathematics. Three questions guide this discussion:

1. What cultural or contextual factors influence program evaluation in the STEM workforce?
2. What are the diversity and equity issues significant to the evaluation of STEM education programs?
3. What are the lessons we have learned in conducting culturally relevant evaluations of STEM programs?

The first two questions explore the critical issues of cultural diversity found within the STEM workforce and education communities. The third question highlights culturally relevant evaluations, which have been used successfully by expert practitioners in the evaluation field. Diversity issues in evaluation are merged with equity concerns in STEM education in the culturally responsive evaluation of STEM education programs.

The chapter begins with a brief overview of relevant literature about contextual issues and the importance of culturally relevant practices in program evaluation. Responses to questions as they have been shared among evaluation practitioners during STEM meetings and focus group sessions will be summarized. The chapter moves from theoretical understanding of how contextual factors in evaluation are considered in the scholarly literature to an appreciation of how to conduct culturally responsive evaluations.[1] Throughout the discussion the chapter addresses unresolved and/or contentious issues that mitigate efforts to employ culturally relevant practices in program evaluation. The chapter concludes with suggestions for future directions.

THE LITERATURE

The use of contextually relevant strategies in STEM builds upon both the background of cultural diversity in evaluation and the recognition of equity concerns in STEM. The evaluation literature has explored the impact of a range of factors including project setting, participant characteristics, stakeholder involvement, the selection of appropriate instruments, and the generation of findings perceived to be relevant by stakeholder groups. The principal evaluation theories that attend to a range of contextual factors include responsive evaluation (Stake, 1976, 1983), participatory evaluation (Cousins & Whitmore, 1998), inclusive evaluation (Ryan, Green, Lincoln, Mathison, & Mertens, 1998), and democratic evaluation (House & Howe, 1999). Kirkhart (1995) discusses cultural sensitivity in the evaluation process within the concept of multicultural validity. The recent literature on cultural context highlights educational evaluation (Frierson, Hood, & Hughes, 2002). Additionally, Hopson's (2004) literature review of cultural context includes lessons learned from other disciplines and provides both a historical and international perspective.

This literature reveals the essential components of context, equity, and culture that underpin all evaluation. Learning experiences and construction of knowledge take place through the shared experiences of the learner in a culture. It follows then that the measurement of learner knowledge requires an understanding and use of culturally relevant practices. To gain this insight, Rodriquez (2003) argues that evaluation practitioners must participate in the cultures they expect to assess. Hopson (2003) emphasizes that the social location of the evaluator matters in shaping and framing the evaluation and that evaluation requires fluency in multiple cultural perspectives.

Furthermore, each community being evaluated needs to participate in constructing the goals and means of evaluation. A participatory approach allows evaluators to address the fundamental differences in the foundational knowledge among the evaluators, the evaluated, and the interpreters of the evaluation (Jolly, 2002). Hopson (2003) adds that the inclusion of culturally and ethnically diverse communities both advances and enriches the evaluation field. Collectively, these arguments underscore the importance of considering contextual factors in the evaluation of STEM programs.

CONTEXTUAL FACTORS INFLUENCING THE PROGRAM EVALUATION OF STEM EFFORTS

The context of the [Rural Systemic Initiative] communities has an enormous influence on the ways educators perceive, design, and implement their reforms.... The most significant contextual factors are (1) geography and size, (2) the social fabric of rural communities, (3) economic viability, and (4) the vision and value of science education.... Rural educators face similar challenges to their urban and suburban colleagues... but cultural relevance and youth out-migration demand equal attention.... Native Americans have traditional ideas and conceptions about science not acknowledged in most western science models. Reform program designs and evaluations must acknowledge and account for these concerns. (Braune Berns, Century, Hiles, Minner, & Moore, 2003, pp. 7–8)

The contextual factors that must be considered in planning and conducting an evaluation fall into two categories: sensitivity to the culture of the program and sensitivity to the culture of the participants. In other words, cultural context plays a critical role in the lives of programs as well as people.

SENSITIVITY TO THE CULTURE OF THE PROGRAM

The design stage of an evaluation is vital because stakeholder groups may not perceive information gathered as valuable or useful without giving attention to the context of the activity under review. The context of an evaluation has been defined as the factors accompanying a study that may influence its results, including geographic location, timing, political and social climate, economic conditions, and other relevant activities in progress at the same time (Frierson, Hood, & Hughes, 2002). The authors emphasize that an evaluation is culturally responsive if it fully takes into account the context of the program being evaluated. Important principles include: (1) the importance of input from all relevant stakeholder groups in framing evaluation questions, including questions that define acceptable evidence; (2) the need to select instruments that are culturally responsive to ensure the validity of inferences drawn from the data about the target population; (3) the importance of training data collectors about the context in which they are working and the potential effect of their behavior on participant responses; and (4) the use of multiple data analysts who represent different stakeholder groups. Some practical examples follow.

A group of evaluators of K–12 STEM education projects who attended a data workshop for urban education reform efforts were asked to describe how context was addressed in the evaluation design. Their responses are summarized below. An italicized phrase precedes the respondents' statements to indicate the cultural context connection.

- *Relevance and diversity.* The evaluation is aligned with the project goals and activities. The evaluation design includes interviews with community stakeholders, for the purpose of gauging the extent to which diverse perspectives are valued by the project staff. (The evaluators believed that since project goals and activities take contextual factors into account, the evaluation does as well.)

- *Collaboration and commonality.* Internal and external teams designed the evaluation collaboratively. The ease of communication and rapport between the core staff of these teams was facilitated because they share the same demographic characteristics (age, race, religion, education level). However, it is yet to be seen if this is a liability given that the characteristics of these teams differ from those of the district teachers and students the program serves.

- *Instrumentation and population culture.* Responding to contextual factors was particularly important in designing the interview protocol for key stakeholders. Teacher culture was the major factor in designing instruments (i.e., instruments for teachers were written to respond to the unique culture in which the teachers work). For example, classroom observation forms should inquire about cultural factors and evidence of attention to diversity in class lessons.

The group also shared comments that mirror the observations of Sylvia Johnson (1995) on developing an evaluation design. They noted that the evaluator is often expected to measure what cannot be measured or observe what cannot be seen. This concern increases the need to broaden the sensitivity, thinking, and powers of observation of the evaluator, so that a more complete and useful appraisal of the program can be made.

An evaluation design requires much attention to the program culture. It involves adequate attention to issues of infrastructure, needs to be addressed, capabilities and resources for intervention/implementation efforts, stakeholder beliefs, and the credible evidence needed for improvement and accountability purposes. Fair reporting of results and concerns about the use of data/results were also mentioned.

SENSITIVITY TO PROGRAM PARTICIPANTS

Culturally relevant evaluation rests in part on the contention that participant characteristics, values, history, and perspectives guide their actions and thus will influence their response to program interventions. In general, sensitivity to the program participants relates to giving sufficient attention to key stakeholders and being aware of learning environments of educators/teachers and learners/students. Evaluators of K–12 STEM education projects emphasized the importance of being sensitive to the impact of participants on the evaluative process and having some awareness of the positive and negative influences of the evaluation on the participants, especially minority populations. Responses about cultural sensitivity for analysis and report writing are characterized below under instrumentation, disaggregation of data, and report writing.

- *Instrumentation.* Instruments should be translated and tested for validity and reliability separately in multiple languages.
- *Disaggregation of data.* All stakeholders expect disaggregated data in all evaluations. It is important to disaggregate the data by multiple categories including race/ethnicity, gender, language proficiency, and poverty level. However, small populations of ethnic groups can skew results.
- *Report writing.* There is a disconnect between preparing different reports for different stakeholders and writing one report to address various stakeholders' perspectives. Various stakeholders often require different formats or presentations of the findings. Evaluation report writers should be trained to analyze disaggregated data/test results. There is an expectation of fairness and balance in reporting disaggregated results to all stakeholders.

It should be noted that the role of culture is not always appreciated or even understood by those who purport to practice culturally responsive evaluation. For example, approximately half of 13 project evaluators who were questioned about the role of cultural context in their evaluations of urban K–12 programs did *not* think contextual factors explicitly influenced data collection, analysis, and interpretation. At the same time, two of these evaluators commented on the importance of sensitivity/diversity training for data collectors.

DIVERSITY AND EQUITY ISSUES IN THE EVALUATION OF STEM EDUCATION PROGRAMS

Equity is not an add-on to a program; it is an essential and inherent component of high-quality mathematics and science at all levels of education.... Reducing achievement differences across groups is valuable, but the longer term goal is to serve all students so that outcomes can no longer be predicted based on gender, ethnicity, class, disability or language group. (Williams, 1998, p. 6)

For the past several decades researchers and evaluators have identified issues that should be addressed in increasing the diversity of the STEM education workforce. These issues are also relevant in the evaluation of programs designed to promote diversity goals and equitable outcomes. This section highlights three themes that emerged during two NSF workshops with minority evaluators. Participants invited to the first workshop included African American, Hispanic, and Native American evaluators; the majority held PhDs in education or related fields; all had experience in teaching, researching, and/or practicing evaluation, particularly in STEM fields. The second workshop was an outgrowth of the first, and based on discussions of ethnic differences in evaluation perspectives and practice, focused on Native American evaluation practitioners. The workshops focused on the evaluation of academic efforts in STEM fields that ranged from pre-college activities through instructional workforce professional development.

In both workshops, the evaluators defined the issues and the critical attention that must be given to them in both planning and conducting culturally relevant evaluation of STEM education programs. Three recurring themes emerged from the NSF workshops: (1) the belief systems of both the project participants and evaluators; (2) the role of expectations of evaluators and educators on opportunities for participants' success; and (3) the resources, bothe materials and personnel, that undergird successful achievement of a diverse workforce.

BELIEF SYSTEMS

Belief systems of program participants, the evaluators, and teaching personnel were characterized as influencing academic success and/or the validity of the evaluation process. Hughes (2001b), for example, points out that math and science achievement among minority students can be greatly inhibited by teachers' low expectations. The belief systems of program participants were seen as vital in the evaluation of education reform efforts. This has particular relevance to Native American cultures, which have a distinct perspective on learning and how to measure achievement (e.g., participatory learning and oral learning mode). Christensen (2003) argues that the native holistic approach, which includes a worldview, values, and learning that are very different from the linear and hierarchical approach of the white majority, *can* be learned and can be utilized in the design of culturally relevant evaluation. There are similar differences between the cultural contexts for African Americans, Hispanics, and the white population. The evaluators of science and technology education programs must attempt to listen and really hear the views of these students and their instructors. Stevens (2001) suggests multi-ethnic evaluation teams.

The validity of evaluation processes comes into question because of persistent myths regarding the appropriateness of instruments and the utilization of results. Basing his discussion on the work of Change, Witt-Sands, Jones, and Hakuta (1999) and Coleman (personal communication, 1999), Rodriguez (2001) summarized some of the more popular and persistent misconceptions and myths articulated in the literature about the impact of race, culture, and language on student learning. These myths address resistance that can plague efforts to sensitize evaluators to the need for attention to contextual factors. One myth is that racial and ethnic groups' past struggles with socioeconomic inequalities no longer exist and no longer require attention. Others include the idea that test scores reflect merit and can alone reveal the quality of the educational experience, fairness can be achieved by ignoring the influence of race in the learning process, and that the goals of excellence and equity cannot be achieved simultaneously.

Conference participants suggested that sensitivity to the issues regarding the belief systems of participants and stakeholders requires "framing the right questions." Additionally, there must be a willingness to define "success" in multiple ways including positive, affective, social, and cultural impacts. There was agreement that a mixed-method evaluation design is needed to give adequate attention to the role of beliefs in understanding the relationship between what was implemented and what was accomplished. Including the examination of beliefs in the evaluation design not only provides missing information about program process and program outcomes, it will also serve as a connector for linking together (via evaluation) policy, practice, and research. Hood (2001) reminds us that evaluation knowledge should contribute to our understanding of the [program participants] and their lived experience. "Observations" and "translation" require both an understanding of the cultural orientation of the group(s) being evaluated at large and the unwritten rules and/or nonverbal behaviors of the individuals that are grounded in attitudes and beliefs.

OPPORTUNITIES

Educators have become more aware that participant success is often dependent, to a large extent, on student opportunity to learn and the quality and intensity of the intervention effort. There is also a need to assess the interaction of the culture of the student with the culture of teaching, learning, and assessment. This allows evaluators and other assessment professionals to develop more effective approaches to determine students' knowledge and ability (Hughes, 2001).

Minority students with weak foundations in basic math and science courses are apt to struggle with high school courses that are prerequisites for college curricula. Furthermore, studies have shown that Hispanic eighth graders are more likely than their non-Hispanic white counterparts receive an education that omits science courses. The result is that Hispanic students lag four years behind their white classmates. Black students have similar issues, with Hispanics and black students more likely than any other groups to be taking remedial mathematics or English courses (Rodriquez, 2001).

Despite the known influences of contextual variables, measures of performance focus on content that underrepresented minorities have *not* learned, rather than on what they *can* do. Jolly (2003) discusses the literature which outlines additional limiting factors facing Native Americans. That is, twenty-three percent of Native Americans speak English poorly, and their native languages often have no written system. The result is that the instruction of children in this community is often "content-rich" with copious verbal instruction that includes a lot of gesturing and visual cues—of which little is ever included in evaluations (Canyon, Gibbs, & Churchman, 1975).

The underlying problem is that these students too often are enrolled in courses that will not prepare them for higher learning. It is difficult for those students to recover valuable instructional time once they move off the college track. It is a common observation among educators that, on average, black and Hispanic students take more vocational courses than academic ones such as algebra, geometry, and science classes—the gateway courses to college. A principal source of the problem is that only six states require Algebra I of all students for high school graduation—and none require geometry (Rodriguez, 2001).

Furthermore, Rodriguez (2001) argues that program evaluation should not just capture the bleak performance of minority students in mathematics and science. Clewell (2001) states that there is a need to measure achievement and to document the factors that may influence achievement outcomes. Collecting this data would not only enhance our understanding of student performance, but would also facilitate the goals of providing equal and equitable learning opportunities. According to Hughes (2001), these factors may include the quality of instruction and teacher quality characteristics, opportunity to learn the material being assessed, and the student's cultural orientation. Hughes also discusses the potential influence of personal and educational experiences of students on teaching, learning, and assessment.

RESOURCES

The resources that undergird the successful achievement of a diverse work-force include both materials and personnel. Evaluators must necessarily be sensitive to how resources impact outcomes. For example, "For many [Native Americans] the schools they attend are under-funded, either because they live in high-poverty urban or rural areas or because they are attending schools under Bureau of Indian Affairs (BIA) operation"[2] (Jolly, 2003, p. 16). It is not surprising that high school dropout estimates for Native Americans reach as high as 50%. Rodriguez describes the systemic cycle of failure as follows:

> If, for example, as we evaluate the loss of our black and Latino students from science and mathematics programs funded by NSF, NASA, the JPL, and the like, we stay at the level that reiterates the deleterious effects of resource-poor educational opportunities, without condemning the insistence of the state or district to perpetuate same, we relegate our greatest resource, our students, to shame. If our program evaluations produce yet more blame-the-victim litanies about minority students' bleak performance in mathematics and science, without also examining the willingness of their interveners to correct same, we do nothing more than subscribe to myopic views. (2001, p. 17)

This section has illustrated the interactions among belief systems, opportunities, and resources. To achieve diversity and equity in the STEM workforce and rigor in the evaluation of programs, stakeholders should be aware of how their belief systems and the resources available for program implementation impact the learning process and program outcomes. Educators and evaluators have additional responsibilities to craft the education/evaluation processes not only to accommodate differences, but to infuse equity in the process through the allocation of resources and the use of diverse teaching styles/evaluation methods. Perhaps most importantly, identifying and building on the strengths of the participants is too often overlooked as a source of energy for desired change. The development of strategies to broaden participation and achievement along STEM pathways should be a component of culturally responsive program development and evaluation as well.

LESSONS LEARNED IN CONDUCTING CULTURALLY RESPONSIVE EVALUATION

Norma Davilla (2001) emphasizes the importance of building cultural sensitivity at multiple levels and the consideration of cultural context in the evaluation of programs. Initial attempts to solicit feedback from practicing evaluators have been instructive. A purposeful sample of eight experienced evaluators of NSF Education Directorate STEM programs were asked to comment in writing on challenges faced in implementing culturally relevant/contextually relevant evaluation practices.[3] The question was open-ended and the respondents were instructed to self-define the term "culturally relevant/contextually relevant" evaluation.

Responses focused on social pressures and the psychometric/design concerns of evaluation. They point out that the political underpinnings of policy, research, and practice are real, yet are not often made explicit or articulated, and are often unexamined when it comes to culturally and contextually relevant evaluation practice. Comments regarding social pressures suggested that cultural stressors that impact evaluation practice and outcomes should be identified and attended to very early in the evaluation planning process. Particular attention was given to staffing issues, such as ensuring that team composition reflects participant demographics, including the use of colleagues who are "native language" speakers. The evaluators also suggested on-site data collectors, well known in the community and fluent in speaking "informal" as well as formal foreign languages, for interactions with participants with varying levels of education. There were also general comments on ensuring stakeholder involvement in the process by establishing trust and encouraging participation, using a point of contact (i.e., work through an organization that knows the stakeholders).

Evaluation design, especially assessment and analyses, was a concern of all the respondents. For example, several commented that contextual data that would better explain the results might be missed if funders do not support the collection of qualitative data because of time and resource constraints. Stakeholders of targeted programs may resist rigorous, evidence-based practice, especially from outside evaluators. The situation is exacerbated when participants mistrust evaluators who are perceived as "authority figures." Also, data collection may not capture and/or reflect participants' views. For example, ensuring validity while "listening" to focus group participants is a concern in qualitative studies. Another example is that results may mask rival explanations that are culturally based and hamper improving policies/practices for participant groups. Economics and geography may seasonally influence program participation. That is, response rates often suffer due to factors like geographic location, participant mobility, poverty and life situation. For example, recent immigrants may withhold follow-up contact information from persons seen as authority figures.

Other responses include the collection of more descriptive information on current contextually relevant practice and findings and translating test instruments into all languages represented among participants. Related to this, respondents suggest triangulating methodologies and perspectives to ensure attention to factors such as expectations, values, constraints, and so on, and sensitivity to the cultural frame of reference of participants. Respondents also found identifying "relevant" comparison groups addressing logistical, contextual, and statistical concerns to be important. In data analysis, advice included comparing focus group data to data gathered through other methods (e.g., interviews) and validating through triangulation of results as well as disaggregating data by student level, race, and gender.

It is apparent that respondents are much clearer in describing psychometric/design concerns and limitations than they are in describing contextual influences that relate to cultural factors. Furthermore, it is not clear whether the observations are uniquely culturally grounded or more broadly grounded in contextual concerns.

One of the issues that these respondents noted in relation to their evaluation experiences is the tendency to "homogenize" individuals or groups or to assume that all members of a particular group are similar (Rodriguez, personal communication, December 18, 2003). Whether this occurs in the data collection, analysis, or reporting phase, its outcome is problematic. Its impact on the entrenchment of cultural, racial, ethnic, and gender stereotypes could be clarified by examples of differences within the group and bring insights to the evaluation. Examples would also clarify "political underpinnings" of policy, research, and practice being "unexamined" and "cultural stressors" impacting evaluation. What is clear, however, is that a language of difference needs to be developed to guide future discussion.

Analysis and recommendations are clearer regarding psychometric/design concerns and could provide a rich source for research and evaluation questions. These include the study of missed interpretations, resistance to practice, listening selectively, not adapting to economic or seasonal realities in sampling, exploring culturally based rival explanations, translation of test instruments and presumably procedures, the interpretation of issues that arise from triangulation results, and data disaggregation. Though some already have a research base (e.g., translation), all provide a set of issues for further investigation to sharpen our understanding of cultural differences in evaluation.

For example, one could develop a descriptive case along the lines of any of the concerns noted in the above listing and gather theorists from different perspectives (e.g., stakeholder, responsive evaluation, democratic evaluation, advocacy evaluation, or empowerment evaluation) and ask them for interpretations or evaluation questions based on the case from their individual theoretical positions. Such an exercise could facilitate the sorting out of the cultural and more broadly contextual issues in evaluation (G.M. Della-Piana, personal communication, August 31, 2004).

There are challenges in all phases of the evaluation process: the design of the evaluation, the development/selection of data collection instruments, the actual data collection, and the analysis of the data. The evaluators recognized these challenges and suggested practices that they found to be effective in culturally relevant evaluation. In summary, while these lessons learned are specific to evaluating STEM programs utilizing culturally relevant practices, they should also be seen as good evaluation practice in general, irrespective of cultural considerations.

FRAMEWORK FOR IMPLEMENTATION OF CULTURALLY RESPONSIVE EVALUATION

The practices and concerns discussed in the previous section were incorporated in the development of a framework to embrace both the culture of the program and culturally relevant evaluation. The goal is to bridge our understanding of the influence of context on evaluation and the implementation of evaluation studies sensitive to the culture of the program and its participants.

Figure 12.1 provides a draft framework for making cultural context in evaluation explicit. It is based, in part, on the strategies described in the *NSF 2002 User-Friendly Handbook for Project Evaluation*. The key premise is that making cultural context explicit is (or should be) a part of every evaluation. The figure illustrates how the principles discussed in the previous section can be applied more broadly in practicing culturally responsive evaluation.

In Figure 12.1, elements in italics describe those features of an evaluation that specifically help an evaluator identify and understand the cultural impact(s) on the program being evaluated, and the response(s) of participants. These elements help to place the program, the participants, the expectations, and the findings in a cultural context. The framework suggests that *every* evaluation should ensure that cultural variables are identified and addressed, that input is solicited from program management, staff and participants; and that assumptions and interpretations are made explicit, so that findings can address what works, for what groups, and in what context.

Issues of cultural context are often subtle. Even the most experienced of evaluators can overlook cultural factors that bear upon the evaluation and its findings. Moreover, evaluators themselves are part of a context. They work within certain constraints, including the resources allocated to the evaluation and the timeframe in which the evaluation must be conducted. These constraints typically mean that compromises to an "ideal" evaluation must be made. The challenge thus becomes one of ensuring that the compromises do not impede the achievement of a culturally responsive evaluation.

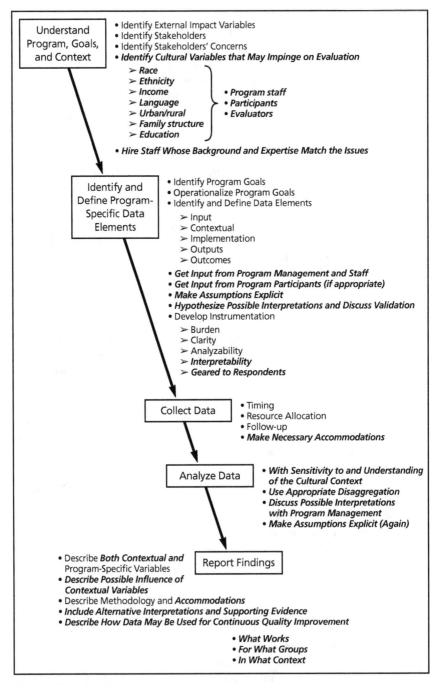

Figure 12.1.   Making cultural context in evaluation explicit. *Note:* Elements shown in **bold italics** are those that are explicitly related to cultural competency.

OUTLOOK FOR THE FUTURE

Hopson (2003) points out that culture shapes worldviews, values, and norms, and thereby impacts the uses of, reactions to, and legitimacy of any evaluation. Furthermore, he claims that evaluation plays a role in furthering social change and social justice. The application of these ideas is appropriate and timely for STEM education. The inequities in performance outcomes and distribution of resources, along with the uneven access to high-quality learning opportunities, continue to be major agenda items for all educational levels, business and industry and science-related professional societies, and the nation at large.

Discussions regarding the status of culturally responsive evaluation as a valid strategy for the profession have prompted the National Science Foundation and the American Evaluation Association to reassess the role of culture in evaluation. The efforts of these organizations have centered on policy review and capacity building. The National Science Foundation (NSF) is a federal agency that supports STEM research and education programs and their evaluation. In recent years, NSF's Directorate for Education and Human Resources (EHR)/Division of Research, Evaluation, and Communications (REC) has broadened its capacity-building efforts in evaluation in order to make context and diversity issues in STEM education explicit in its evaluation. Activities have included productive meetings with professional evaluators of color to identify needs and priorities in training and education. This has resulted in a capacity-building initiative focused on career exploration and mentoring for graduate students and professional development for practicing evaluators. REC has created a formal grants program for capacity-building and evaluative research that will facilitate studies to address research methodologies and evaluative techniques to further the development of contextually relevant evaluation.

To date, resource development has included the addition of a chapter pertaining to strategies for culturally responsive evaluation to the NSF publication *User-Friendly Handbook for Project Evaluation.* As a result of these efforts, NSF has a small portfolio of projects focused on capacity building (professional development/training) and model development within the framework of culturally relevant evaluation. A recently funded project focuses on the development of an indigenous model of evaluation for the assessment of Native American student achievement in STEM programs. Additional initiatives continue to be explored. For the NSF, the ongoing goal is increased diversity in STEM fields.

The American Evaluation Association (AEA)—an international professional association of evaluators devoted to the application and exploration of program evaluation, personnel evaluation, technology, and many other forms of evaluation—implemented a *Building Diversity Initiative* (BDI) funded by the Kellogg Foundation (2000–2003). Under this initiative, AEA:

- Developed a plan to increase diversity in AEA and in evaluation through a set of recommended actions;
- Queried minority evaluators about barriers to involvement; and
- Surveyed foundations and government agencies on how they identify and use diverse and culturally competent evaluators, and the strategies used by professional associations, to increase diversity among their members.

The AEA board accepted the BDI recommendations in 2003, and has initiated implementation activities.

The Multicultural Issues in Evaluation Topical Interest Group (TIG) of AEA continues to emphasize cultural context through its conference program and mentoring activities for new evaluators, in addition to a range of other activities. In 2003 *Evaluation Methodology* was selected as the theme at the 2003 Annual Meeting Presidential Strand because, "[Evaluation] methodology is being affected by technology, social pressure, legal forces and an increased awareness of the need for cultural sensitivity" (Krueger, 2003).

The membership of AEA recently approved revisions to the language in the organization's Guiding Principles for Evaluators after an extensive review process, guided by the Ethics Committee of the Board. The current document includes attention to the role of cultural context in the evaluation process. AEA is also involved in the review of the Joint Committee Standards for Program Evaluation, which provides guidance for the evaluation of education and training programs (Joint Committee on Standards for Educational Evaluation, 1994). AEA provided comments to the Joint Committee based on a "cultural reading" of the Standards. Future actions by NSF and AEA are dependent on continued pressure from the field for training and professional development that informs appropriate strategies for culturally relevant evaluation. Guiding these efforts will be feedback from evaluators on the effectiveness of these strategies for ensuring the validity of findings for the participant population as well as the funding source.

FUTURE CHALLENGE

The increasing awareness of the complexity of the issues of parity, equity, diversity, and increased participation confronting STEM educational efforts is encouraging. Also encouraging is the parallel development of culturally responsive evaluation approaches to education. One can sense a synergy in the two movements, but considerably more effort is required. It would be disingenuous to conclude that the parallel movements are at present widely embraced in the education community. They are not and probably will not be in the near future. But to abandon the effort is not a choice. STEM and culturally responsive evaluation deserve our robust, sustained, and honest efforts. They represent the best available avenues for pursuing the one principle that undergirds our democracy and to which we can all pledge our allegiance, the principle of equal rights. The challenge for evaluators is to conduct culturally relevant evaluation in such a manner that they advance evaluation methodologies and promote social justice.

NOTES

1. The major data sources for this discussion are proceedings from two workshops with minority evaluation professionals sponsored by the NSF Education Directorate Evaluation Program in June 2000 and April 2002; the *NSF 2002 User-Friendly Handbook for Project Evaluation*; and the reflections of an available purposive sample of 13 project evaluators of urban K–12 programs who shared with the author during an informal meeting their views of how contextual factors inform the evaluation process and how their evaluation activities are influenced by the culture of the projects being evaluated.

2. The BIA allocates a little more than $3,000 for each Native American (NA) student annually, while the average U.S. public school expenditure per pupil is more than $6,000.

3. These were experienced practitioners who had evaluated different types of STEM programs addressing diversity/equity concerns.

REFERENCES

Brauner, B. B., Century, J.R., Hiles, E., Minner, D. D., & Moore, G. (2003). Science education reform in rural America: A snapshot. Newton, MA: Center for ScienceEducation,EducationDevelopmentCenter,Inc.

Canyon, L., Gibbs, S., & Churchman, D. (1975). Development of a Native American evaluation team. *Journal of American Indian Education, 15*(1), 23–28.

Change, M., Witt-Sands, D., Jones, J., & Hakuta, K (Eds.). (1999). *The dynamics of race in higher education.* Stanford, CA: AERA, Center for Comparative Studies in Race and Ethnicity.

Christensen, R. A. (2003). Cultural context and evaluation: A balance of form and function. In Proceedings of *The cultural context of educational evaluation: A Native American perspective.* (pp. 23–33). Arlington, VA: National Science Foundation.

Clewell, B. (2001). Evaluation of educational achievement of underrepresented minorities. Discussion highlights. In Proceedings of *The cultural context of educational evaluation: The role of minority evaluation professionals.* (p. 8). Arlington, VA: National Science Foundation.

Cousins, J. B., & Whitmore, E. (1998). Framing participatory evaluation. In E. Whitmore (Ed.). *New directions for evaluation,* Vol. 80. Understanding and practicing participatory evaluation. San Francisco: Jossey-Bass.

Davilla, N. (2001). Participation of minority professionals in educational evaluation. Discussion highlights. In Proceedings of *The cultural context of educational evaluation: The role of minority evaluation professionals.* (pp. 26–28). Arlington, VA: National Science Foundation.

Frierson, H.T., Hood, S., & Hughes, G. B. (2002). Strategies that address culturally responsive evaluation. In *The 2002 user-friendly handbook for project evaluation.* (pp. 63–73). Arlington, VA: National Science Foundation.

Hood, S. (2001). New look at an old question. In Proceedings of *The cultural context of educational evaluation: The role of minority evaluation professionals.* (pp. 29–31). Arlington, VA: National Science Foundation.

Hopson, R. (2003). Synthesis of multicultural/culturally competent evaluation: Five basic tenets. In *Overview of multicultural and culturally competent program evaluation issues, challenges and opportunities.* Woodland Hills, CA: California Endowment Multicul-tural Health Evaluation.

Hopson, R. (2004). An analysis of evaluation within a cultural context. Literature review for the National Science Foundation. Unpublished paper.

House, E. R., & Howe, K R. (1999). *Values in evaluation and social research.* Thousand Oaks, CA: Sage.

Hughes, G. B. (2001a). Evaluation of educational achievement of underrepresented minorities. Discussion highlights. In Proceedings of *The cultural context of educational evaluation: The role of minority evaluation professionals.* (pp. 8–11). Arlington, VA: National Science Foundation.

Hughes, G. B. (2001b). Evaluation of educational achievement of underrepre-sented minorities: Assessing correlates of student academic achievement. In Proceedings of *The cultural context of educational evaluation: The role of minority evaluation professionals.* (pp. 12–15). Arlington, VA: National Science Foundation.

Johnson, S. (1995). Searching near, far and wide: A plan for evaluation. In *FOOTPRINTS: Strategies for non-traditional program evaluation.* (pp. 15–23.) Arlington, VA: National Science Foundation.

Joint Committee on Standards for Educational Evaluation. (1994). *The Program Evaluation Standards* (2nd ed.). Thousand Oaks, CA: Sage.

Jolly, E.J. (2003). On the quest for cultural context in evaluation: Non ceteris paribus. In Proceedings of *The cultural context of educational evaluation: A Native American perspective.* (pp. 14–22). Arlington, VA; National Science Foundation.

Kirkhart, K. E. (1995). Seeking multicultural validity: A postcard from the road. *Evaluation Practice, 16,* 1–12.

Krueger, R. (2003, November). Evaluation 2003 President's Welcome Address. In American Evaluation Association Annual Conference Program. Reno/Sparks, NV.

Rodriguez, C. M. (2001). Assessing underrepresented science and mathematics students: Issues and myths. In Proceedings of *The cultural context of educational evaluation: The role of minority evaluation professionals.* (pp. 16–23). Arlington, VA: National Science Foundation.

Rodriguez, C. M. (2003) Closing remarks. (NSF 03-032). In Proceedings of *The cultural context of educational evaluation: A Native American perspective.* (pp. 77–79). Arlington, VA: National Science Foundation.

Ryan, K, Greene, J., Lincoln, Y., Mathison, S., & Mertens, D. M. (1998). Advantages and challenges of using inclusive evaluation approaches in evaluation practice. *American Journal of Evaluation, 1*(1), 101–122.

Stake, R.E. (1976). A theoretical statement of responsive evaluation. *Studies in Educational Evaluation, 2*(1), 19–22.

Stake, R.E. (1983). Responsive evaluation. In T. Husen and T. N. Postlewaite (Eds.) *International encyclopedia of education: Research and studies.* New York: Pergamon Press.

Stevens, F. I. (2001). Reflections and interviews: Information collected about training evaluators of math and science projects. In Proceedings of *The cultural context of educational evaluation: The role of minority evaluation professionals.* (pp. 41–46). Arlington, VA: National Science Foundation.

Williams, L. S. (1998). Overview. In B. Anderson, P. Campbell, Y. George, E. Jolly, J. Kahle, N. Kreinber, J. Lopez-Ferrao, & G. Taylor. *Infusing equity in systemic reform: An implementation scheme* (pp. 4–7). Arlington, VA: National Science Foundation.